Christian Radio

Christian Radio

The Growth of a Mainstream Broadcasting Force

BOB LOCHTE

McFarland & Company, Inc., Publishers
Jefferson, North Carolina, and London

Scriptures referenced by author are taken from the
King James Version of the Bible.

LIBRARY OF CONGRESS CATALOGUING-IN-PUBLICATION DATA

Lochte, Robert H.
    Christian radio : the growth of a mainstream broadcasting
force / Bob Lochte.
        p.   cm.
    Includes bibliographical references and index.

    ISBN 0-7864-2239-4 (softcover : 50# alkaline paper)

    1. Radio in religion — United States — History.   2. Religious
broadcasting — Christianity — History.   3. Religious broadcasting —
United States — History.   I. Title
    BV656.L53   2006
    269'.260973 — dc22   2005025413

British Library cataloguing data are available

Cover illustration ©2005 Brand X Pictures

Manufactured in the United States of America

McFarland & Company, Inc., Publishers
    Box 611, Jefferson, North Carolina 28640
        www.mcfarlandpub.com

To Kate.
She made me do this

Contents

Acknowledgments: Let Us Give Thanks

Although there is one author named on the title page of this book, that is no indication of the true number of people who contributed to its contents. For without all the folks mentioned below, this project would never have been possible. I am deeply indebted to them all.

Darrell Gibson at Heartland Radio Ministries in Hardin, Kentucky, helped me get started. I also thank Brandon Karstetter, Darrell's promotion director and my former student.

At Moody Radio in Chicago, John Hayden took the better part of a day to answer my questions and show me around. Phil Shappard, a fountain of information, checked facts for me and filled in many gaps in the narrative.

Mike Miller at Salem Radio Network in Nashville gave me a tour and patiently helped me with information. Denise Davis in California reviewed the manuscript, improving my accuracy.

Many thanks to Matt Austin and Dusty Rhodes at WAY-FM and to former staffer Doug Hannah.

Ditto to former WAY-FM promotion manager Andrea Kleid, another student of mine, who is now with EMI Christian Music Group, for helping me make contacts and looking over some early drafts.

Marvin Sanders and Pat Vaughn at American Family Radio were most helpful, not only about the AFR operation but in pointing out background issues and sources of information that I would have missed.

I never got to meet Mike Novak at K-LOVE in person, but I've spoken with him on the phone often and exchanged enough e-mails to feel like I know him well, and with his help, learned a good bit about Christian radio.

Janet Simonsen at the Foursquare Gospel Church in Los Angeles was most helpful with background information on Aimee Semple McPherson.

Jack Houghton and Kelly Crane at Bott Radio Network opened some doors for me and helped me revise the sections detailing their organization.

Two more of my students, Andrea Keen and Regina Clark, assisted me ably in various phases of my research.

The Reverends Mark and Karen Welch looked at an early draft and had many useful suggestions.

And finally, without the support, encouragement and indexing skills of my wife, Kate, I doubt I would even have begun this project.

Many thanks to one and all and to the rest of the people who helped along the way but whose names I fail to recollect.

Preface:
Preachers and Politicians
Pay Cash Upfront

In a way, I began my professional career in Christian radio. Back in 1966, a friend worked for a local radio station in my hometown of Nashville, Tennessee. One of his jobs was originating the broadcast of the Sunday service from the large Presbyterian church that we both attended. I started hanging around the radio room off the sanctuary, learned the basics, and took over the job the next year when my friend went away to college. Although there wasn't much to it — making sure that the remote console was on and hooked up to the telephone line, setting up and testing the microphones, riding gain on the two channels during the service, and packing up the gear afterwards — it got me started in radio. And I was able say that I worked for WKDA, one of the two Top 40 rock stations that were hot with my social set.

So why did a Top 40 radio station, formatted for teenagers, broadcast a Presbyterian church service on Sunday mornings? It paid the bills. At that time, local "blue laws" restricted most retail business on Sundays, and many regular advertisers considered it improper to advertise on the Sabbath. Many radio stations broke format on Sunday mornings to sell program time to churches and evangelists because it was the only time they could sell all day. Some broadcasters even considered this practice a community or public service to listeners. Besides, there wasn't much audience, period, on Sunday mornings.

After college and a quick run through the garden of educational TV,

I got interested in owning a radio station. It was the 1970s, and FM was just beginning to take off. So my wife Kate and I and another couple pooled our resources, borrowed more than we should have, got the owner to finance two-thirds of the purchase price, and bought a struggling FM in Pulaski, Tennessee, in Giles County, where James David Vaughan was born.

At that time, there were no local marketing agreements, so the old owners had to wait at least three months, until the Federal Communications Commission approved the license transfer, for us to actually buy the station and take over operations. While we were waiting, my partner and I traveled to Pulaski frequently to listen to the station, get to know our listeners and potential advertisers, and formulate strategies for our new business. We had never discussed a policy regarding religious broadcasting until an incident with a local retailer.

She was a pleasant lady who managed a five-and-dime store on the town square. It was one of the few regular advertisers, and she one of the few people around the square who had our future station playing in her business. The layout was typical—a large display floor with cases and tables full of merchandise stretching its entire length. The cash register was by the front door, and the office in a mezzanine suspended above the main floor at the rear. We were chatting with her by the cash register when a local preacher came on the radio, as he did for 15 minutes every weekday morning at 9:30. She politely excused herself, walked all the way to the back of the store, up the stairs to the office, and turned the radio off. My partner and I looked at each other with the realization that she probably was not the only one doing this. Despite the regular revenue from the broadcasts and the goodwill from having a respected member of the clergy from a large local church on the radio, we knew that this was bad business.

The broker who arranged the station purchase was a nice guy who had many years of experience as a radio owner and operator in towns like Pulaski. We sought his advice, and he told us, "The first rule to follow is: Preachers and politicians pay cash up front. Then think about your audience. If your regular listeners turn the radio off, and his congregation tunes in to hear him and then turns the radio off when he stops, who's still listening?" So we set a policy of paid religious broadcasting only on Sunday mornings. The preacher was upset, took his daily program and the Sunday service to our competition, and chided us from the pulpit on his last broadcast. But we survived and took comfort in the thought that although our competition got the revenue, they also got the tuneouts.

We had been in business a month or two when a Pentecostal preacher named Brother Ted came by and wanted to buy a half hour every Sunday morning. He worked in a plant during the week and pursued his calling of faith in the evenings and on weekends. Because Brother Ted didn't have a regular church, we asked him for references. He told us that we should check with a radio station in Lawrenceburg where he used to have a Sunday morning program.

I called the station manager and heard a curious story. One Sunday morning, the Sunday-morning operator, a 16-year-old kid, called the manager in a panic. Brother Ted was talking in tongues and had gone into a trance very much like an epileptic fit, and the boy couldn't get him out of the control room. The manager rushed to the station, carried Brother Ted out, and cancelled his contract.

Although I was uncertain about dealing with Brother Ted, he had asked me to contact the manager and was not trying to hide the incident. He assured us that he had better self-control, and we let him buy the time. In the five years that Brother Ted kept the program, he never got a congregation. Twice a year, however, he organized weeklong camp meetings for which he pitched a big tent near a creek where he could conduct baptisms. For these events he brought in local gospel singing groups and part-time evangelists like himself. Although the crowds rarely exceeded a few hundred people, Brother Ted collected enough love offerings to pay for the airtime.

Our main competitor was the old-line AM in town — the traditional favorite for news and sports, with established personalities and a strong base of advertisers. There was another station in the county, however — a 500-watt daytime-only AM in Ardmore, a tiny community that straddled the Tennessee-Alabama line. It was a commercial station, but the owner was a minister for a church that bought large blocks of time and solicited donations to pay for it. The rest of the time, the station played southern gospel music and sold commercials as usual. Its audience was quite small, often not measurable in the annual Arbitron estimates.

But I listened to this station occasionally, as I did to all the competition, to see what they were doing and who was advertising. To my surprise, I once heard a substantial campaign for a Goodyear Tire dealer in Pulaski. The next time I saw the store's owner, I mentioned that his budget would get better results with us because the Ardmore station only had a few hundred listeners, mostly older women who were not the primary target audience for tires. He countered with, "Yeah, but when they get on the radio and say, 'We know you like this good gospel music, but we can't afford to play it for you if you don't go down and get a set of those Goodyear Tires,' every one of those little old ladies will come buy tires from me whether they need 'em or not." I had no ready reply.

Although my recollections are anecdotal and limited to my own experience, they are indicative of the situation for Christian radio in the 1960s and 1970s. There were few Christian radio stations on the air, and most of them had very small audiences. National programs were almost nonexistent, and local radio stations begrudgingly sold time to Christian broadcasters when they could not sell commercials. The second generation of electronic evangelists, like Billy Graham, Oral Roberts, Jerry Falwell, Kathryn Kuhlman, Jimmy Swaggart, and the Rev. Ike, had moved on to the Promised Land of television. The National Association of Religious Broadcasters (NARB) held annual conventions, but most of the topics of discussion dealt with televangelism, not the older medium of radio. Yet changes were on the way.

In 1988, Kate and I moved to Kentucky and bought a house near the lake. It didn't take us long to learn that the roof leaked, so I hunted around and located a carpenter to repair it. John was tall, slender and strong, and spoke with an East Coast urban accent. He and his family had just moved to the area too, but they came to find a more wholesome place to raise their kids. Among the disorderly pile of tools, notepaper, and fast-food debris on the front seat of his truck was a well-thumbed Bible. A crucifix hung from the rearview mirror.

One afternoon, I came home to check on John's progress. To my surprise I heard loud heavy metal rock music spewing from a cheap cassette recorder beside John on the roof. Turning the volume down so we could talk, he said, "Hey, man, like the music?" "I'm not really sure," I replied. "What is it?" "It's Christian rock," he said. "They play like Jimi Hendrix but sing about Jesus."

That was my first exposure to the genre. I had been aware of Christian rock since its inception within the Jesus Freak movement of the 1970s, but had never paid much attention. Occasionally a song like "Spirit in the Sky" would hit the pop Top 40. The Christian rock musicals *Jesus Christ Superstar* and *Godspell* were still popular, and a few Christian artists like Amy Grant gained wider appeal among pop-music audiences. But I always thought of Christian rock as an underground phenomenon. I could not have been more mistaken.

Then I noticed many new radio stations going on the air, most of them on non-commercial FM channels, and all of them in the general category of Christian radio. Some of these were overtly evangelical, with a combination of syndicated national programs and local preachers who reminded me of Christian radio of the past. But more often what I heard was music — some rock, some contemporary pop, some acoustic — in a reasonably pleasant mix. When you listened closely to the lyrics, however, you heard an intensely personal testimony and evangelical message.

By the early 1990s, some of my students began to get part-time jobs at local Christian radio stations. I really took notice when, late in the decade, two of my very best ones went into Christian radio as a career after graduation. Something was happening here, something that I sensed was very important to the radio industry. But I learned next to nothing about Christian radio by consulting standard trade publications and information sources. And people that I knew in both commercial and non-commercial radio were either as ignorant as I was or strangely reluctant to discuss the subject. The only way I was going to find out about this radio phenomenon was from the folks who were making it happen.

So I embarked on a research project that involved many conversations and communication with many people in Christian radio, over a period of almost two years. Along the way, I jettisoned my misconceptions about this being a fringe activity in the radio business and developed a profound respect for the professionalism, insight, effort, and sincere dedication that these individuals and many like them possess and bring to the industry. In reviving interest in Christian radio, moreover, they may be reviving interest in radio, a medium that desperately needs new ideas.

Once my curiosity got me into this, I discovered very little had been written about Christian radio in the past ten years and nothing of a comprehensive nature that put its present development and growth into context with its history and with other social, political, and cultural trends. That's when I decided to write this book. So here we are.

Bob Lochte
Fall 2005

1. In the Beginning

"This is a ministry. It just happens to be radio." As he talks, Darrell Gibson sits in an office cluttered with mementos of his days as a sportscaster — coffee cups permanently stained a burnt umber, FCC applications, spare parts, and scripture passages on calendar pages. His bulletin board is covered with snapshots of family, dogs, and fishing trips. There's a collapsible playpen on the floor for when his daughter, the receptionist, brings his grandchildren to work. On one wall is a framed autographed poster from a Red Skelton performance with two ticket stubs glued to it.

The office is in a non-descript building that could be a modest ranch-style home. The comparison is ironic. "I designed this place when we started the business," Gibson says. "Back then, I thought we might have to live in it." The hallway is partially blocked with boxes of Bibles, videotapes, CDs, and Sunday school books. They collect these from listeners and donate them to a missionary organization that distributes them to churches in 39 countries. So far, they've sent out more than 100,000 items. The other offices and control rooms are decorated with photos of recording artists, many with autographs, and concert and movie posters. In the lobby, there's a crate with a new antenna for a power upgrade on one of the stations.

Gibson's broadcasting career goes back more than 30 years. Since 1989 he's run a non-commercial Christian radio business in a small town in west Kentucky. He has five stations, each with a different format, a network of translators, and construction permits for more. He talks about audiences, hard drives, voice tracking, control-room design, coverage maps, regulations, finance, disc jockeys, and programming philosophy.

"We're not evangelistic. Our objective is to strengthen and encourage the body of Christ. We have Presbyterians, Methodists, Baptists, Pentecostals, Foursquare Gospel — it doesn't matter. All we have to agree on is Jesus."[1] He sums up his strategy with a New Testament verse:

> Whatsoever things are true, whatsoever things are honest, whatsoever things are just, whatsoever things are pure, whatsoever things are lovely, whatsoever things are of good report; if there be any virtue and if there be any praise, think on these things [Philippians 4:8].

Darrell Gibson loves radio, and he loves Jesus. And he's not alone. In the United States today, there are thousands more like him.

For the oldest electronic medium, the 1990s were a turbulent time. As the decade began, the commercial radio industry faced its greatest financial peril since the 1950s, when the combined forces of the loss of network programming, audience erosion to television, and the rapid expansion of new radio stations forced survival strategies based on smaller audiences and smaller slices of a declining advertising pie. By 1990, once again there were too many radio stations, too little advertising revenue to support them, and too much debt leveraged against those revenues. The crisis was especially acute with AM stations whose share of the total audience dropped below 20 percent, clustered mainly in the older demographics not favored by advertisers. The decade saw the number of AM licenses drop for the first time ever. At one point, the FCC was concerned that it was unable to keep track of all the AMs that were going dark.

The situation for FM stations was little better. Overall, in 1995, the National Association of Broadcasters (NAB) estimated that one-third of all the commercial radio stations in the U.S. were effectively bankrupt, another third existing hand to mouth. To cope with the economic realities, the FCC begrudgingly allowed numerous Local Marketing Agreements (LMAs) whereby a struggling broadcaster would lease his station to a stronger competitor. By combining operation function to lower costs and utilizing superior management and marketing skills, the competitor turned the struggling station around and paid its owner a monthly fee. Although LMAs became common, they presented regulatory issues for the FCC. If there were rule violations, it was unclear whether the commission should take action against the owner who held the license or the operator who did not. And there was the philosophical problem that

LMAs concentrated more control and power in local radio markets in fewer hands.

Nevertheless, the FCC put up with the LMA situation until the Telecommunications Act of 1996 allowed it to remove ownership caps nationally and change the rules so that owners could have multiple licenses (up to eight in the larger markets) in the same community. This brought on an unprecedented wave of consolidation as companies like Clear Channel Communications, Viacom, Citadel Communications, Cumulus Media and others jumped at the opportunity to expand and grab control of individual radio markets, often moving vertically into related businesses like outdoor advertising and concert venues as well. Consolidation brought financial stability to the radio industry for the first time since the Golden Era, but economic progress came at the expense of live, local programming.

The way to dominate an individual radio market is to develop program formats that appeal to the key demographic groups sought by advertisers. The large groups have distinct advantages. They can pay top dollar for on-air personalities who cut daily voice tracks to appear on stations in several markets, thus spreading the expense. They can maintain an extensive programming research staff that develops programming, playlists, and new personalities for all stations in the group. They can make big deals directly with the music conglomerates to assure that artists get maximum exposure. And they, or their national representatives, can negotiate shares of all major advertising buys.

The big guys quickly staked their claims to the "monster" formats — adult contemporary, contemporary hit radio, country, news/talk, classic rock, and urban contemporary. In the large and medium radio markets, the big groups own these formats and audiences. The downside is franchised programming — the same thing in every city — that is not especially innovative. This formula approach to commercial radio has limited appeal to younger listeners. Although the total radio audience remained strong throughout the 1990s, commercial radio's share of Average Persons Rating (APR), a measure of listener loyalty, declined nearly 17 percent, most precipitously among teenagers and young adults. Many of these listeners were choosing public and other non-commercial radio stations, but many were gravitating to the Internet, video games, and other media alternatives.[2]

Commercial radio fought this trend by experimenting with boutique

formats like smooth jazz, new age, and triple A (adult acoustic alternative). For the mammoths, these promised to add a few more share points
to the total. For the broadcasters who tried to compete with them, they
could be a way to reach alternative audiences who didn't like the homog-
enized monster formats. Although each of these came forth with plenty
of promotional hype, the audience was not interested. As of 2003 there
were only 8 smooth jazz, 35 new age, and 69 triple A stations still
around.[3]

   Nevertheless, in the early 21st century, despite some problems, the
mainstream radio industry in the U.S. is healthy. Moreover, as table 1
indicates, the total number of radio stations continues to grow, as it has
in the past 30 years. The most substantial spurt has happened since the
Telecommunications Act of 1996 when more than 1,700 new radio stations

TABLE 1
RADIO STATION GROWTH, 1973–2002

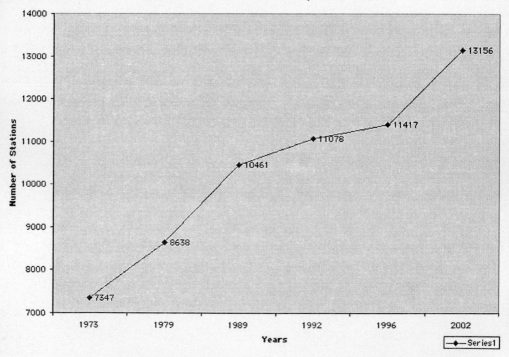

Table 1 created from information in *Broadcasting Yearbook* 1973 and 1979, and
Broadcasting and Cable Yearbook 1989, 1992, 1996 and 2002–2003.

have signed on. But most of these new stations do not fit the traditional molds of commercial and non-commercial radio. They are part of a current phenomenon called Christian radio, and it is moving rapidly from the backwaters into the mainstream.

For the purpose of this study, all radio stations that define their formats or are classified by Arbitron and other radio industry sources as Christian, Contemporary Christian, Christian Hit Radio, Christian News/Talk, Gospel, Southern Gospel, Inspirational, and Religious are lumped together as Christian radio. There is substantial discussion below about the meaning and value of these various format labels.

As an alternative to radio-as-usual, Christian radio is booming. As table 2 indicates, there are now more than 2,500 stations across the nation with Christian, religious, gospel, or inspirational formats. Most of them

TABLE 2
CHRISTIAN RADIO STATION GROWTH, 1973–2002

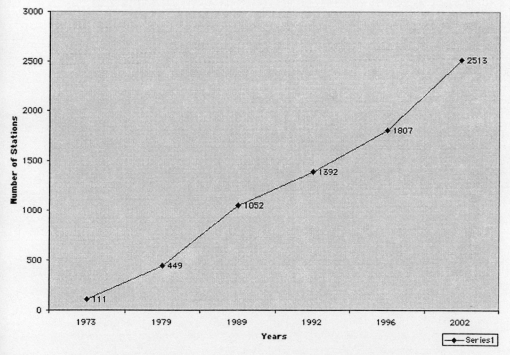

Table 2 created from information in *Broadcasting Yearbook* 1973 and 1979, and *Broadcasting and Cable Yearbook* 1989, 1992, 1996 and 2002–2003.

were not on the air in 1989. That's more than the total number of radio stations that program most of the monster formats. And while the growth in the number of Christian radio stations has paralleled the trend in the radio industry as a whole, table 3 shows that proportionally this expansion is even more impressive. Clearly, Christian radio has characteristics that suggest a mainstream media phenomenon. Yet it is one that people in the radio industry in general, even within the subset of religious broadcasters, do not fully understand.

Many Christian radio stations are low power, and so far audience growth has not kept pace with the explosion of new stations. But there are signs that this is changing. The Barna Group estimates that more than half of adult American radio listeners (109 million people) tune into Christian radio programs each week, but many of these shows air on

TABLE 3
CHRISTIAN RADIO STATIONS AS PERCENTAGE
OF ALL RADIO STATIONS, 1973–2002

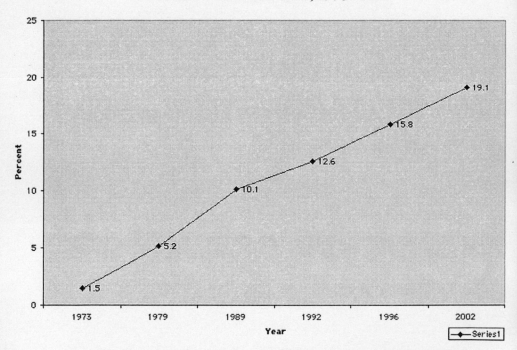

Table 3 created from information in *Broadcasting Yearbook* 1973 and 1979, and *Broadcasting and Cable Yearbook* 1989, 1992, 1996 and 2002–2003.

commercial radio stations that have various formats. The same study claims that 43 percent of the adult audience listens to stations that play Christian music, one of the fastest growing categories in the music industry. Slightly fewer listeners tune into traditional teaching and preaching, inspirational, and news/talk shows. Audience penetration is highest in the South and Midwest, among Protestants, and in African American households.[4]

Other audience estimates, measuring only listeners to radio stations that have Christian religious formats, are more conservative. Arbitron states that these stations have 557,200 listeners at any time, 6:00 A.M.– Midnight, seven days a week. Although the numbers look small, this is a larger audience than better-known formats like Soft Adult Contemporary, Middle-of-the-Road, Album-Oriented Rock (AOR), and All News. And the Christian radio audience has grown by 38 percent since 1998, while many other formats are in decline. The most significant growth for Christian radio has been in the ages 12–17 web-surfing and video-game-playing demographic, which has doubled in the time period.[5] Table 4 charts this audience growth among young and middle-aged adults, adult women and teenagers.

The average quarter hour share, stated in percentage of the total audience that is tuned into all radio stations is a measure of listener loyalty. This table uses the results of the winter Arbitron surveys, when radio listening tends to be the highest, and the broadest possible day part,

TABLE 4
CHRISTIAN RADIO AUDIENCE GROWTH, 1999–2004
ARBITRON WINTER ESTIMATES, MON.–SUN.,
6:00 A.M.–MIDNIGHT, TOTAL U.S. AQR SHARE

Demo	1999	2000	2001	2002	2003	2004
Adults 25–54	2.1	2.5	2.6	2.7	3.0	3.1
Adults 25–34	1.6	1.9	1.9	1.9	2.2	2.3
Adults 35–44	2.4	2.8	2.7	3.1	3.2	3.4
Women 25–34	1.9	2.6	2.5	2.7	3.0	2.8
Women 35–44	3.0	3.7	3.6	4.1	4.2	4.5
Teens	0.9	1.2	1.3	1.8	1.8	1.9

Table 4 created from information taken from www.arbitron.com

essentially sign on to sign off. Although the shares are not as large as the number of Christian radio stations would suggest or as station operators would like, the audience growth is substantial in all of these target demographic groups. This is an encouraging trend.

There's probably a lingering stereotype that the Christian radio audience is mostly old women, but analysis of audience data dispute that supposition. While the Christian radio audience is 65 percent female, only 18 percent is in the 65-plus age demo. Further analysis reveals surprising strength among younger listeners. The largest audience group is ages 35–44, at 21 percent, with slightly more men than women. Teens and young adults ages 18–34 now comprise a quarter of the total audience. In these younger demographics, women lead men by a considerable margin. In all, Christian radio has a 5.2 Average Quarter Hour (AQH) share of radio listeners ages 12 and older. That share is highest in morning drive time (6:00–10:00 A.M.) during the week, but remarkably stable across all weekday dayparts, indicating substantial listener loyalty to individual favorite stations. The number of Christian radio listeners grows by more than 10 percent on the weekends. The highest shares are in the South Atlantic and South Central regions of the United States, basically from Maryland, West Virginia and Kentucky across the south to Texas. But there are also higher than average shares in the Midwest and Great Plains states.[6]

Recently, contemporary Christian–formatted stations have moved past traditional religious stations to become the top Christian radio format. Two-thirds of the audience for stations that program contemporary Christian music are under age 45 with significant growth since 1998 in girls ages 12–17 and men ages 35–44. A new music format, Christian hit radio, is proving even more successful with women ages 18–34 in radio markets as large as Houston and Dallas, Texas.[7] This younger audience is the dynamic force behind the growth of Christian radio in the United States. Whether they seek encouragement, enlightenment, companionship, an oasis in the radio desert of sameness and smut, or good music with inspirational lyrics, an expression of faith is part of their media experience. All radio listeners have emotional attachments to their favorite stations. It's what makes radio work. But this audience has a double dose of loyalty.

Black radio listeners are an interesting subset of the larger Christian radio audience. Christian radio reaches more than 11 percent of black radio listeners, with distinct preferences for stations with Gospel music or traditional religious formats. They listen an average of 11 hours per week. While the entire black audience for Christian radio skews older than the white and total American audiences, nearly two-thirds of the female listeners are age 44 or under. Among black females, who make up 70 percent of the audience, Christian radio is the second most popular format.[8]

Although its current manifestation seems miraculous, Christian radio has been around almost as long as the medium has. Of the 709 initial station licenses issued by the Federal Radio Commission (FRC), churches, Christian organizations, and Christian schools held 60.[9] Many of these early licensees, however, fell by the wayside, victims of the budgetary woes of the Great Depression and regulatory policies that favored commercial broadcasters. But Christian radio programs, both network and local, and the evangelists who hosted them, sustained by donations from their audiences, remained popular. So did gospel music among African American and rural Southern and Midwestern white listeners. Commercial radio stations saw paid religion alternately as sustaining programming for times when listening levels were low and as sources of income when advertisers were unlikely to buy time.[10]

In the 1970s, social, political, technical, and demographic trends provided Christian radio with new audiences, and opportunities. By the next decade, it surfaced from the fringes of radio and advanced to become the industry's fastest-growing segment today. With the growing number of Christian stations came new sources of programming, format concepts, networks, and business models. The first few chapters chart this remarkable history.

After that, there is a detailed look at the operations of several Christian radio businesses. They range in size from more than 200 stations to just a handful. There are some of the oldest Christian broadcasters, one that is controversial because of its political interests, and many with fresh programming concepts that take a contemporary spin on an evangelical mission. Most are non-profit and non-commercial, but one is a profitable corporation whose stock is listed on the NASDAQ. Their objectives are similar, but their approaches uniquely different. While these case studies cannot cover the breadth and depth of the subject, they can provide insight into the variety, energy, and faith that define Christian radio today, and demonstrate that Good News can also be good radio.

In the process, this study attempts to answer several pertinent questions: What is Christian radio? How did it develop into what it is today? How has the mission of Christian radio changed over time? What people and organizations are responsible for this development? Why is the growth in Christian radio happening now? Is Christian radio a momentary fad or an important trend for the mainstream radio business? Where is Christian radio headed in the future?

The story begins in the early days of the radio era.

2. Sowing the Seeds

It probably began in Lawrenceburg, a quiet, unassuming town in middle Tennessee, near the Alabama line. It's a place where they hold beautiful baby contests on the courthouse square. Davy Crockett lived in Lawrenceburg when the citizens of Tennessee elected the colorful frontiersman to Congress. And James David Vaughan moved there in 1902 to work as a clerk for his cousin, the Lawrence County register of deeds. But Vaughan had more lofty aspirations.[1]

A native of nearby Giles County, James David Vaughan showed early promise as an educator. He taught school for a while in middle Tennessee, then moved to Cisco, Texas, in 1890 where his uncle, a Methodist minister, helped him find a new position. Vaughan flourished in the new environment until a cyclone wiped out the town and forced him and his family to return to Tennessee. He quickly found a job and rose through the ranks of public education to become a school principal before he changed careers.

But it was Vaughan's love of shape-note singing, the forerunner of southern gospel, that led him to start the James D. Vaughan Music Company, an enterprise that became his full-time occupation by 1905. From his childhood, Vaughan had evidenced an aptitude for singing, a popular family activity. He attended two sessions of a traveling 10-day singing school conducted by the popular Ruebush-Keiffer Company, a powerful gospel music publishing house from Dayton, Virginia. By 1882, Vaughan combined his musical talents with his developing skills as an educator and started his own singing school at the local church. To publicize his school, he organized a family gospel quartet to appear at other area churches and social gatherings.

In the late 19th century, most gospel music companies used education as their primary marketing mechanism. They organized traveling singing schools, like the one Vaughan attended, to encourage interest in performing the music that they published. In addition, they established residential schools, called normals, where church choir directors and individuals could get more extensive training in shape-note harmony. The music companies often persuaded students to return to the schools for more advanced studies and updates on the latest songs. About the time that Vaughan got involved, a new promotional possibility emerged. Throughout the South, rural Midwest, and Southwest, evangelists were drawing large crowds to tent revivals and singing conventions. Vaughan and others correctly perceived that performing their compositions at such events would be a good way to publicize and sell the songbooks. The quartet proved to be the most cost-efficient–sized group to showcase the rich harmony.

While he was in Texas, Vaughan met Ephraim Timothy Hildebrand, a music publisher and teacher from Virginia, and attended one of Hildebrand's advanced normals. Hildebrand encouraged Vaughan to begin writing gospel songs and helped him get the first ones published. After he returned to Tennessee, Vaughan continued singing and writing, and by 1900 had enough of his own compositions to publish his first songbook, *Gospel Chimes*. It went into a second edition, and Vaughan followed it with five others. In 1910, with sales of 60,000 books a year, he put his first Vaughan Gospel Quartet on the road. Then he established the Vaughan Normal School of Music in Lawrenceburg and began publishing a monthly magazine, *The Musical Visitor*, which quickly grew to over 5,000 subscribers.

Vaughan's love of the music, business acumen, and flair for promotion paid off. Sales of his 1915 songbook *Crown Carol* topped 100,000. There were multiple Vaughan Quartets touring the heartland. The normal school increased its term from four to six weeks and then to two sessions a year. Former students sold Vaughan songbooks and subscriptions to *The Musical Visitor* as they worked the circuit of rural singing schools. In 1920, Vaughan changed the name of the school to The Vaughan Conservatory of Music and Bible Institute to emphasize evangelical work as well as continuing musical education and lengthened the term to five months.

Vaughan knew that marketing was the key to his success and was willing to try new technologies to advance his ideal of using music to spread the Christian gospel throughout rural America. He launched Vaughan Phonograph Records in 1921 to introduce his music to a wider audience. He promoted the records in the magazine, by then *Vaughan's Family Visitor*, and at performances of the Vaughan Quartets. This enterprise continued until 1935 when decline in sales brought on by the Great Depression made this form of promotion less attractive.

Vaughan's next media foray was radio, and here his activity is relevant to this narrative. A friend from Lawrenceburg who had been in the Army Signal Corps during World War I convinced Vaughan to apply for a broadcasting license from the U.S. Department of Commerce in 1922. In early 1923, WOAN in Lawrenceburg, Tennessee, signed on the air at 150 watts. Like many other early radio stations, WOAN changed frequencies and output power several times. Eventually, the station increased power to 500 watts and occupied the advantageous 600-kHz slot on the AM dial. With few radio stations on the air to interfere with its signal initially, WOAN had surprising nighttime coverage, and soon was getting mail from as far away as California and Canada. The license was non-commercial because Vaughan saw WOAN as a public educational service and as a vehicle to feature his music publications and school, expose them to a wider audience, and increase songbook sales.

The programming emphasis was, understandably, southern gospel music. Although Vaughan himself and members of the Vaughan School faculty taught Bible lessons, the majority of the airtime was devoted to performances by the various Vaughan Quartets, students and instructors from the school, and the 12-piece WOAN orchestra. Selections ranged from hymns and other inspirational music to old favorites from the Vaughan songbooks to the latest compositions that would be published in the next volumes.

Ultimately, WOAN did not prove as effective a marketing tool for the Vaughan Music Company as the direct sales approach did. More radio stations on the air meant more interference that limited nighttime coverage. By the end of the decade, it was also clear that a non-commercial radio station in a small town, unaffiliated with any network, was not economically viable on its own. Vaughan sold the station in 1929 to a group that changed the license to a commercial one and moved the transmitter to Memphis. Although WOAN was not a successful venture, James David Vaughan correctly foresaw the important symbiotic relationship between radio and music — in which popular music attracts listeners and listeners get to sample new music that they may want to buy — that ultimately became the driving force in the radio business, and the programming strategy that would bring many new listeners to Christian radio by the end of the 20th century.

In the early days, no one really knew what radio would turn out to be. Large technology-based companies like Westinghouse, AT&T, RCA, and Crosley developed a national business model, while retailers, insurance companies, and publishers saw the new medium as a promotional tool to exploit local markets. With the exception of AT&T's brief attempt at subscription service, their model was based on selling enough advertising time to pay the bills and earn profits. Meanwhile, educators, religious organizations, and labor unions argued that some channels should be reserved for non-commercial public service broadcasting. And government oversight was uncertain at best. In the 15 years after World War I, regulatory responsibility for radio passed from the U.S. Navy to the Department of Commerce to the FRC and finally to the FCC in 1932. By then, radio's chaotic survival-of-the-fittest era had ended. Those left standing included commercial broadcasters with powerful stations in cities and the national networks that owned or were affiliated with those stations. Educational and religious broadcasters were relegated to the fringes of the radio industry.[2]

This period was important for Christian radio, however, because the people involved with it created two operations models that remained viable for subsequent generations. The first model, station and network programming strategies, eventually became the archetype for today's Christian radio business. But the development of policies regarding religious broadcasting by networks, stations, and the FCC and the economic climate of the 1930s effectively curtailed the expansion of Christian radio stations. Determined to fulfill their mission of establishing a ministry of the airwaves, Christian broadcasters bought whatever blocks of time were available to them and asked their listeners for donations to support the effort. These evangelists who appeared on the radio networks and local and regional stations were by far the most successful Christian radio pioneers. They created the blueprint for their successors, on both radio and television, and fixed the image of their profession in American popular culture.

Early Christian Radio Stations

In December 1921, the Church of the Covenant in Washington, D.C., received the first radio broadcast license issued to a religious organization. Early the next year the Calvary Baptist Church, one of New York City's oldest congregations, began radio broadcasts with a 250-watt transmitter. Pastor John Roach Stratton expounded on his objectives: "I shall try to continue doing my part ... tearing down the strongholds of Satan, and I hope that our radio system will prove so efficient that when I twist the Devil's tail in New York, his squawk will be heard across the continent."[3]

By 1923, 10 churches and Christian organizations were operating radio stations. There are various estimates of the number of licenses issued to Christian radio stations in the 1920s. The accounting is complicated somewhat by the practice of sharing frequencies with other broadcasters in the same city. In 1928, the FRC listed 60 Christian radio licensees, most of them evangelical churches, especially Baptist. Few were full time, and the channels and output power allocations made it difficult for these operations to reach large audiences.[4] Among the notable early Christian radio stations were:

1922　WCAL: St. Olaf College, a Lutheran school in Northfield, Minnesota. St.Olaf's continues its radio operations today on WCAL-FM, which signed on in 1968. The college ceased broadcasts on the original AM frequency several years ago.

1923　KFSG: International Church of the Foursquare Gospel, Los Angeles, California. KFSG was the radio base for evangelist Aimee Semple McPherson. Her story follows.

1924　WWBL: Grace Covenant Presbyterian Church, Richmond, Virginia. WWBL continued operations until the early 1980s.

1924　KPPC: Pasadena Presbyterian Church, Pasadena, California. KPPC is still on the air, but its current owner no longer has a Christian format.

1924　KFUO: Missouri Synod of the American Lutheran Church, Clayton (St. Louis), Missouri. KFUO was the brainchild of evangelist Walter Maier and was operated by Concordia Seminary. It added KFUO FM in 1948. Both are still on the air.

1926   WMBI: Moody Bible Institute, Chicago, Illinois. WMBI and WMBI-FM (which signed on in 1960) continue operations today as the foundation of the Moody Radio Network, described in a later chapter. The stations also serve as training facilities for students at the Institute.

1927   KPOF: Pillar of Fire, Denver, Colorado. The fundamentalist denomination continues to operate KPOF today.

1927   KFGQ, Boone Biblical Ministries, Boone, Iowa. KFGQ and KFGQ-FM (which signed on in 1950) continue to operate as outreach services of Boone Biblical College. KFGQ has the historical distinction of employing Lois Crawford, who received the first FCC operator's license issued to a woman, in 1927.[5]

Although regulatory and commercial broadcasting policies did not encourage Christian broadcasters to continue station operations, probably the dire economic conditions of the Great Depression did the most damage. The mainstream churches could no longer afford full-time radio ministries. Most of the evangelists had already decided that producing individual programs funded by donations from listeners made more financial sense. By placing these on powerful radio stations and networks with established audiences, they could reach more people at less cost. So interest in Christian radio stations dwindled in the 1930s. By 1933, half of the original 60 licensees remained on the air, and only 12 survived into the 1980s.[6] But by then, social, political, technological, and cultural changes in America afforded Christian radio broadcasters a new opportunity to try station operations again.

Regulations and Network Policies

In the 1920s, Americans were more concerned about the effects of propaganda campaigns than they are today. World War I and the Bolshevik Revolution were still fresh memories. At home, there had been violent labor disputes. Using the media to distort public opinion and foster unrest was a common technique in all these events. When the FRC began establishing the criteria for proper programming by licensees, it favored the interests of the broad, general public over those of small groups, like labor unions, political parties, and religious organizations.

In the latter category, the FRC was especially concerned about evangelists like Father Charles Coughlin (described at length later in the chapter) who spewed anti–Semitic and/or anti–Catholic rhetoric and used their electronic pulpits for political diatribes. Although these radio preachers were in the minority, both then and now, the mere existence of that behavior led the FRC to classify many Christian radio stations as propaganda outlets. Instead, the commission favored a "well-rounded program to best serve the public. In such a scheme, there is no room for the operation of broadcasting stations exclusively by or in the private interests of individuals or groups. As a general rule, particular doctrines, creeds or beliefs must find their way into the market of ideas by the existing public-service stations."[7] In 1929, the FRC effectively ceased issuing licenses to religious groups.

The other shoe dropped for Christian Radio broadcasters when the FRC and its successor, the FCC, refused to support channels reserved for public service stations. Educators and Midwest land-grant universities advanced the argument for reserved channels. But commercial broadcasters countered with general promises of free sustaining time for educational programs. This split the educational radio lobby into two groups — one that wanted separate non-commercial channels and one that sided with the commercial stations and networks. In addition to this philosophical division, neither group had a clear programming strategy. By 1933, the fight was over. The FCC established an allocation policy that favored commercial broadcasters.[8]

So educational and religious broadcasters were for the most part at the mercy of commercial radio. Although religious programming was an option to fulfill FCC-mandated public service requirements, in practice most stations only offered such sustaining time in periods when there weren't many people listening. Most evangelicals decided to buy blocks of program time in better dayparts, produce their own programs, and solicit donations from listeners to support their ministry. Many learned that this practice was more effective, less costly, and subject to less government intrusion than radio station operations.

NBC, the dominant radio network, was the first to deny access to evangelicals for paid time broadcasts, but CBS and many affiliates of both networks soon adopted the same policies. NBC decided to offer free airtime to non-sectarian and non-denominational broadcasts that avoided indoctrination and controversial subjects. Further, the network only offered the airtime to the "central or national agencies of great religious faiths, as for example, the Roman Catholics, the Protestants, and the Jews, as distinguished from individual churches or small group movements."[9] NBC formed a Religious Activities Committee, consisting of representatives from the Federal (later National) Council of Churches, the National Council of Catholic Men, and the Jewish Theological Seminary in America, to oversee the policy. This led to mildly spiritual and non-controversial programs like *The National Radio Pulpit* and *The Catholic Hour*. Since few evangelical churches belonged to the Protestant Federal Council, they were effectively eliminated from consideration.

The Scopes trial of 1925 had showcased the fundamentalist Christian movement as distinctly anti-modern and marginalized evangelical Christians. The NBC and CBS policies on religious broadcasts moved them further to the fringes. And the networks' collusion with the Federal Council of Churches drove a larger wedge between the "liberal" mainstream Protestant denominations and the "conservative" fundamentalists, evangelicals, and Pentecostals.[10] But NBC and CBS did not totally control the radio industry. By the 1930s, large cities had many radio stations not affiliated with either network. And when the fledgling Mutual Radio Network came along in 1935, it welcomed the business from evangelical preachers. Within a few years, Mutual earned more that a quarter of its income from those accounts. When Mutual changed its policy and began to phase out these programs after 1945, the new ABC Radio Network came along to pick some of them up.[11]

Paid-time Christian radio programs in popular dayparts were quite common until the U.S. economy began to expand after World War II, and with it advertising revenues for radio stations. As stations became more prosperous, they needed the income from radio evangelists less. In the 1950s, the creation of format radio made these programs less desirable still. Format radio promised the listeners consistent programming targeted directly at their tastes, usually based on popular music. It was contrary to the "something for everybody" block-programming strategy of network radio, and later network television. Individual programs were not as important as continuity. The point was to create a program flow that encouraged listeners to stay tuned to only one radio station. Whether the music was pop, country, rock, or middle-of-the-road, preachers interrupted the flow. Many stations cancelled these programs outright, while others restricted the blocks available for them. But there were also many new radio stations going on the air, mostly in small towns, that were hungry for business. So it was still possible for an enterprising radio evangelist to cobble together a "network" of stations.

The Radio Evangelists

Early radio pioneer Reginald Fessenden was also the first Christian broadcaster. On Christmas Eve 1906, he tested his new voice transmitter at Brant Rock, Massachusetts, by reading the Christmas story from the Gospel of Luke. Following the scripture, Fessenden's wife sang Handel's "Largo" from *The Messiah* and the inventor played "O Holy Night" on the violin. Ship's radio operators all up and down the East Coast, monitoring the air for Morse code signals, were astonished at what they heard.[12]

As far as we know, the first complete religious broadcast originated from Calvary Episcopal Church in Pittsburgh, Pennsylvania, on January 2, 1921. Westinghouse station KDKA had been on the air about two months. A station engineer who sang in the church choir convinced the manager and his pastor that broadcasting the first Sunday evening vespers of the New Year would be an appropriate program. The Rev. Lewis B. Whittemore conducted the service and thus became the first Christian broadcaster.[13] Since that event, remote broadcasts of church services from mainstream denominations have been a significant component of Christian radio programming, especially on commercial stations.

Since the evangelical movement of the late 19th century, stem-winding, fire-and-brimstone preachers had been part of American culture. Tent revivals, camp meetings, and similar gatherings were important events that drew large crowds in cities and small towns alike. The movement also established many common social institutions like Sunday school and chautauquas. As radio became popular, many revival preachers tried out the new medium, some, like former baseball star Billy Sunday, who used radio near the end of his life. His sermons were colorful, fervent and memorable. "America didn't need repeal; she needed repentance. She didn't need rum; she needed righteousness. We don't need jags; we need Jesus," he preached in an early broadcast on Chicago's WMBI.[14] But Sunday and other itinerant preachers used radio primarily as an adjunct to and a promotional device for personal appearances. Other evangelists, however, found a new mission for radio — a miraculous invention that would allow them to create an electronic church without walls, spreading the gospel to millions at one time.

PAUL RADER

In Chicago, evangelist Paul Rader, pastor of the Chicago Gospel Tabernacle, accepted an invitation from the mayor to preach a sermon on the city's radio station sometime during the summer of 1922. Rader soon realized radio's potential to spread his fundamentalist message. He arranged to use the idle transmitter of WBBM for fourteen hours each Sunday, where he set up his own radio "station" WJBT (Where Jesus Blesses Thousands). Rader broadcast live from the Tabernacle, complete with hymns, gospel songs, and inspirational music performed by the orchestra and choir, and dramatized Bible stories. Soon Rader was attracting large audiences to his own church and to the many crusades that he led throughout the United States. His popular broadcasts were on all Chicago stations. In 1931, he created the daily network program *Breakfast Brigade* for CBS. Rader's programming was non-denominational, evangelical, fundamentalist, and entertaining — a significant concept for Christian radio. And it was popular. In 1932, Rader's Gospel Tabernacle sent out more than 250,000 pieces of literature to radio listeners. By the early years of the Great Depression, Rader was spending up to $1,700 per week to purchase radio time, an expense his ministry was having difficulty meeting.[15]

Paul Rader was a burly, athletic evangelist who spoke in plain language that his audience could understand. Radio suited his friendly and personal masculine style. He often acted out conversations with non-believers:

> Here is someone that says, "I am so lonely."
> "Say, Buddy, wake up, don't you know there is such a thing as a radio? Some of your neighbors hear all of the day long singing and preaching, stock reports and the like."
> "Well, I did hear about that, but I don't know, I don't pay enough attention to it. You know, I intend to some of these days, but I am just so lonesome and I don't hear anything."
> "Stop your false fears. You could have had a radio and you didn't get it."

"I did not know whether it would work."

"What do you suppose all the rest of the folks did?"

There are some of you folks who have no radio in your heart. You could have heard glorious harmonies from heaven. In your bosom God's pipe organ of grace could have been playing.... He's not going to let you stand there and bawl and cry, as an excuse, "Oh, Lord. I was so lonesome, so discouraged. The devil fought me so hard. Oh Lord, it was so dark."

Won't you yield here and kneel here and say, "Lord, you are calling me to this deeper fellowship and I will come."[16]

Rader's most important contribution to Christian radio was probably his influence on a group of young preachers who followed him into radio evangelism. Clarence Jones was one such disciple. He and partner Reuben Larson founded the World Radio Missionary Fellowship and went to Ecuador in 1931 to put shortwave station HCJB on the air with an antenna high in the Andes, near the equator. Today HCJB and its affiliated, AM and FM stations can reach more than 90 percent of the world's population.[17]

CHARLES FULLER

Another Rader admirer was Charles Fuller, who gave up his business career after he heard Rader preach in 1916. Fuller entered the Bible Institute of Los Angeles (Biola College) to train for the ministry, made his first radio broadcast and began teaching Bible lessons over the school's radio station in 1923, and founded a Presbyterian church in Placentia, California. After his ordination in 1925, he created the non-denominational Calvary Church and quickly started a radio ministry.[18]

By 1933, Fuller's weekly broadcasts on KGER in Long Beach attracted wide audiences on the West Coast, but the elders in his church considered them inappropriate. Fuller resigned as pastor and took up radio evangelism full time with a non-profit corporation, the Gospel Broadcasting Association. He created the weekly *Radio Revival Hour*, later renamed the *Old-Fashioned Revival Hour*, and moved to clear channel KNX in Los Angeles. In 1937, Fuller went national on Mutual, and within a few years was the network's best customer with a tab of more than $1.5 million a year, all paid by donations from listeners.[19]

On the strength of his Mutual Network broadcasts, Fuller became a nationally recognized religious leader with a following of millions of listeners. Fuller's evangelism was very effective. He stressed the voluntary acceptance of Christ. Although he preached against evil and played on the audience's guilty conscience, he offered friendly advice rather than the threat of damnation. His message and soothing delivery offered hope and went over well with Americans during the Great Depression. Young broadcast evangelists like Billy Graham and Jerry Falwell emulated Fuller's presentation style and carried his message onward.[20]

Dr. Walter Maier

When Dr. Walter Maier addressed a convention of young Lutherans in Louisville, Kentucky, in 1922, a local radio station broadcast the event. He was so impressed with the numerous favorable comments from listeners that he convinced the Missouri Lutheran Synod to start a radio station at Concordia Seminary in St. Louis. After KFUO (Keep Forward Upward Onward) signed on in December 1924, Maier devoted his life to spreading the message of Christianity through this miraculous medium. By 1930, he was ready to create a weekly network program called *The Lutheran Hour*. But he encountered obstacles with new broadcast policies.[21]

Maier first approached NBC, the largest radio network, with an offer to purchase time for his program. The network countered with an offer of free sustaining time, provided that he paid his own production costs, and that the messages be non-sectarian, free of doctrine and controversy. Maier's offer was caught up in two struggles. First was the ongoing tussle between liberals and conservatives over the correct approach to Christianity. The second was the desire of radio broadcasters to attract large audiences for advertisers, which often meant compromises for producers whose programs might be considered offensive. As explained previously, NBC opted not to sell time to the conservatives, but to include religious programs during sustaining time, when audiences were too small to attract advertisers or on Sundays when many advertisers did not find it appropriate to purchase time.[22]

Barred from NBC, Maier took his program to CBS, which continued to sell time for religious broadcast for another five years. At a cost of $200,000 a year, Maier purchased the hour immediately following the popular mystery series *The Shadow* on Thursday night, and *The Lutheran*

Hour debuted on October 2, 1930, from the studios of WHK, Cleveland. Maier was the principal speaker, with musical interludes from the Cleveland Bach Chorus. In 1935, the program moved to Mutual and began origination from KFUO. Maier also convinced General Motors to underwrite the broadcasts that now had a substantial audience. In 1939, he began to syndicate the program on transcription to individual radio stations and initiated worldwide shortwave service. At its peak, *The Lutheran Hour* had more than 10 million listeners in the United States alone. At one time, Maier got more fan mail than *Amos 'n' Andy*.[23]

Maier's secret was that he concentrated on the message of his sermons with a low-key approach unlike most Christian radio personalities of the era. Although his approach to Christianity was close to the conservative evangelicals, he was carefully non-denominational and inclusive. Over time, donations to *The Lutheran Hour* broadcasts made it possible for the Missouri Synod to create other radio programs and branch out into television.

Aimee Semple McPherson

In contrast to the self-effacing Walter Maier, Aimee Semple McPherson was perhaps the most flamboyant radio evangelist in the history of the medium. A licensed Baptist and Assemblies of God minister, McPherson founded the fundamentalist International Church of the Foursquare Gospel in Los Angeles, California, in 1923. Already famous as a powerful preacher, a highly effective evangelist and fundraiser, and motivator, McPherson competed successfully with Hollywood in the show business world of Southern California. Services at her Angelus Temple were pure theater with staged revues, outlandish costumes and skits, a full orchestra, and of course the star of the show, Aimee Semple McPherson, healing the sick and preaching the gospel.[24]

Radio was a natural extension of McPherson's ministry and the medium that made her both famous and infamous. She first preached on radio at a revival in Oakland, California, in 1922, then delivered occasional sermons over KHJ in Los Angeles. When she founded her church, McPherson also applied for and received the third radio license issued in Los Angeles — KFSG for Kall Foursquare Gospel — and built the station with donations from live audiences and subscribers to her magazine *Bridal Call*. To McPherson radio was

like some fantastic dream! Like a visionary tale from the Arabian Nights!
Like an imaginary fairy tale is the Story of Radio. These are the days
of invention! The days when the impossible has become possible! Days
more favorable than any that ever have been known for the preaching
of the blessed Gospel of our Lord and Saviour, Jesus Christ! Now, the
crowning blessing, the most golden opportunity, the most miraculous
conveyance for the Message has come — The Radio![25]

In the loosely regulated early radio era, KFSG often changed output power and frequency to improve coverage. This practice raised the
ire of the federal government, but McPherson boldly replied to Secretary of Commerce Herbert Hoover's complaint with a telegram: "Please
order your minions of Satan to leave my station alone Stop You cannot
expect the Almighty to abide by your wave length nonsense Stop"[26]

KFSG was unique in the early days of Christian radio because it
originated programming in an extensive schedule around the clock. By
contrast, most of the other radio evangelists of the period, like Paul Rader,
could only afford a few hours a week, devoted primarily to sermons, with
broadcast equipment that was often unreliable. McPherson's signal was
strong and the technology competitive with commercial broadcasters of
the era. The schedule included not only church services but also drama,
entertainment, long blocks of music, and features targeted at specific
audiences like women, children, and African Americans.

By 1926, Aimee Semple McPherson was a legitimate national radio star.
But then she suddenly disappeared, and rumors began that she had drowned.
About a month later, she surfaced, wandering in the desert, the victim of
an alleged kidnapping plot. Believing the incident to be a crude publicity
stunt, authorities in Los Angeles charged McPherson with fraud and tried
to put her on trial. Like the Scopes trial, McPherson's hearing before the
grand jury was the subject of nationwide news broadcasts. The grand jury
found that she had not actually tried to cheat anyone out of any money
and refused to return an indictment. At that point, the district attorney
dropped the charges. McPherson emerged from the incident with her public image bruised but her fame enhanced. Later, more rumors surfaced that
her disappearance was a tryst with an employee, but Sister Aimee never
wavered in her testimony of kidnapping and no evidence materialized to
prove otherwise. In her defense, her life indicates that although she was
fallible, McPherson tended to make her mistakes public and thus present
a human side to her ministry that made it more appealing and effective.[27]

McPherson was a creation of the Roaring Twenties, and her popularity waned during the early years of the Great Depression. She suffered from illness, the breakup of her third marriage, and a parting of ways with her mother and daughter, Roberta, whom she had groomed to be her successor. Throughout this difficult period, she and her son, Rolf, remained close. McPherson staged somewhat of a comeback in 1939 and was on the verge of mounting a television ministry when she died in 1944 from heart failure due to an accidental overdose of sleeping pills.[28]

Although Aimee Semple McPherson was not a traditional role model for a Christian lifestyle, her show-business style became perhaps the most widely copied practice for subsequent evangelists. Her ability to draw and hold crowds, the sophisticated promotional machine that included radio, and the injection of her personality into her ministry were her hallmarks. Even Sister Aimee's funeral was a media event, attracting more than 10,000 mourners to the Angelus Temple. From faith healers like Oral Roberts to the many Charismatic preachers today, you see a little bit of Aimee in every service. In acknowledgement of her contribution, the National Religious Broadcasters inducted Aimee Semple McPherson into its Hall of Fame in 2000.

FATHER CHARLES COUGHLIN

Although McPherson and her escapades were the subject of prurient interest and curiosity, she was not the most controversial or outrageous radio evangelist of the early era. That dubious honor probably belongs to Father Charles Coughlin, a Catholic priest from Michigan who mixed conservative religion with politics and economics in his sermons. By 1930, Coughlin had a spot on CBS, but the network dropped him the next year after he made personal attacks on President Hoover. Moving to an ad hoc network of independent radio stations, Coughlin stepped up his rhetoric to include anti–Semitic remarks and a protracted assault on President Roosevelt, whom he had actively supported in the 1932 election. At his peak, Father Coughlin was receiving a half million dollars in donations from listeners a year, a fantastic sum during the Great Depression. But when he began to speak out in favor of the Nazis during World War II, the NAB censured him, and the Bishop of Detroit ordered Coughlin to cease his broadcasts.[29]

GERALD WINROD AND GERALD L. K. SMITH

Among the fundamentalists who seized the opportunity that radio afforded to reach a larger congregation were Gerald Winrod and Gerald L. K. Smith. Winrod was a full-fledged anti–Semite and anti–Catholic who blamed the Jews for the Great Depression and denounced the New Deal as a Communist plot. He gained some notoriety when he ran for the U.S. Senate in Kansas in 1938, but lost by a wide margin in the Republican primary. Later the Justice Department charged him with "conspiracy to cause insubordination in the armed forces" for his endorsement of Nazi policies, but the case ended in a mistrial.[30]

Smith, a Disciples of Christ preacher, became a devoted follower of Louisiana Governor Huey Long and left his pastorate to get involved in politics. After Long's assassination in 1935, Smith became disillusioned with socialism and turned into a reactionary bigot, much like Winrod. In 1937, Smith moved to Detroit and began Sunday-night broadcasts over the ad hoc radio network that Father Coughlin used. He soon became a mouthpiece for right-wing extremism and a friend of Henry Ford. After an unsuccessful run for the U.S. Senate in 1942, he lapsed into obscurity but continued his anti–Semitic and anti–Communist crusade for another 30 years.[31]

For the public at large, Coughlin, Winrod, and Smith were probably as representative of early Christian radio as the many sincere and legitimate evangelists who used the airwaves in less controversial fashion. In addition, there were a few outright charlatans like Dr. John Romulus Brinkley, who used religious broadcasts among his many schemes to sell worthless medications and surgical procedures.[32] The behavior of this small minority of miscreants made it easy for the radio networks, the NAB, and public policymakers in Congress and at the FCC to discriminate against all Christian radio programming.

Southern Gospel Music

While the radio preachers and evangelists enjoyed a loyal following, their popularity was equaled and perhaps exceeded within the rural heartland of the United States by that of the many singing groups whose music is called southern gospel. James David Vaughan, Virgil Stamps and other songwriters and publishers established these groups, mostly quartets, to tour the region selling songbooks and singing lessons. Despite Vaughan's premature and unsuccessful experiment with a southern gospel radio format, individual quartets performed daily programs on local, regional, and network radio, including early syndication of recorded transcriptions, throughout the 1920s, 1930s, and 1940s. These broadcasts, coupled with the budding recorded-music business, provided a boost to both the sale of songbooks and the musical genre itself.

Most radio in this era was live. A small singing group, accompanied by someone playing the piano that was already in the studio, was a relatively simple and inexpensive production to stage. Although the music was religious, the singers were not evangelists and hence did not provoke the criticism leveled at radio preachers. And the audience liked the music. So radio-station operators had no problem with this variety of Christian radio, especially when it came with lucrative contracts from big advertising accounts. Roy Carter, second-generation member of the Chuck Wagon Gang, explained the appeal of southern gospel music on the radio this way:

> People enjoy and like what they understand. Dad told me one time, "Son, there's 10,000 farmers out there plowing on a plow and listening to a radio ... that sincerely believe that they can sing bass just as good as you can. It's because they understand it. It's simple."[33]

In addition to Vaughan's WOAN in Lawrenceburg, Tennessee, one of the earliest gospel music broadcasts originated in Atlanta, Georgia; Nashville, Tennessee; and Ft. Worth, Texas. WSB in Atlanta had a religious variety program featuring the Jenkins Family as early as 1922 and regularly scheduled other local quartets like Smith's Sacred Singers, who landed a recording contract with Columbia Records after a talent scout heard one of their broadcasts. In 1927, the Vaughan Recording Quartet appeared widely on radio, including broadcasts from Aimee Semple McPherson's Angelus Temple and at the Grand Ole Opry on Nashville's WSM. By the mid–1930s, the group had a daily show on WSM, which like WSB had become a 50,000-watt station.[34]

In 1935, the Carter Quartet successfully auditioned for a spot on 50,000-watt WBAP in Ft. Worth. This quickly became a daily program sponsored by Morton Salt. Although the Carter's were a secular group, they always included at least one gospel song on the program. Soon a new sponsor, Bewley Flour Mills, approached them with an offer. The flour company had a regular group named the Chuck Wagon Gang that played regularly on WBAP and toured the area to promote its products. Bewley needed a second Chuck Wagon Gang to do the live radio show when the first one was on tour. Within a few weeks, the Carters changed their name and sponsor. Slowly they also modified their repertoire to include more gospel music until that was all they performed. The audience soon forgot that they were not the original group, and the Carters' Chuck Wagon Gang became one of the most widely known southern gospel groups, largely due to their exposure on radio.[35]

There were numerous other southern gospel quartets on the radio in the years before World War II. The Stamps-Baxter company alone had groups who performed on KRLD in Dallas, Texas; WMAZ in Macon, Georgia; WAPL in Birmingham, Alabama; KWKH in Shreveport, Louisiana; KRAK in Little Rock, Arkansas; WBBB in Burlington, North Carolina; and KGER in Long Beach, California. The Speer Family, originally associated with James David Vaughan, got their start on WSFA in Montgomery, Alabama, performing daily shows in both the morning and afternoon. The LeFevres were popular on Atlanta's WGST where the NuGrape and Orange Crush Soft Drink Company sponsored their daily broadcast and paid for transcriptions to air on radio stations throughout the South. The Blackwood Brothers Quartet began their radio career at WJDX in Jackson, Mississippi, but soon moved on to 50,000-watt KWKH in Shreveport, where they had both morning and noon daily shows. The Swanee River Boys began on WNOX in Knoxville, Tennessee, moved on to WDOD in Chattanooga, Tennessee, and eventually landed a regular spot on the widely heard WSB Barn Dance from Atlanta.[36]

One of the more interesting gospel groups of the era was the Rangers, who had earlier been called the Texas Rangers Quartet and the Cycling Rangers. The latter title came from a 1936 publicity stunt, sponsored by Montgomery Ward, Justin Boots, and Stetson Hats, where the quartet planned to ride bicycles from Texas to New York and appear on the radio network program *Major Bowe's Amateur Hour*, appearing in concerts along the way. But when they reached Louisville, Kentucky, WHAS offered them a regular spot on the morning farm report. In January 1937, disastrous floods swept through Kentucky, and WHAS became the hub of network broadcasts, a connection that gave the Rangers national exposure.

They moved on to 50,000-watt WBT in Charlotte, North Carolina, where they performed on a morning show twice a week and on a program sponsored by BC Headache Powders for the regional CBS Dixie Network several evenings a week.[37]

By the late 1940s, it was obvious that radio and recorded music were the future for southern gospel music. Radio in particular became more important during the Great Depression when the economic downturn reduced the sales of songbooks and limited the ability of publishers to mount tours and singing conventions and operate singing schools. Once they built a following on radio, either local or regional, the quartets were a bigger draw at concerts and sold more records. But radio also provided competition for the professional quartets that the music publishers supported, as Charles Vaughan, James David's brother, noted:

> A male quartet in the country is not looked upon as it was years ago. Then it was an unfailing attraction that people would pay money to hear sing, because it was rare. Now while people like to hear a good male quartet they can hear one over the radio for nothing and they do not go any great distance out of their way to hear one.[38]

Another popular venue for promoting southern gospel music was the All-Night Sing, a concept that V. O. Stamps had created in the late 1930s as all-night radio broadcasts. By the late 1940s and early 1950s, concert impresarios had turned these gospel songfests into traveling shows featuring the stars of the genre, who were familiar to the audience through their radio performances. Wilmer Nowlin in Texas called his shows the Battle of Songs and urged the audience to come out and give their favorite groups audible support. Wally Fowler in Nashville arranged for radio station WSM to broadcast a few hours of some events live from the Ryman Auditorium, home of the Grand Ole Opry. By the mid–1950s, Fowlers was staging All-Night Sings in up to 200 cities and towns across the South, attracting two million fans a year. Another successful promoter of southern gospel music was the Rev. J. Bazzel Mull of Knoxville, Tennessee. Mull produced a radio program called *The Mull Singing Convention of the Air* and syndicated it on several high-power radio stations throughout the South, and used it to promote his concerts. He attracted top-name talent like the Chuck Wagon Gang to his venues.[39]

These concerts soon replaced singing conventions, singing schools, and songbooks sales as the primary sources of revenue for the gospel groups fortunate enough to make the tours. But the majority of local groups were not included, settling instead for performances at churches and revivals and donations or "love offerings" from the crowd. Southern gospel music gained a loyal following, but the fans were largely regional and rural and of little interest to the larger recording industry. Several gospel groups established modest national reputations by singing backup for country music stars like Eddy Arnold, Red Foley, and Hank Snow. Notable among them were the Jordanaires and J. D. Sumner and the Stamps Quartet, who both sang harmony for Elvis Presley.[40]

While southern gospel was primarily music for a southern white audience, the black gospel music genre was perhaps older and enjoyed just as loyal a following among African Americans. Black gospel music also migrated successfully to the urban areas of the United States as its audience left the South and Southwest to seek better jobs and lives. But other than a few groups like the Golden Gate Quartet, the Dixie Hummingbirds, and the Five Blind Boys of Alabama, most of this music never found its way to radio. Despite its being an underground music phenomenon, black gospel music was a training ground for many artists like Sam Cooke, Aretha Franklin, and Lou Rawls who went on to substantial careers in secular music. Later in the 20th century, black gospel music and artists became more prominent in the music industry.[41]

With the shift to multi-artist venues like All-Night Sings, the nature of southern gospel music changed with some controversial results. The interactivity of the audience-response format, which may have had its roots in the growing Pentecostal movement, created a need for the acts to have more stage presence and visual appeal. They still had to sing with energy and harmony, but the audiences began to react more enthusiastically to the more flamboyant groups like the Statesmen and the Blackwoods. Costumes, lighting, movement on stage, and other theatrical elements of the performance were just as important to the audience, who had, after all, paid to see a show. By the 1970s, gospel groups were dressing in leisure suits and sporting long hair and flashy jewelry, looking very much like any other pop music personalities.[42]

As southern gospel became more entertainment oriented, however, it moved farther from its roots in churches, tent revivals, and singing conventions — too far to suit some fundamentalist Christians who felt the music was losing its focus as a means to spread the Gospel in favor of becoming a worldly activity that pandered to the excesses of popular culture. The popular song "Gospel Boogie," also called "Wonderful Time Up There," by the Homeland Harmony Quartet was an example. It put gospel lyrics to a boogie-woogie piano tune, a musical style associated in the fundamentalists minds with aberrant social and sexual behavior. This debate about the proper role for gospel music continues today and has become more prominent as contemporary Christian music and the Christian radio stations that play it have become mainstream cultural phenomena.

The visual style of southern gospel music lent itself more to the new medium of television than to radio. As television stations went on the air in the South, Southwest, and rural Midwest in the 1950s and videotape technology emerged, promoters like Fowler and Mull soon began to produce syndicated television shows. They found that one weekly television hour or half hour on a Saturday or Sunday could reach as large and audience as multiple radio stations and attract more income from sponsors. So the promoters began to de-emphasize radio. At the same time, more radio stations were moving from block programming strategies that tried to reach different audiences in the various day parts to consistent formats, usually based on popular music and targeted at one or two demographic audiences throughout the day. As with programs from the radio evangelists, fewer radio stations were willing to interrupt their formats to schedule southern gospel music blocks except on time periods like Sunday mornings when there was very little audience. And it was rare that a commercial radio station could survive with a southern gospel music format. By the late 1960s, this genre remained on the radio mainly in syndicated programs, and was generally less prominent than it had been only a decade earlier.[43]

Format radio, however, was advantageous to black gospel music. Beginning in the late 1940s, new radio stations in the South and elsewhere began to target African American listeners. Black gospel music appealed to a large segment of this audience, especially female listeners. So it ended up on the regular play lists for many of these stations, either in rotation with secular music or in separate blocks.

One of the most important artists to emerge from southern gospel music was Bill Gaither. As a child growing up in Indiana, Gaither listened to the Rangers, the Statesmen, the Blackwoods and other gospel groups on the radio and knew he wanted to have a career in music. In the early 1960s, Gaither, his brother Danny and his sister Mary Ann formed a family singing group in Indiana, performing songs that Bill and his wife, Gloria, wrote. Eventually Gloria replaced Mary Ann in the trio, which came to be called simply The Gaither Trio (and was also known as the Gaithers). Unlike other groups, however, the Gaithers were part of a growing movement in the genre that used contemporary idioms and style to return the music to its original evangelistic mission of spreading the Gospel. Instead of preaching, they offered the message through their lyrics. Their music was immensely successful. The 1968 album *Alleluia* sold more than 250,000 copies, and their concerts drew crowds of 10,000 or more, all without the support of a major recording company. Bill Gaither is considered largely responsible for creating the Christian music genre called praise and inspiration, one of the cornerstones of today's contemporary Christian music business and the basis for Christian radio formats.[44]

NRB — National Religious Broadcasters

Part of the challenge for religious conservatives in their quest for better access to the radio airwaves was that their opponents, the liberals, were organized and they were not. Because so many fundamentalist, evangelical, and Pentecostal churches were independent or part of small, loosely structured denominations, it was almost impossible to form a conservative counterpart to the National Council of Churches. Nevertheless, by 1940, as the Mutual Radio Network began to have second thoughts about its policy that permitted paid religion, many Christian radio broadcasters saw the need to mount an organized effort, even if the result was only better communication among each other.

In 1942, fundamentalist preacher Carl McIntire called a convention in St. Louis, the result of which was the formation of the National Association of Evangelicals for United Action (now the NAE). This group was the first to address the plight of Christian radio broadcasters and the discriminatory policies of the FCC and the commercial broadcasting industry. It sought to protect the rights of Christian radio broadcasters to preach whatever the speakers deemed appropriate, to purchase time to do so, and to share the free sustaining time with the liberals.[45]

Two years later, some NAE members invited about 150 Christian radio broadcasters to a conference in Columbus, Ohio, to form a separate organization for their benefit. On April 12, 1944, the conference attendees founded National Religious Broadcasters (NRB). With respected theologian William Ward Ayer as its first chairman, NRB moved quickly to establish a code of ethics that governed program content, technical quality, and financial disclosure and sought to distance NRB members from the charlatans, con artists, and hucksters who existed on the fringes of Christian radio.

In its early years, NRB was most valuable at raising the standards of Christian radio broadcasting and eventually became the legitimate political voice for conservatives and their millions of radio listeners. By the 1950s, NRB was a recognized and influential lobbying group, both in Washington and within the broadcasting industry. By the 1970s, U.S. presidents were giving speeches at NRB conventions.

3. Jesus Christ Superstar

In the final decades of the 20th century, American Christianity and the nature of worship underwent profound changes. Profession of faith became more open and less tied to dogma and doctrine. At the same time, there was growth in both Fundamentalist and Pentecostal Christian churches, and Christians were likely to speak out in moral outrage against what they saw as the deterioration of traditional family and American values and to vigorously support politicians and parties who agreed with their point of view. It is therefore logical that Christian media, including radio, would reflect and advance these changes.

Contemporary Christian and Gospel Music

By the 1980s and '90s, a whole generation was growing up listening to modern Christian music, written and performed in every style imaginable, from acoustic rock to metal to rap and over-produced pop. The music was the hook that got their attention, but it was the lyrics that made them want to hear more. Artists like Amy Grant, Steven Curtis Chapman, Kirk Franklin, Jars of Clay, Michael W. Smith, and Point of Grace were as familiar to their fans as Madonna and Michael Jackson were to the wider audience of teens and young adults. Yet for the most part, the Christian stars got very little airplay on secular radio stations. Instead, they became popular through concert tours and personal appearances, often at churches with large congregations and auditoriums. They sold CDs and cassettes at the shows and through the ever-increasing network of Christian bookstores throughout the United States. In 1995, *Billboard* magazine added these retail outlets to its database that determines song and artist popularity, and several Christian artists began to get attention from the music industry and the media. *Radio and Records*, one of the key trade magazines that researches and establishes the popularity of current music, now publishes four regular surveys for Christian music — Christian hit radio (CHR), inspirational, Christian rock, and Christian adult contemporary (AC). Major music companies like EMI, BMG, and Warner Brothers bought out independent labels to establish Christian music divisions. Contemporary Christian music is now considered a mainstream genre.[1]

In a 2001 speech at the Golden Gate Baptist Seminary, John Styll, publisher of *CCM* magazine, described the groundswell support for the new Christian music:

> It didn't start in the church. [It] started as a countercultural response to the counterculture of the '60s. Many of the young people who were rebelling against the establishment structures of the 1960s found something they hadn't counted on: a relationship with Jesus. By 1970, there was a full-scale revival taking place in the counterculture. It became known as the Jesus Movement. The movement made the cover of *TIME* magazine, spawned at least two Broadway musicals and created an avenue for new songs about Jesus on the secular music pop charts. With music being a big a part of the counterculture, it was only natural that the newfound faith of young people would find musical expression. So they just wrote and played the popular rock music they knew, giving it lyrical content about Jesus. What began as a movement from the long haired, barefoot worshipers eventually became an industry, with most large contemporary Christian music labels now owned by mainstream entertainment companies.[2]

The 1980s and 1990s also brought renewed interest in gospel music. In reality, it had never retreated into the background of radio programming to the extent that evangelical preaching and teaching had. Throughout the rural South and Midwest, southern gospel music was part of the white popular culture. In the early part of the 20th century, traveling Gospel groups like the Vaughan, Stamps, and Daniel Quartets, the Speer Family, The LeFevres, and the Blackwood Brothers became famous entertainers. Contrary to the discrimination that they practiced with preachers, radio stations and networks welcomed gospel singers into prime-time program slots because they drew large audiences that advertisers wanted to reach. The simple harmonies and familiar lyrics that promised a better life in the hereafter appealed to more than country folk during the Great Depression. After the live-radio era ended, many individual stations continued to air syndicated gospel programs or blocks of recorded gospel music hosted by local disc jockeys. Radio remained a key promotional platform for southern gospel music into the 1960s, well beyond the beginning of the television era.[3]

Black gospel music, which some call spirituals, has also retained its popularity and roots within African American popular culture. In the segregated world of 20th-century America, only a few black gospel artists like the Golden Gate Quartet, Mahalia Jackson, and songwriter Thomas Dorsey gained wide acclaim outside of African American communities, primarily in cities in the eastern half of the country. Radio listeners heard very little black gospel music until the late 1940s when a new generation of radio stations created formats that targeted the African American audience. Throughout the 1950s and '60s, these stations carried blocks of black gospel programming within their daytime programming, as well as programs sold to local black preachers, right alongside blocks of rhythm and blues and soul music. Some popular urban contemporary stations continue this practice today, and many African American pop music stars came out of the black gospel tradition and return to it on occasion. On the whole, black gospel music is a much larger business than southern gospel is.[4]

Many new southern gospel groups have emerged that blended the old-style shape-note harmonies with a contemporary Christian sound. Today there is so much crossover that it is hard to place a particular artist or group into one genre of Christian music. The crossover between black and white gospel music has been more tentative. Although some black gospel artists are widely popular with all audiences, there are still plenty of Christian radio stations whose playlists are segregated, both all white and all black.

While there are many styles of contemporary Christian music, what is called Christian adult contemporary (AC) is the most popular, but the praise and worship category is quickly growing. John Styll elaborated on this trend:

> The church, too, has become hungry for contemporary praise choruses. It has become known: do contemporary worship and your church will grow; resist and die, or at least stagnate. Praise choruses are often

defined by music that is contemporary in style but with shorter texts than hymns. The music that is today called modern worship is a mix of contemporary Christian music and praise choruses. Today there are worship bands using extremely contemporary musical idioms but worship-oriented lyrics. Worship music is now popular and commercial. What contemporary Christian music has done is make the worship experience more relevant and therefore more meaningful to a new generation. But the danger is contemporary music is very performance-oriented. The line between worship and entertainment can very easily get blurred. Music in worship should draw our attention toward God, but contemporary music often draws attention to itself. Congregations can take on a consumer mentality, evaluating whether worship was good today based on how well the performances pleased us. Things could change in the future. Emerging generations of young people already may be rejecting some elements of contemporary worship. A recent interdenominational survey of people in their 20s revealed their deepest desire is to have a genuine encounter with God and they seek to recover depth and substance in worship. The demand for depth and substance speaks to us of the need to find those biblical and transcultural principles of worship that have endured through 2,000 years of history and to incarnate deep principles into a new style demanded by the cultural patterns of a postmodern world. If we can achieve this, then the new generation will have taken us beyond the contemporary worship of yesterday into the contemporary worship of tomorrow.[5]

The popularity of contemporary Christian music accelerated in the 1990s as the music industry discovered its fan base. In a 1992 article for *CCM* magazine, Michael Janke described the growth and maturity that the Christian music business had attained in the last decade.

When you consider that Christian music has only been around since about the mid–1970s, 10 years is all of a sudden a significant amount of time. It's about a third of the genre's history. It becomes an even bigger number when [you consider] the fact that many of today's fans are very new to the scene and don't have much of a sense of the genre's history.... Ten years ago, worship music had no "modern" in front of it. Praise and worship sold well but was dominated by the likes of the more conservative sounds of Hosanna! Music, Vineyard Music, and Maranatha.... Anyone seeking passionate, contemporary worship music with an edge was generally out of luck.... Ten years ago, crossing over was still highly controversial. Amy Grant, Michael W. Smith, and Kathy Troccoli had all done it to varying levels of success by now, but the subject was a sore one for many in the church. Today it's more or less an acceptable thing, with just the how's of it all being debated.... Ten years ago, inspirational music was a much greater force.... Today inspirational artists struggle to find homes on the major labels, they sell in smaller quantities, and the big sound that defined so much of what Christian music used to be is largely dead.... Ten years ago, danceable pop was still almost unheard of in Christian music. For some, of course, dancing was still a sin.... [I]t would be about eight years before Christian music would finally get it right on a large scale.... Ten years ago, the debate about business and ministry in the genre was still being debated, as it is still being debated today. And the "what is Christian music?" debate was raging at full force as well. [*CCM* publisher John] Styll poignantly wrote in the April [1992] issue of *CCM*: "Hopefully by now you can see that contemporary Christian music can be defined as any music by a believing artist which testifies to the Truth as found in scripture, knowing that the scriptures address all aspects of life. Thus, contemporary Christian music is not always 'gospel' music because it is not always about the Gospel. You might want to think of it as a 'soundtrack to everyday life....'" Ten years ago, the consolidation of the Christian music labels by large mainstream conglomerates was still in the future.... The entire market was more fragmented. Today we have the consolidation, and the money (and problems) that the big corporate parents bring to the table.[6]

Contemporary Christian music attempts to combine the forces of popular culture with the practice of a basically fundamentalist form of Christianity. This amalgamation is not without critics from within traditional and conservative Christians. Mark Allan Powell, publisher of the *Encyclopedia of Contemporary Christian Music*, framed the debate this way:

"Why should the devil have all the good music?" Martin Luther is reputed to have once asked, endorsing the notion of using secular tunes to promote sacred themes. But would Luther have approved of the Christian rap group Gospel Gangstas, or could he have endured the heavy-metal screaming of Christian rock band Tourniquet? Can anyone imagine him getting down and rocking to Christian dance fave Joy Electric? Christian rock, you may have noticed, is huge — bigger than it's ever been. *Newsweek* did a cover story on the phenomenon in 2001, and HBO's *The Sopranos* introduced a humorous subplot about the mob family trying to get in on the action. Some pundits in the Gospel Music Association maintain that the field now generates close to a billion dollars a year in business, with sales that continue to rise while pop music in general takes a downturn.[7]

Dr. H. T. Spence, writing in *Confronting Contemporary Christian Music*, decried the music and the pop culture intrusion into fundamentalist Christianity:

> In 1973 a Neo-Evangelical movement swept across America called "Key '73." Many of the evangelical denominations, including the Pentecostals, joined this movement, believing it would be the strongest evangelistic thrust to date in our country. An extensive invitation was sent out for new music to be written that promoted the message of "Key '73" with several stipulations: the words *righteousness, judgment, holiness, repentance,* and several other biblical terms were not allowed to be used, and the lyrics were to be of a positive nature. There was an intentional effort made to write non-offensive songs. A number of these were produced that year through this evangelical effort, strengthening the move away from biblical, doctrinal standards in the music.
>
> By 1972, Bill Gaither, a member of the Nazarene Church who started his public music career in southern gospel, was experimenting with a disco form of music, and because of the reaction from the more moderate element of the evangelical spectrum, he started the Bill Gaither Vocal Band in order to further his music in the strong contemporary vein. It has only been in the last few years that he has returned to his southern gospel roots and conventional style, especially in his reminiscing gospelsing videos. He is the man who promulgated the "praise" music which was at its height during the mid 1980s and early 1990s. Its influence is now affecting the borders of the fundamentalists' music with the charismatic sound in a number of choruses sung in the churches and youth camps. No, we are not against praise, but such an emphasis with certain types of music can be a ploy to make us leave off taking a stand against the apostasy of our time. Gaither's song "Get All Excited" was written to pull the people away from speaking against anything that would cause division among "God's people," specifically doctrine and biblical concepts of separation. It truly intimidates the child of God in taking a stand in his church that is drifting away from the Word of God. The Charismatic leaders are regularly reminding us that the Book of Psalms is truly a hymnbook dedicated to praise. But we must carefully read this precious book: praise is often in the context of battle themes, imprecatory prayers, overcoming those who are against God, and instruction of godly living in opposition to carnal living. The battle theme in present-day fundamentalist music compositions is conspicuously absent. The term *apostasy* is never mentioned. The melodies and arrangements are progressively lacking strength and literally creating the "soft sound" in church music.
>
> One of the characteristics that should be upon the hearts of fundamentalist music leaders is the hope for balance in the repertoire. When the

"easy listening" and the "soft sound" flow steadily from the pens of the music composers, the music will definitely produce soft and weak Christians. We were told back in 1969 that the "music is the message," not just the lyrics. Much of this soft and pretty sound is coming from female arrangers teaching in our Christian colleges and universities. God made the feminine gender soft and pretty. And her tendency in history has been to write from that perspective. A few women in the past have written lyrics with strength and fewer have written melodies with strength. In this age when love and softness on apostasy have practically become the perfume of the modern Church, our dear Fundamentalist ladies who are part of the music ministry must be careful that they do not contribute to this "falling away" with their published, weak arrangements of once strong hymns. Such music encourages passivity on the battlefield. We are in desperate need of strong melodies bearing along strong lyrics, feeding strength to the warriors for Christ.[8]

In the foreword to Spence's book, the Rev. John Ashbrook wrote:

Contemporary Christian music — it is the innovation of the hour in our age of church history. It has taken the Bible-believing church by storm. When a fundamental church adopts CCM as its musical style, it always moves into the new evangelical orbit. Where CCM comes, new evangelism follows, as certainly as the tail follows the dog. Reverent worship disappears, sound doctrine declines, and holy living is despised. Why is it so?[9]

Dial-the-Truth Ministries, a "Christian resource ministry" whose purpose is "presenting the truth and exposing error with the light of the Word of God, with emphasis on the King James Bible, prophecy and Christian music," issued the following "Bible Guidelines for Christian Music":

- Christian music should praise the Lord Jesus Christ — not man.
- Christian music is a new song — not an old song.
- Christian music's message should be clear — not vague or deceptive.
- Christian music should emphasis [sic] the message — not the music — nor the musician.
- Christian music is in the local church — not concert halls, night clubs.
- Christian music should feed the spirit — not the flesh.
- Christian musicians should be dedicated to the Lord — not worldly (pursuits).[10]

But Powell offered a defense of the music from its critics.

> Of course, if you don't like pop music at all, there may be nothing for
> you. But otherwise, the variety is overwhelming, from the Celtic
> strains of Iona to the friendly pop of Steven Curtis Chapman to the
> screaming rap-core of P.O.D. The group Switchfoot does alternative
> "nerd-rock" (similar to Weezer) and The Newsboys have perfected a
> retro/new-wave sound (compare with Smashmouth). If you like loud,
> buzzing guitars with almost indecipherable vocals, try Starflyer 59, or
> if you prefer intelligent, sensitive music with poetic lyrics, go for The
> Choir or Sixpence None the Richer. There's also Christian goth and
> Christian reggae and Christian disco. As for the theology, one should
> not expect profound insights from pop songs, but heresy is rare, and
> much of the material is less simplistic than one might suppose. As the
> Christian rock band Daniel Amos once put it, "There may be noth-
> ing new to say / But I'm fond of finding words that say it in a different
> way." And even the simplistic stuff can be harmless fun. When
> DeGarmo & Key did a tune called "God Good, Devil Bad," they didn't
> intend to offer the kids anything of theological substance, but it had
> a beat and you could clap your hands to it. So, what's wrong with that?
> Remember singing "Do Lord" and "Give Me Oil in My Lamp" at
> summer camp?[11]

Despite its critics, contemporary Christian music is still growing in
popularity, especially within younger demographic groups that have traditionally not tuned into religious broadcasts. For Christian radio, these
dynamic and successful trends in the music business were godsends. They
gave radio stations the basis for new formats — Christian AC, CHR,
Southern Gospel, Black Gospel, Praise and Worship, Inspirational and
others — that conveyed the message through music, and came with a
built-in loyal audience. By minimizing the preaching and teaching that
dominated traditional Christian radio, these new formats widened their
appeal to teenagers and young adult women. They could also effectively
counterprogram secular radio with clean lyrics, spiritual inspiration, and
family values as the fundamental imperatives of their programming philosophy. As a unique selling proposition to attract new listeners, prom-
ising wholesome radio programming that kids can enjoy and parents need
not fear has proved to be an excellent marketing concept.

The New Evangelists

Another external factor to the growth of Christian radio in the late 20th century has been the evangelical movement that began approximately in the 1970s. Depending on which historian you favor, this is the third or fourth such event in American history, the last three of which occurred at roughly 100-year intervals.[12] The current movement manifests itself in many ways. There has been tremendous growth in both the number of non-denominational churches and the size of congregations that describe themselves as fundamentalist, evangelical, Pentecostal, and/or Charismatic. Although most of these churches function independently, some are affiliated with denominations such as the Assemblies of God in Springfield, Missouri. By featuring contemporary Christian and gospel music in their services and stressing an upbeat message, these congregations increasingly attract young families with children.

Many, but not all, new evangelicals have often been active in politics, especially in support of socially conservative causes such as banning abortion, promoting prayer in schools and other public assemblies, denying special rights and privileges to homosexuals, and fighting against government programs that they consider antithetical to the traditional values of the nuclear family. Groups like the Moral Majority and the Christian Coalition, the creations of evangelists Jerry Falwell and Pat Robertson respectively, became quite influential in the Republican Party, especially in the South. Although both organizations have now effectively disbanded, their leaders are still active in mainstream politics and continue to advance their socially conservative agendas.[13]

Currently, the most successful writers in America are Tim LaHaye and Jerry Jenkins, a pair of evangelical Christians who write suspense novels about the Rapture, Armageddon, Jesus and the Antichrist, and other subjects taken mainly from the Bible Book of Revelation. LaHaye is a co-founder of the Moral Majority and Jenkins an author of inspirational biographies of Christian athletes. Beginning with *Left Behind* in 1995, they have published 12 novels in the series, all of which were instant bestsellers. The final book, *Glorious Appearing,* sold nearly two million copies before publication. Both a sequel and prequel to the series are in the works. The primary buyers are born-again middle-aged Christian women with children, with most sales in the South, Southwest, and

Midwest heartland of the United States, but nearly one out of every eight American is reading these techno-thrillers about the Apocalypse.[14]

Unlike their counterparts in earlier evangelical movements, these Christians are media consumers, and the evangelists who lead the movements are media savvy. So there has been a proliferation of Christian media content — books, magazines, recorded music, television, radio, and websites — to serve the cause and reach the audience, using the same marketing concepts and channels that the secular business world does.

It was natural that Christian radio stations, like Christian bookstores, should grow in numbers, to meet the content demand that commercial radio, like mass-market bookstores, was not prepared to service. As the pioneers of Christian radio realized, it was an excellent medium for evangelical work. Inexpensive to produce, compared to television and the rising cost of direct mail, radio programming was free to the audience — unless, of course, listeners wanted to send in a donation to support the ministry. An intimate medium, radio allows personal contact with the listener and encourages loyalty to a particular station or program. Radio's broad reach at low cost made it economically efficient for both outreach and fundraising.

Contemporary Christian Radio Personalities

While there are many new radio evangelists on the air, following in the footsteps of Walter Maier and Charles Fuller, new types of Christian radio personalities have also emerged. The development of the Christian News/Talk format has created opportunities for journalists, political and social commentators, and hosts for live phone-in talks shows. The new Christian music formats have spawned disc jockeys and on-air personalities who can relate to the music and the audience. But the most intriguing new Christian radio personalities are the ones who promote and reinforce Christian lifestyles.

A quick trip to a major bookstore will reveal the popularity of self-help as a topic in America. Christian radio is responding to this market with talk shows that emphasize the value of Christian behavior and perspective in coping with the challenges of contemporary life. The hosts of these shows, however, are markedly different from the evangelists who preach and teach and from the political and social commentators who host the more controversial talk shows. Their objectives are unlike those of the evangelists as well. The point of these Christian advice programs is not to convert listeners, because they are already Christians, but to reinforce the Christian behaviors that they espouse.

DR. JAMES DOBSON

By far the most popular Christian radio personality is Dr. James Dobson. A child psychologist and son of a Pentecostal minister, Dobson hosts the daily program *Focus on the Family*, broadcast on more than 1,500 Christian radio stations, with an estimated audience of 22 million listeners per week. *Focus on the Family* airs on many secular, commercial radio stations too.[15]

After completing his education, Dobson took a faculty position at the University of Southern California School of Medicine, which he held for 14 years, and served on the staff at the Children's Hospital of Los Angeles as a child development specialist. In 1970, he published the bestseller *Dare to Discipline* where he advocated an end to the Dr. Spock era of permissive child rearing and a return to old-fashioned parental authority and supervision, including corporal punishment under certain circumstances. Dobson is also a staunch advocate of preserving the nuclear family. He became immensely popular with social conservatives and more controversial than perhaps he had intended. In 1977, Dobson gave up his faculty job to launch the *Focus on the Family* series, initially on a local radio station in Arcadia, California, and devote more time to speaking engagements, publishing and his own family.[16]

Today, Dobson's enterprise is based in Colorado Springs with an 81-acre campus and 1,300 employees. The business includes a variety of radio programs, a syndicated newspaper column, television, magazines and newsletters, and books. Dobson's center gets about 400,000 visitors a year, he receives more than 250,000 letters, calls, and E-mails from listeners each month. By any definition, this is big business.[17]

For the radio market, Dobson and his organization offer several programs. The original half-hour program *Focus on the Family* is still the best known and among the most popular programs on radio. The vast radio network carrying the daily *Focus on the Family* broadcast continues to expand in the number of facilities and programs offered. Every week it is aired on nearly 2,000 facilities, both Christian and secular commercial, throughout the U.S. with hundreds more around the world. These timely programs cover concerns facing today's families and provide a welcome source of encouragement and direction. From the daily English program, a daily 15-minute program is excerpted, scripted and then translated into French, Russian and Spanish airing on hundreds of stations across Europe, the Commonwealth of Independent States (CIS), and Latin America. In addition to its daily broadcast host, Dr. James Dobson, this broadcast features a lineup of guest hosts that include psychologist-in-residence Dr. Bill Maier, physician Dr. Walt Larimore, *Life on the Edge* host Susie Shellenberger, and Heritage Builders representatives Kurt and Olivia Bruner. This daily broadcast is offered as a resource in cassette and CD format. Since 1983, a weekly variation of the *Focus on the Family* daily program has aired on the Armed Forces Radio & Television Services Network (AFRTS). This feature is released in AFRTS's regular block of programming (as opposed to the Sunday religious block) and is distributed from their headquarters by satellite, compact disc, and short-wave radio to every U.S. military installation around the world and to all ships at sea.

The daily half-hour program has generated several spinoff features like *Focus on the Family Weekend!* Airing on over 1,400 facilities nationwide, this weekly feature replays the finest moments from the daily broadcasts in a fast-paced, one-hour magazine format aimed at those unable to tune in during the week. Besides the excerpts from the daily program, *Weekend!* also features reports from *Family News in Focus* and short feature commentaries designed to keep families informed on issues that matter to them.

The *Focus on the Family Weekend Magazine* provides general-market radio stations with a pre-produced hour-long program that airs once a week. Creative elements such as on-the-street interviews, dramas, and music are combined with studio interviews Dr. Dobson has held with different guests on a wide variety of topics. The result is an entertaining and informative program that brings valuable information on a specific topic each week, designed to reach audiences who may not be Christian but are in need of solid, morally based advice and information to strengthen their marriages and families.

Focus on Your Family's Health is a 60-second feature that airs on general-market television and radio stations across the country. The feature runs during newscasts on FOX, ABC and CBS affiliates, and radio stations including WABC in New York City, the top-ranked talk-radio station in the country. *Focus on Your Family's Health* is hosted by Dr. Walt Larimore and delivers breaking health information for mind, body and spirit. Issues from safe pregnancies, to child and teen health to caring for older adults are addressed. *The Focus on the Family* commentary broadcast is a 90-second practical family-help spot, featuring commentary by Dr. James Dobson. It is now carried every day by more than 325 general-market radio stations. Eight out of the top 10 national markets broadcast this feature, including secular news/talk stations KNX in Los Angeles and WOR in New York City.

Family News in Focus is a daily radio news and commentary program that informs citizens about current events and challenges them to take action on pro-family matters. Over 1,550 facilities carry this feature, which is released via three formats: daily two-minute or five-minute versions, and a weekly 30-minute version. News segments are posted daily online and archived for over six weeks.

Every Saturday night teens all across the country can tune in to *Life on the Edge—Live!*, a call-in show heard on over 175 radio affiliates. Hosted by popular youth speakers and authors Joe White and Susie Shellenberger, *Life on the Edge* sets a lively, down-to-earth tone that speaks to the hearts of young people and says, "Hey, no question is too stupid to ask!" Teens listen to this one-of-a-kind, two-hour, live program that is relevant, spontaneous, entertaining and challenging. *Life on the Edge* is also broadcast live on the Internet, available to teens the world over.

Renewing the Heart is another one-hour live radio call-in program, a conversation about women's lives — their work, family, and spiritual needs, hosted by author and mentor Janet Parshall every Saturday. It airs on more than 250 facilities nationwide.

A unique half-hour radio drama airing daily and on weekends, *Adventures in Odyssey* has been an audience favorite since its beginning in 1987. Utilizing professional actors from Hollywood, top-notch writers, and state-of-the-art production, this series appeals to young and old alike. In fact, children and adults from all over the U.S. and the world have responded enthusiastically to the way in which comedy and drama are combined with biblically-based morality to tell compelling, enjoyable stories that teach a lesson.

Focus on the Family Radio Theatre began as a series of special broadcasts with the acclaimed production of *A Christmas Carol* and the

Peabody Award–winning *Bonhoeffer: The Cost of Freedom*. It is now a weekly broadcast featuring classic and original stories. *The Chronicles of Narnia, Les Miserables, Ben-Hur, Silas Marner, The Father Gilbert Mysteries, The Luke Reports*, and *Billy Budd, Sailor* have currently been produced, and others are under production. In a groundbreaking move, the adaptation of *The Lion, the Witch and the Wardrobe* is being made available to National Public Radio (NPR). There are more than 470 facilities nationwide that are currently airing this series.

James Dobson's appeal is that he does not overtly preach, evangelize, or advance fundamentalist Christian doctrine. Instead, he leads a growing crusade in the ongoing culture war against societal trends that he finds antithetical to healthy family life:

> As the 21st century progresses, it is clear that our culture is at war with the institution of the traditional family like never before. Parents who wish to instill biblical values in their children — or even just teach them a basic sense of right and wrong — face an uphill battle. It's difficult, after all, for moms and dads to instruct their children in what it means to be moral when the culture is telling them that morality doesn't exist. But what is the root cause of this conflict? I believe that the single greatest threat to family stability ... is the prevalence of postmodernism. It is the sickness from which all of the other symptoms grow: sexual immorality, abortion, divorce, pornography, etc. This system of thought teaches that truth is unknowable — whether from God (whom postmodernism perceives as a myth) or from man (who has no right to speak for the rest of us). In fact, for the postmodern mind, "truth" varies according the perceiver. Nothing is right or wrong; nothing is good or evil; nothing is positive or negative. Everything is relative. All that matters is "what's right for me and what's right for you."[18]

Occasionally Dobson brushes up against politics, and many conservative Republicans consider a pilgrimage to Colorado Springs mandatory.

> Thankfully, there have been encouraging signs over the past couple of years that families might not have to "go it alone" in the battle to defend morality and preserve traditional principles. Many of our elected leaders are demonstrating a renewed willingness to listen to the concerns of American families and to enact laws that respect the Judeo-Christian values upon which our nation was founded. I believe that the situation in Washington is more encouraging now than it has been in the past 30 years. This renewed commitment on the part of our leaders to

embrace policies that clearly distinguish between "right" and "wrong" can be seen in a number of arenas, such as the rise in federal funding for abstinence-based sex education programs. The most encouraging progress, however, has been made in the battle to defend the sanctity of human life. For the first time since *Roe v. Wade*, some leaders in Congress and the White House are together taking a long, hard look at issues such as abortion and euthanasia, and concluding that such concerns do have moral implications, after all.[19]

Yet Dobson counsels his listeners not to depend on politicians to solve sociological problems. Instead he urges a return to traditional American virtues like strong nuclear families and self-reliance.

Even so, I'm sure most would agree that it's not primarily the government's responsibility to teach children about moral absolutes. That job rests with Mom and Dad. But what are parents to do when the pendulum of public policy is only beginning to swing back in their favor while the rest of the culture is still blissfully wallowing in moral relativism? Let me encourage you with the thought that, even though you're fighting an uphill battle — it is a battle well worth fighting! Thankfully, there are steps we can take to help our kids navigate the postmodern wasteland that is festering all around them. First, let's give priority to our children. In days gone by, the culture acted to shield them from harmful images and exploitation. Now it's open season for even the youngest among us. Let's put the welfare of our kids ahead of our own convenience and invest the time and effort to teach them the difference between right and wrong. They need to hear also that God is the Author of their rights and liberties. Let's teach them at an early age that He created them, loves them and holds them to a high level of moral accountability. Second, let's do everything in our power to reverse the blight of violence and lust that has become so pervasive in America. Let's demand that the entertainment industry stop filling our eyes and ears with an endless barrage of debauchery. Let's support legislators who will stand on principle, rather than cater to passing trends and political correctness. And let's hold ourselves to the highest standards of personal accountability. The mantra "If it feels good, do it!" has filled too many hospitals with drug-overdosed kids, too many prison cells with sex offenders, too many abortion clinics with teenage mothers and caused too many tears for bewildered parents.[20]

His popularity is based on his commonsense advice, his sincere dedication to the well-being of children and families, and his ability to use radio to communicate personally with every individual in the audience. Dr. Dobson is clearly the most respected Christian radio personality in the marketplace today and probably has developed programming concepts and a presentation style that others will emulate for years to come.

Crown Financial Ministries

Another important category for lifestyle advice shows is financial planning from a Christian perspective. Crown Financial Ministries, based in Gainesville, Georgia, is a leader in this area of Christian radio. Crown Financial Ministries is the result of the merger between two earlier organizations, Crown Ministries and Christian Financial Concepts, in 2000, making it the world's largest financial ministry. Its mission is "teaching people God's financial principles in order to know Christ more intimately and to be free to serve him. Crown's vision is to teach 300 million people — 30 million Americans and 270 million people internationally — to handle money from God's perspective by September 2015."[21]

All of the principal personnel at Crown came from the world of business. Howard Dayton was born October 7, 1943, and was raised in Daytona Beach, Florida. He graduated from the School of Hotel Administration at Cornell University in 1967, then served two and a half years as a naval officer. In 1969 Dayton developed The Caboose, a successful railroad-themed restaurant, in Orlando, Florida. In 1972 he began his commercial real estate development career, specializing in office development in the Central Florida area. In 1974, a business partner challenged Dayton to study the Bible to discover what God teaches about handling money. What he found profoundly changed his life and gave him a passion to share these life-changing principles with others. He wrote *Your Money: Frustration or Freedom*, and for 10 years he invested about 30 percent of his time doing further research, writing, and conducting financial seminars for churches. He is also the author of *Your Money Counts* and *How to Get Out of Debt.* Dayton founded Crown Ministries in 1985 and developed a remarkably effective small-group financial study program that he marketed through churches. Dayton has served full time as president of Crown and as an unpaid volunteer since its inception.[22]

Larry Burkett, who passed away in 2003, was born in Winter Park,

Florida, on March 3, 1939, the fifth of eight children. After completing high school in Winter Garden, Florida, he entered the U.S. Air Force, where he served in the Strategic Air Command. Upon completion of his military duties, he and his wife, Judy, returned to central Florida, where he worked in the space program at Cape Canaveral, Florida. He spent the next several years at the space center in charge of an experiments test facility that served the Mercury, Gemini, and Apollo manned space programs. While working at the space center, Burkett earned degrees in marketing and finance at Rollins College in Winter Park, Florida. Burkett left the space center in 1970 to become vice president of an electronics manufacturing firm. In 1972 he put his trust and faith in Jesus Christ to guide his life — an event that had a profound effect. In 1973 he left the electronics company to join the staff of a nonprofit ministry, Campus Crusade for Christ, as a financial counselor. It was during this time that he began an intense study of what the Bible says about handling money, and he started teaching small groups around the country. In 1976 Burkett left the campus ministry to form Christian Financial Concepts, a nonprofit organization dedicated to teaching the biblical principles of handling money.[23]

Burkett and Dayton had been acquaintances for years and friends since the early 1990s. Dayton recognized that Crown Ministries was doing an excellent job one church at a time with small study groups in many parts of the country and the world. However, he had a vision to reach millions, not thousands. Something was missing. Burkett had seen phenomenal growth in the outreach of Christian Financial Concepts, but the one area he wanted to impact with small study groups was the local church. His radio broadcasts had given him ready recognition all around the country and in many parts of the world. But again, something was missing. After a radio interview, Burkett felt compelled to ask Dayton, "Why don't we merge our organizations together?" This led to personal talks between the two CEOs and, later, to serious discussions with the boards of directors of both ministries. After much study, discussion, and a lot of prayer, the boards of both Crown Ministries and Christian Financial Concepts unanimously agreed to merge into a new organization, Crown Financial Ministries, in September 2000.[24]

After Burkett died, Steve Moore replaced him on air. Moore was born and raised in Rochester, New York. He began his broadcasting career in his hometown at WGMC after pursuing a career as a professional musician. He worked for four years at WYRD in Syracuse, New York, as program director and then for seven years as a legislative reporter and program director at West Virginia Public Radio. During his time in public broadcasting, Moore hosted and produced a nationally syndicated music program, *Love Song*. In 1985, Moore joined Christian Financial Concepts to head up the broadcasting department, and now serves as the vice president of broadcasting for Crown Financial Ministries. He manages a staff of 12 people and oversees the production of Crown's award-winning syndicated radio programs.[25]

Dave Rae, president of Crown Financial Ministries, was born in Toronto, Ontario, Canada, on June 18, 1950. He graduated from the University of Toronto in 1973 with a bachelor's degree in physical education. In 1972, while attending the university, he began serving as youth leader at Bayfair Baptist Church in Toronto. He continued in this role until 1981. From 1985 to 1992, Rae served as president of Apple Canada, Inc., where for three years he was recognized as Apple's Manager of the Year. During his tenure, Apple of Canada grew from $80 million in annual sales to more than $400 million. Under Rae's leadership, Canada enjoyed the highest percentage of market share for Apple in the world.

Rae was selected for fast-track leadership development and completed the Advanced Management Program at Harvard Business School. In 1988, he was promoted to vice president of Apple Computer Worldwide and was involved in the quarterly strategic planning team. During Rae's tenure as vice president, Apple grew its revenues from $10 billion to $13 billion, with a worldwide employee base of 13,000.

From Apple Computer, Inc., Rae went to EDiX Corporation, in Manhattan Beach, California. While there, he developed a business concept plan for a medical transcription company that used unique, long-distance technology to provide nearly instantaneous transcription of a patient's medical records.

In 1996, on the advice of a number of former professional hockey players concerned by the low number of Christians involved in hockey, Rae started the Hockey Network International in Colorado Springs, Colorado. He used his professional and spiritual background, as well as other executive business contacts, to provide life-skills mentoring for professional athletes in a Judeo-Christian context. Eighteen professional hockey players and 46 business mentors were recruited to the program. Rae served with the Business & Professional Ministries, a division of The

Navigators in Colorado Springs, Colorado, from 1992 until he joined Crown Financial Ministries in 2000.[26]

Crown Financial Ministries produces several radio programs that present biblical truths relating to stewardship, ethics, practical money management, and God's ability to meet financial needs. Radio stations in all 50 states, the District of Columbia, Canada, the Caribbean basin, and elsewhere around the world air these programs. The half-hour program *Money Matters* gives listeners an opportunity to talk with expert guests. Heard on 456 stations, *Money Matters* also includes consumer-oriented features, financial news, and commentaries aimed at helping people become good and faithful stewards. *Money Matters* is also available in the 48 contiguous U.S. states via XM Satellite Radio, on FamilyTalk-XM 170, at 10:00 PM Eastern.

How to Manage Your Money is a daily four-minute program, aired on 700 radio stations in the United States and overseas, that focuses on plain-spoken, practical advice and biblical guidelines that relate to money management. Often culled from presentations that Dayton, Burkett and other members of the Crown staff have made on location at church-sponsored workshops or from the audio tracks of videos produced for those sessions, these features offer a combination of information, financial planning guidance, and stewardship counseling from a biblical perspective. An announcer, usually Steve Moore, introduces each program and wraps it up at the end with a sales pitch for services like Crown Financial Ministries 10-week small-group study for churches or Money Matters Financial Planning Software. In a recent broadcast, Howard Dayton recounted the financial state of the average American:

> Debt in the United States and many countries is escalating rapidly. In the United States alone, debt has gone up 20 percent in the last two years. The second area is the area of saving. In 1992 Americans saved over eight percent of their income. Now it's less than half that amount. Another trend that I see happening everywhere is in the area of gambling. Gambling in the United States has grown incredibly. We now have five and a half million people who basically spend everything they can get theirs hands on to gamble. And that often results in divorce in the family. Bankruptcy is something that's expanding in the United States. There will be 1.6 million personal bankruptcies this year alone. And unfortunately giving has been impacted as well. Giving — the percentage that people give — has declined almost every year for the past 30 years. In fact, in the recent surveys they have found that only seven

percent who come to church give 10 percent of their money to Christ. Thirty-seven percent of the people who go to church regularly give nothing at all. So what we see is giving declining, savings declining, while more people gamble, while more people go into debt. It's affecting Christians as well as those who don't know Christ because Christians haven't learned what God says about handling money.[27]

How to Manage Your Money also utilizes archival material from past workshops, like a recent re-broadcast of a September 2001 Larry Burkett presentation on "God's Financial Principles":

God's people need to realize that we are here but for one purpose. We serve a lot of functions in this life. Your function may be to run a computer company. Mine may be to write a book, and somebody else's may be to run General Motors. That's your function in life. Those are the things you do, and you can steer through life using the principle of dealing with things. But our purpose in life is to lead other people into the Kingdom of God. Satan's greatest tool in our generation is materialism. Nothing wrong with material things; now don't get me wrong. And God's got a different plan for every human being here. Whether you drive a Chevette or a Mercedes is irrelevant to God. He owns it all. He's just going to recycle it when you're gone anyway. But what is important is what God chose you to do with the resources He's given you to affect the society around you. And we aren't doing a very good job. And until we are, we will not see revival in America. And I believe that's what God — I know that's what God wants. He'll put us through a real testing period maybe to get our attention. I said before, and I do believe it, that if I could do one thing for God's people that would benefit them the most, I would give them a terminal illness. Then I'd put them in remission so they'd never know when it was going to start up again. Because it would force God's people to rethink what they're doing with their lives — what's important and what's not important. And whether or not you need to store up enough money to live a thousand years. Whether you think you do or not, you're not going to make it. So you might as well not do it. And there's got to be a balance to everything. I understand that. But our purpose in being here is to fund the Kingdom of God and to lead other people into the Kingdom of God.[28]

Among the most popular Crown radio productions is *A Money Minute*, a series of acclaimed public service announcements. Airing on 902 stations, *A Money Minute* uses both wit and wisdom to communicate biblical financial principles. Some of the spots offer straightforward advice with supporting evidence from the Bible:

> When you see the rich and famous on TV, maybe you feel a touch of envy, wishing you could have what they have. But the Bible says amassing riches without righteousness is a dead end street. Listen to the words of Psalm 49: "They trust in their wealth and boast of great riches, yet when they die they will carry nothing with them. Their wealth will not follow them into the grave. In this life they consider themselves fortunate, and the world loudly applauds their success, but they will die like all others before them." The Apostle Paul put it this way: "We brought nothing into the world, and we can take nothing out of it." And he goes on to warn Christians, saying: "Some people craving money have wandered from the faith, and have pierced themselves with many sorrows." Money isn't ungodly, and you can have lots of money and be a fine Christian. But worldly wealth should never be the goal of your life nor the object of your hope. Never trade righteousness for riches. It's a bad deal. *A Money Minute* from Crown Financial Ministries.[29]

But other *Money Minute* spots are dramatized vignettes with little or no biblical reference, like the 1940s-style script for "Harry Slade, Private Accountant":

> *Rain sound effects, up full then under.*
> SLADE: The rain was coming down in sheets, and I'd just put my head on my pillow when ... (He picks up the phone.) Harry Slade, Private Accountant.
> WOMAN ON PHONE: Mr. Slade, you must help me.
> SLADE (on phone): Sure, it's your nickel, lady. Keep talking.
> WOMAN ON PHONE: Meet me at the café at 9th and Maple in 10 minutes.
> *Rain segues into piano music in background.*
> SLADE: It was the kind of invitation that was difficult for a guy to resist. Rescuing damsels in distress is nice work if you can get it.
> WOMAN (in person): Mr. Slade, I'm so glad you're here.
> *Restaurant ambience under, mixed with piano.*
> SLADE: Well that makes two of us. Now what's the trouble?
> WOMAN: It just doesn't add up. My checkbook, I mean.
> SLADE: Ah, now you're talking my language, sweetheart.
> WOMAN: Please help me, Mr. Slade.
> SLADE: Call me Harry.

WOMAN: Harry.

SLADE: Say, when was the last time you used an ATM, an automated teller machine?

WOMAN: I don't know. Yesterday, maybe the day before. Why?

SLADE: Did you write down the transaction?

WOMAN: Oh no, I don't believe I did.

SLADE: Well, there's you problem right there, dollface. When you get money from an ATM, you need to write it down in your checkbook just as soon as you can. If you don't, things are never gonna add up.

WOMAN: Oh, Harry. You've really got my number.

SLADE: That's just part of what I do.

Background ambience fades out.

ANNOUNCER: *A Money Minute* from Crown Financial Ministries.[30]

The Crown Financial Ministries radio productions stand alone as useful additions to a variety of Christian radio program strategies. Like *Focus on the Family*, they come from a lay ministry that offers particular appeal to today's evangelical and charismatic Christians. Just as important, they fit within the overall objectives of the ministry, driving traffic to the website and toll-free telephone numbers to support the other activities and services that Crown provides.

ALISTAIR BEGG

There is also a place for traditional radio preachers who concentrate on Bible-based evangelism and are able to communicate with young adult listeners. Alistair Begg, the pastor of Parkside Church, a large non-denominational body of believers located in a southeast suburb of Cleveland, Ohio, is a good example. The church had its origins in 1968 when a small group of businessmen came together for weekly prayer meetings on Cleveland's east side. Attendance grew, along with a conviction to consider the formation of a local church. Parkside Church, originally known as the Chapel, formally became a church in 1972. It continued to grow and in 1983 after the original pastor was called to the mission field and interim pastors filled the role for three years, Begg accepted the call to be the senior pastor and arrived with his wife and children from Scotland.

Begg was born in Glasgow in 1952 to Christian parents, graduated in 1975 from London Bible College, and lived in Edinburgh for two years where he was assistant pastor at Charlotte Chapel. From 1977 to 1983 he was pastor of Hamilton Baptist Church. In the summer of 1983 he accepted the invitation to come to Cleveland and has been there ever since, except when he is traveling on his many speaking engagements. Begg has a charming Scottish accent and sincere, relaxed delivery, with the result that everyone in his audience feels that the preacher is speaking directly to her or him. This oratory skill makes Begg's sermons especially effective on radio, and they are the basis for the syndicated program *Truth for Life*. This 25-minute daily broadcast began on February 27, 1995, and the program can now be heard throughout the week by radio listeners all across the United States and throughout the world on the internet. All programs feature the Bible teaching of Alistair Begg. The core content for each program is relevant and clear Bible teaching. Whether it is a study from the book of 1 Peter, a "How to..." on evangelism, a study on Church authority, or one on the doctrine of God's providence, Begg guides listeners to see how God's Word applies to our lives and often brings us to the ultimate question "Who is Jesus?" His frequent charge to "open your Bible to see if what I'm telling you is really there" serves as a challenge to study the truth of God's Word and a cue for interaction by the audience. Currently *Truth for Life* airs on more than 700 Christian radio stations.[31]

Deregulation, the FCC, and New Technology

Unlike opening a bookstore, which you can do with enough capital, a sound business plan, and hard work, starting a radio station requires a license that may not be readily available. That's where the third external factor — the politics of deregulation — becomes important. Beginning with the Carter administration in the late 1970s, the FCC took a new look at its role as overseer of the nation's airwaves and made several significant changes. It reconfigured the FM radio band, effectively creating room for more than 1,000 new stations. It simplified the applications for construction permits, the licensing, and the annual reporting procedures. And in a 1977 policy reversal described in detail in the profile of the Moody Bible Institute later in the book, the FCC became more liberal in its interpretation of "non-commercial educational use" in assigning licenses for the numerous channels already allocated for that purpose for which a construction permit had never been issued. Churches and religious organizations now qualified more readily.

Coincidentally, advances in technology made Christian radio more feasible. The development of inexpensive computer programs to plot potential radio signal–contour maps made it possible to put together an application for a construction permit without a costly engineering study. The same software proved useful at identifying new channels not listed in the FCC table of allocations where radio signals could exist without interfering with existing stations. This led to further growth in the number of FM stations on the air. Satellite networks that carried live and syndicated programming began to proliferate, primarily for television. Each satellite television transponder, however, contained a minimum of two additional audio channels that could be used for radio networks. The advent of digital satellite transmission increased this capacity, making a wide array of radio services available and inexpensive. Finally, the quality of remote-signal monitoring equipment improved to the point that the FCC permitted radio stations to operate without people present. Now a network of satellite radio stations, each fed from a common origination site, is both technically and economically feasible.

Within the radio industry, the demographic shift from AM to FM has had important implications for Christian broadcasters. As FM has become the choice of more and younger listeners, AM stations have lost revenue and become less valuable. In addition, the AM audience that remains has a large portion in the 55-plus demographic that is not in demand by most advertisers. But this is precisely the audience that traditional Christian radio broadcasters, who rely on preaching and teaching programs for income, are trying to reach. So many Christian radio stations are AM, on channels that the owners have picked up at bargain-basement prices.

Programming Innovations

While this combination of phenomena created the opportunity for Christian radio to flourish in the last decades of the 20th century, it took innovative programmers and perceptive entrepreneurs to make it happen. Until the 1980s, Christian radio had one format or overall programming strategy. It consisted mainly of sermons, devotionals, Bible lessons, talk shows about Christianity, an occasional drama, and enough inspirational or gospel music to fill the gaps between the spoken word programs. This is generally known as Preaching and Teaching and is still a major format for Christian radio.

The new evangelism has brought forth many new radio evangelists ready and willing to purchase time for their broadcasts. With an expanding audience of evangelical Christians and the potential for a steady revenue stream from paid programming, many Christian radio entrepreneurs have chosen to stick with an updated version of Preaching and Teaching. Radio evangelists have seized the opportunity to buy time on Christian radio stations, often moving the programs from commercial radio stations, for several reasons. There are generally no restrictions on dayparts and fewer adverse policies about program content. Moreover, because Christian radio stations are formatted to offer the audience a steady stream of similar programming, the evangelists are more likely to reach and attract loyal listeners. Most of this audience remains in the 50-plus age demographic, with a preponderance of female listeners.

The growing interest in Christian lifestyles and the involvement of conservative Christians in politics and social issues have afforded other opportunities for spoken-word programming on Christian radio stations. For many years, the News/Talk radio format has been popular in commercial radio, especially on AM stations, because it appeals to adults 35 and older and skews to a male audience. Christian radio stations are now experimenting successfully with a Christian News/Talk format, complete with exclusive news networks and a wide array of live, syndicated programming. The USA Radio Network, based in Dallas, is one example of a programming source created to serve these stations. It currently has more than 900 affiliates and provides hourly newscasts, talk and interview programs, sports, features, and business news updates.[32]

Probably the most vibrant and diverse segment of Christian radio is the growing array of music formats. Still works in progress, these include traditional Praise and Inspirational music, Southern Gospel, Black Gospel, Christian Rock, Contemporary Christian, Christian Adult Contemporary, and more. Although some of the music stations still include as much as 30 percent talk and preaching and teaching, an increasing number are sticking to the commercial radio model that stresses all music, all the time. Program directors for these music stations are often quite savvy about ways to present and promote their formats to a young-adult audience (ages 18–34), with a secondary emphasis on teenagers.

In a very short period of time, Christian radio programming strategies have created formats targeted at all the key demographic groups that exist in the radio audience. They are also using the same programming, promotional, and marketing strategies that have worked for mainstream secular, commercial radio. And there are tentative signs that Christian radio stations are reaching and attracting the listeners they are targeting. It's no longer just little old ladies tuning in to hear their favorite preacher. And the mission is not just the conversion of unbelievers and the spread of fundamentalist doctrine. It is rapidly becoming the encouragement and support of healthy Christian lifestyles.

defined by FOTF

4. Advancing the Cause of Christ — The Moody Broadcasting Network

Dwight Lyman Moody was one of the most respected evangelists in 19th-century America. Born in Massachusetts in 1837, Moody worked in his uncle's shoe store and attended a Congregational church where a Sunday school teacher influenced him to accept Jesus as his personal Savior. In 1856, Moody moved to Chicago with dreams of making his fortune in the shoe business. But he also maintained his religious zeal and soon set up a Sunday school for children in a converted saloon. President-elect Lincoln attended Moody's Sunday school on a stop during his trip to Washington. The venture proved so popular that Moody soon outgrew the building. His friends encouraged him to begin his own church. On February 28, 1864, the Illinois Street Church opened in its doors, with Dwight Moody as its full-time pastor.

Upon leaving the business community, Moody engaged in religious work with salesman-like fervor. He was the founder and early booster of the YMCA in Chicago. During the Civil War, he traveled with General Grant and ministered to the soldiers at Ft. Donelson, Shiloh, and elsewhere in the western campaign. After a few years, he relinquished the pastorate, moved back to Massachusetts, and became immersed in an energetic schedule of mass evangelism that covered America and Great Britain until his death in 1899. But at a distance, Moody remained active in the management of his Chicago operation.

Meanwhile, Moody's Chicago church grew steadily and branched out further into the field of religious education. In the aftermath of the 1871 Chicago Fire, Moody hired Emma Dryer, principal and teacher at Illinois State Normal University, to minister to the needs of thousands who were left homeless and to develop a program of Bible study, teaching and home visitation. Dryer encouraged Moody to start a permanent training school for young men and women. He agreed with the idea and in 1886 established the Chicago Evangelization Society to train young men and women to do city missionary work. Upon Moody's death in 1899, the society changed its name to the Moody Bible Institute.[1]

Today, the Moody Bible Institute (MBI) is a group of ministries that seek to advance the cause of Christ. The primary objective of MBI is education, with three different divisions: undergraduate school, graduate school and distance learning. In addition to education, the ministries of MBI include Moody Publishers, Moody Radio, and conference and church ministries.

Early Radio Broadcasts

As an adjunct to its educational mission, MBI began broadcast service in 1925 with a weekly program on WGES in Chicago. The institute also applied for and received a license for a radio station, and WMBI in Chicago signed on July 28, 1926, with this announcement:

> Good afternoon, radio friends. This is the Moody Bible Institute of Chicago, the West Point of Christian service, radio station WMBI, a station which is dedicated fully to the service of our Lord and savior Jesus Christ.[2]

During the Roaring Twenties, WMBI was not exactly in the forefront of public attention, but it steadily gained a loyal audience and added more programming throughout the decade. Early programs featured evangelists, hymns and instrumental Christian music performed by one of the many Moody ensembles and orchestras, and church services. Despite the stock market crash of 1929 and the onset of the Great Depression, the Moody Bible Institute kept WMBI on the air for at least a few hours a day. Throughout the 1930s, the staff often worked without pay.

A favorite early program on WMBI, and one that continued until

2002, was the *Radio School of the Bible*, an outgrowth of the Moody Bible Institute External Studies, in operation since 1900. The idea actually came from listeners who often wrote letters addressed to the Radio School of the Moody Institute. On September 9, 1926, the institute sent out a questionnaire to listeners to assess interest in a series of organized lessons on the books of the Bible. Response was so immediate that WMBI began the program on September 26, with lessons taught by professors at the MBI. During these years when there were fewer AM stations on the air and less interference, the signal carried much farther. A regular feature called *The Question Box* invited listeners to write in. Within two years, the *Radio School of the Bible* got mail from all 48 states, plus Hawaii and several foreign countries. This led to WMBI's first foray into multilingual programming. Official enrollment in the radio school grew from 2000 in 1932 to more than 22,000 in 1943.[3]

In 1939, WMBI moved into its present facility with studios constructed specifically for radio broadcasting. Studios A and B were the primary sites for the live programs that comprised the vast majority of the schedule. In between them was the small Studio C, an announcer's booth to cut away for station breaks while the engineers changed the setup to the alternate main studio. When a program originated in Studio A, the cast and crew of the next program rehearsed in Studio B, ready to go live when the time came. The WMBI studio arrangement mirrored that of commercial radio stations and networks of the era. Studio B was especially well equipped for large scale productions like live drama, choir concerts and orchestral recitals. There was a Kimball pipe organ, a piano, and a glassed in gallery for an audience. The sign on the wall read: "Your song may be used to save a soul."[4]

By 1941, WMBI filled its entire sunrise-to-sunset schedule with a variety of programs, many suggested by listeners. That same year, the institute filed a successful application for a new FM channel in nearby Addison, Illinois, where the AM transmitter had moved in 1927. Although FM was experimental at the time and receivers were scarce, the new technology would allow 24-hour broadcast service. After the FCC granted a rare construction permit during World War II, the institute signed on WDLM-FM (for Dwight Lyman Moody) at 50,000 watts on October 1, 1943. During daylight hours, WDLM simulcast programming with WMBI. However, although the FM experiment was useful, ultimately there were not enough listeners to sustain the service — a common plight for early FM operators. Moody ceased WDLM operations in 1952, but returned to FM a few years later.[5]

Wartime operations were complicated. For security, the Chicago police department stationed guards at the studio and transmitter. Three regular WMBI operators were deputized and carried firearms to work. Through all this, the station staff of over 100 employees produced 250 programs per week, about 80 percent of them live. Typically, it took a month of preparation and rehearsal to create one week of programming. And the programming was slowly progressing from the traditional preaching, Bible study, devotionals, and church music to include more popular drama, gospel music, lifestyle advice, and listener-response shows.[6]

Expansion of Service and Programming

Moody Radio was the first significant producer and distributor of syndicated Christian radio programming and one of the few sources of recorded Christian music throughout the 1930s and 1940s. Beginning with the 15-minute program *Miracles and Melodies*, WMBI recorded electronic transcriptions that aired on radio stations across the nation.

After World War II, WMBI refocused its programming effort on its core evangelistic mission. That meant more radio drama, music, and talk shows to attract a new generation of Christian radio listeners. There were action shows like *Sailor Sam*, kids shows like *The Sugar Creek Gang*, and the ever-popular *Stories of Great Christians*. The latter program was a series of dramatized biographies of men and women of faith. Its goal was "not to elevate man but to magnify God's great working in the lives of those who are fully yielded in faith and obedience to Him." Throughout the 1940s, these solid dramas combined with teaching, preaching, and music to make WMBI "a relevant and powerful force in the lives of Christian radio listeners."[7]

In addition to its own productions, WMBI began to air programs from other evangelistic radio missions. It was one of the first stations to pick up Charles Fuller's *Old-Fashioned Revival Hour*, described in detail in Chapter 2. Another favorite was one that originated at the Midwest Bible Church in a nearby suburb. Called simply *Songs in the Night*, the Rev. Torrey Johnson began his broadcasts of music and devotional commentary in 1943. It featured the sounds of pipe organ music and a regular choir — the King's Karollers. On WMBI and other stations, the program generated a worldwide audience and became most noteworthy as the place where evangelist Billy Graham launched his career. Late in 1943, Johnson had to give up the broadcasts and chose Graham, a recent graduate of Wheaton College, to succeed him. Graham also added inspirational singer George Beverly Shea, a regular performer on WMBI, to his retinue, beginning a working relationship and ministry that would last into the 21st century.[8]

The MBI was committed to radio evangelism. It added technical courses in radio to the Institute's curriculum for missionaries in the 1950s, and many future employees of WMBI, the network, and other stations came out of this program. Also in this period, Moody grew outside its broadcasting base in Chicago to establish new radio stations in Cleveland, Ohio; Spokane, Washington; and East Moline, Illinois. The institute had received mail from potential listeners in both cities and felt that there would be enough support for and interest in the new stations. The Cleveland operation marked Moody's return to FM broadcasting on a commercial channel. At the time, the FCC restrained religious organizations from getting non-commercial educational licenses unless they operated schools in the community. In 1960, Moody successfully received a non-commercial license for the new WMBI-FM in Chicago.

By the 1960s, Moody had an interest in new programming targeted at women. One program was *Sugar and Spice*, hosted by Ruth Dimwiddie. Ruth was a secretary at Moody's WCRF in Cleveland who came up with the idea for a 15-minute women's show in 1964. It was a lighthearted, practical program that dealt with everyday issues women faced, from choosing the right kitchen thermometer to what to look for in sunglasses to tips on how to manage your time. Regardless of the topic, there was always light music, often secular, from orchestras like the Boston Pops.[9]

Frances Nordlund, and later Dollie Meredith, hosted a different program called *Woman to Woman*, which had a stately feel. The introduction described it as "talks from the heart of one woman to another. Out of her many years of experience as a pastor's wife and mother, Frances Nordlund shares with you thoughts to help you become a more effective Christian woman." Here again, music was a regular feature but was devotional in nature, often from a well-known choir. The goal was to help women develop their spiritual lives, which would then affect the world around them, and to provide practical information and advice that would help women lead successful, satisfying Christian lives. Like Ruth Dimwiddie, Nordlund also solicited and responded to questions from listeners.[10]

Music styles today have changed and tips have less to do with kitchen thermometers than how to balance the responsibilities of 20th-century life. But while programs like *Sugar and Spice* and *Woman to Woman* were not truly groundbreaking and resembled other series on local commercial radio, they nevertheless foreshadowed programming strategies of future Christian radio broadcasters for whom women would be the primary audience.

Legal Issues and a Fledgling Network

By the 1970s, Moody had an interest in further expansion of its radio service and began to dream of a radio network. It was already active in the syndication market, both as a supplier and consumer of Christian radio programs. But most full-service AM licenses were taken and having to compete with commercial enterprises for FM licenses was difficult and expensive. So Moody decided to petition the FCC to reconsider its restrictive policy on religious organizations qualifying for non-commercial educational FM licenses. In a 1977 decision that opened the doors for the current expansion of Christian radio, a majority of the commissioners agreed with Moody and issued MBI new FM licenses in Boynton Beach, Florida, and East Moline, Illinois, where Moody revived the WDLM-FM call letters. In her concurring statement on the decision, Commissioner Margita White described the legal issue and the commission's policy considerations:

> Over the years, the Commission has articulated the principle that organizations which are primarily religious in nature, even though they may have some educational aspects, will not be allowed to operate on channels reserved for educational use. [*Keswick Foundation, Incorporated,* 26 FCC 2nd 1025 (1970); *Christ Church Foundation, Inc.,* 13 FCC 2nd 987 (1968); *National Educational Foundation, Inc.,* 15 FCC 2nd 1032 (1968)] We have recognized an exception to this general principle in that a religious organization which operates a school may be found to be qualified as an educational applicant for the community in which

the school is operated. [*Pensacola Christian School, Inc.*, 41 FCC 2nd 74 (1973)]

The application of local school requirement *solely* to religious educational organizations is clearly discriminatory. It adds burden to "religious" applicants which other applicants need not meet. The Commission has granted several licenses to the Pacifica Foundation which maintains no school at all, much less one in each community of license. Poor Peoples Radio (San Francisco), The Chicago Boys Club, and the Virgin Islands Council of the Boy Scouts, all may serve their communities, but they were accorded preferred treatment over their "religious" counterparts since none of them was required to show that it operated a school in the community. This disparate past treatment of "religious" and other applicants is impermissible.[11]

During the its first 55 years, the Moody Broadcasting Network (MBN), expanded deliberately as finances and the need for radio service permitted to include the following properties:

- 1926 — WMBI-AM in Chicago, IL
- 1958 — WCRF-FM in Cleveland, OH (commercial channel)
- 1960 — WDLM-AM in East Moline, IL
  WMBI-FM in Chicago
- 1973 — WMBW-FM in Chattanooga, TN (acquired)
- 1974 — KMBI-AM and FM in Spokane, WA (commercial channel)
- 1979 — WRMB-FM in Boynton Beach, FL
- 1980 — WDLM-FM in Moline, IL

Between 1988 and the present, Moody added 24 owned-and-operated (O&O) stations, 13 of them since 1996. Many of the new stations are satellites or repeaters of existing ones, an expansion strategy called *clustering*. Acquisitions became increasingly expensive, including $5.5 million for WGNR-AM and FM, in Anderson, Indiana, in 1997, $5 million for WKES-FM, in Lakeland, Florida, in 1996, and $2.3 million for WAFS-AM, in Atlanta, Georgia, in 1989 (which Moody sold to Salem Communications for $16 million in 2004).

Satellite Connection and National Programming

Until 1982, the MBN was a loose association of O&O stations and affiliates who received taped programs by mail. In that year, MBN established satellite interconnection. Program Director Wayne Shepherd described the change:

> It was revolutionary for Christian radio. Suddenly we could do live programs. We could do live call-in programs, and we could produce a live newscast specially tailored for the Christian audience that we were trying to serve. Moody was a pioneer. Programs like *Prime Time Live*, *Open Line*, and the *Midday Connection* now have immediacy for a nationwide audience of more than 1,000,000 listeners.[12]

Music Through the Night, hosted by Mike Kellogg, began in 1982 and became a mainstay of MBN programming. Kellogg's voice is deep, soothing, and reassuring, yet capable of great drama. Former WMBI Manager Bruce Eberhart said this about the show and its success:

> When people are looking for answers, maybe for a friend on the radio, Mike has been able to add that companionship, that relationship, that friendship to countless people and really anchors our radio station overnight. His voice represents what Moody Broadcasting is all about.[13]

Kellogg added:

> We live in a secular culture, and the things of the Lord are very far away from people. And I would say a lot of people don't really care until the hard times come. And then they want something really substantive. And what's substantive is not the meanderings of some old guy talking behind a microphone. It's the word of God that's so powerful. They hear that word, and it cuts to the very quick of their soul.[14]

Another important MBN program was *Saturday Night Alive*, a program for teenagers created in 1985 by host, minister, and activist in Youth for Christ Ron Hutchcraft. A radical idea at the time, *Saturday Night Alive* lasted for more than 10 years and was the precursor for many similar Christian radio programs to come. Producer Todd Busteed described the show:

> It was about youth ministry, also about modeling to youth ministers. It was about encouraging kids to do youth ministry. Ron believed teens were more likely to trust other teens. He had kids reading Scripture, kids commenting, kids talking. That was a model that he maintained, and it was quite effective because kids enjoyed hearing other kids.[15]

An excerpt from the show, with techno dance music in the background, demonstrates how Hutchcraft drew in his target audience:

> RON: Hey we can do our own Top Ten lists here, right guys. Can we do a Top Ten list? OK, let's go for it. Let's do our Top Ten list of ... uh.... Let's see if we can come up with 10 things that parents don't want their kids to know.
> KID 1: They don't want you to know that they did exactly the same dumb things that you're doing now.
> RON: That's number one.
> KID 2: How my family's doing financially.
> RON: Two.
> KID 3: Maybe they were a loser in school.
> RON: Three.
> KID 4: If you were born an accident.[16]

Saturday Night Alive also went out of the studios and on the road to get kids perspectives on things like walking around the streets of New York City. It aired around the world, notably in South Africa, Lebanon, and Latin America. Hutchcraft was not afraid to deal with complex issues from a teenager's perspective.

During this era, Moody also expanded its outreach to ethnic and multilingual audiences in Chicago. Radio Esperanza, a service for the Hispanic Christian audience begun by Jim "Jaime" Shedd, came from the suggestions from Chicago-area Latino pastors. It began with one Saturday program on WMBI-AM in 1974, grew to a three-hour block and then to the entire day. With the addition of programs produced for missionary work by HCJB, Trans World Radio and other organizations and Spanish-language versions of popular syndicated shows like *Insight for Living* and *Back to the Bible*, Radio Esperanza has grown since 1980. It now occupies the 10:30–3:30 block daily on WMBI-AM. Program Director Gersón Garcia described Radio Esperanza this way:

> In the mind of the listener, it is not just a provider of Christian music, Bible studies and preaching programs. It is a meeting place, a place to talk about personal concerns, to look for guidance, a place to pray and to develop personal relationships.[17]

Present and Future

The MBI is a substantial, dignified campus stretching from Chicago to Walton in the blocks between Wells and LaSalle on Chicago's Near North Side. A short distance north is the Moody Memorial Church and Sunday school, a round brick tabernacle occupying the block across the street from the Chicago Historical Society. In all, MBI owns 25 acres in the downtown area, making it one of the largest urban real estate holders in the United States.

MBI occupies the upper three floors of an understated brick tower on the campus. You approach the lobby through an interior glass corridor overlooking a garden courtyard. On the ground floor is the Dwight Lyman Moody Museum with exhibits tracing the history of the institute. The overall impression is one of long-lasting stability.

The radio studios are vast but conscientiously arranged to use every square foot. You pass by the regular photos of MBN personalities and Christian recording artists, plaques and other symbols of recognition. A simple mission statement adorns the walls and the banner on the MBN website:

> Think Biblically
> Live Christianly
> Serve Effectively
> Evangelize Consistently

There are now 36 MBN O&O stations, 10 studio locations, and 400 affiliates who carry some MBN programming. In Chicago, WMBI-AM, WMBI-FM, and MBN have separate staffs and production facilities. The target audience is evangelical females ages 35–54, but MBN and stations are changing their morning-drive programming to attract more males. The 2004 budget for MBN and the O&O stations was $13 million. Moody sells block time to other organizations on both the network and individual stations. And it began soliciting business underwriting in 2003. In addition to its evangelical function, MBN helps the MBI raise funds and attract students.[18]

Most of the on air personnel have a background in Christian radio, and many trained at the MBI. WMBI FM Program Director John Hayden worked for Bott and was station manager at KLJC in Kansas City, licensed to the Calvary Bible College where he earned a master of ministry.

Currently, more new hires are coming from secular radio. As it has done since the beginning, Moody is revising programming to meet the needs and changing lifestyles of its Christian audience. But the focus remains on the core mission, as Hayden explained:

> Moody is bucking the trend in Christian radio by concentrating on preaching and teaching. But we have moved to a 60/40 mix of music to spoken word. The change has been gradual. Our music is primarily light Christian AC with an emphasis on Praise and Worship. But we will not add music just to get higher ratings. The mission is still the growth of the believer. Bible teaching is still first and foremost. We're always looking for Bible teachers whom God is using. We recently added a daily program with James McDonald, pastor of the Harvest Bible Chapel, one of the fastest-growing suburban congregations in Chicago.[19]

At the same time Moody is constantly tweaking the production style of its traditional spoken-word programs. Radio listeners have personal attachment to their favorite personalities and know them as real people and real friends. For radio preachers and teachers, the goal is to develop this connection and give the listeners something that goes beyond what they can get out of the sermons. Network Program Director Wayne Shepherd sees this trend as a natural outgrowth of the psychographic appeal of radio, which more ministries are coming to understand: "Listeners develop a sense of trust in the teachers they listen to, and over time, [the teachers] have opportunity to challenge them spiritually. That challenge might be to purchase a product that will help them grow, or to take a specific life action step."[20]

Promotion, both on air and off, has been an ongoing effort since Jim Wick, WMBI general manager at the time, began Sunday Night Rallies back in the 1970s. Wick and on-air personalities would go to local Chicago churches, make presentations about WMBI and the institute, and lead the congregation in singing. But in the contemporary and competitive world of Christian radio, promotion has become more important. John Hayden elaborated:

> Marketing is a relatively new concept, but one we have developed within the past five years. We now have a marketing and promotion director and the network has a marketing staff primarily to sell programming. Recently we bought an SUV and painted it with the logos and a mural

of the Chicago skyline. We call it The Skyliner, and it travels around to churches and public events. We give out bumper stickers, do some giveaways, even an occasional trip. Other stations do direct mail. The network gets coverage in *Today in the Word*, the institute's monthly magazine.[21]

What does the future hold for MBN? Network Program Director Wayne Shepherd believes that new technology means new opportunities:

> As I think of the future for Moody Broadcasting via the Internet or any other technology we haven't even thought of yet, I'm reminded of the importance of the message. The content of what we say and what we do at Moody Broadcasting hopefully will always remain the same — focused on the Word of God, the authority of the Word of God. I'm convinced that as we grow wider in or distribution, we want to grow deeper in what we offer to our listeners at the same time so that the Gospel is always there in the front of people's minds.[22]

WMBI-FM Program Director John Hayden thinks that programming is still the most important consideration:

> Digital audio and the Internet are factors for the future, but emphasis on the local markets, the listeners, is more important. There are too many good programs available and too few time slots. There is pressure on producers to shorten programs, from 58 to 28 minutes, and from 28 to 14, and to provide breakaways for spots.[23]

Dr. Joseph Stowell, past president of the MBI, is willing to consider any and all changes in technology, programming or any other facet of the broadcasting effort, so long as it remains true to the vision of the founder, Dwight Lyman Moody. As Stowell speaks, you can almost hear the voice of the 19th-century street-corner evangelist, preaching amid the ruin of the Chicago fire and echoing his words:

> One of the new frontiers that technology is opening up to Christian broadcaster is that listening to your radio in your car will not only be done through local stations, but there will be this little satellite dish on your back windshield that will pull down hundreds of streams. With the technology of the Internet, Christian broadcasting can go anywhere, anytime to anybody on the face of this planet. Technology is a

moving train. Instead of having to buy different stations to do classical Christian music, or contemporary Christian music, or 24 hours a
day of great Bible teaching, now the future will give us the opportunity to actually stream those different formats on the Internet. The
mission remains the same. Seek every opportunity we can to advance
the cause of Christ through broadcasting to maximize the power of the
Gospel to a lost and dying world.[24]

5. The Undisputed Leader — Salem Communications

In a letter to shareholders, written for the 2003 annual report for Salem Communications Corporation, Stuart Epperson and Edward Atsinger said:

> We are pleased to report that Salem Communications' 2003 performance was a great success. We continued to deliver on our mission of being the market leader in providing religious and family-themed content across our radio, Internet, and publishing platform. At a time when national attention is focused on programming quality and broadcast standards, this strategy is increasingly relevant.
>
> When we launched our contemporary Christian music radio format in 2000, the logical positioning that set us apart was "Safe for the whole family." In fact, we are trademarking that specific phrase and it has become the principal identity for these radio stations. Given the content concerns as a result of the Super Bowl halftime programming issue, our positioning has proven to be more than fortuitous. Adults with families are motivated more than ever to find quality programming that they know never will be offensive to their personal values and those they desire for their children. Family-friendly programming targeting the values-driven audience has been our strategic focus for more than 30 years. More than 40 percent of Americans attend church at least once a week and more than 60 percent are members of a church or synagogue — statistics that have remained consistent for more than 40 years. The religious radio audience is large and, in fact, is the fastest-growing format in radio with a 38 percent growth in listenership over the past five years.[1]

79

Salem Communications is the result of a long-term vision by two men — Stuart Epperson and Edward Atsinger — developed over four decades in Christian radio. Epperson is from North Carolina, where he was active in conservative Republican politics and twice ran for Congress. He built his first radio station in 1961 in Roanoke, Virginia, and acquired a second two years later in Winston-Salem, North Carolina. Atsinger was born in Honolulu, grew up in Southern California, and attended Bob Jones University and the University of Southern California where he earned a graduate degree in communications. For several years, he taught at Los Angeles City College where he served as the college's director of forensics and as an associate professor of speech. Atsinger bought his first station in Raleigh, North Carolina, in 1967, and entered into the first joint venture with Epperson in 1972 to buy a station in Bakersfield, California. Along the way, Epperson married Atsinger's sister Nancy. In 1974, Atsinger put his first full-time Christian radio station on the air — KDAR-AM in Oxnard, California. Three years later, Epperson and Atsinger sold all their secular stations to devote their efforts exclusively to developing commercial Christian radio stations.

They formed Salem Communications in 1986 with 13 radio stations, including outlets in New York, Los Angeles, and Boston. Within a few years, Salem added properties in Seattle, Portland, San Diego, Chicago, and Washington and began to establish clusters of more than one station in many major radio markets. Salem funded most of its acquisitions by selling stations whose value had increased under its management. It also purchased many undervalued AM stations in large markets that Epperson and Atsinger thought were suitable for Salem's programming concept and capable of serving its target audience. When the Telecommunications Act of 1996 and subsequent FCC policy changes liberalized ownership rules, Salem was positioned for expansion both into new markets and by adding more stations to existing clusters.

The company went public in 1999, but Epperson, Atsinger and their families still control the majority of the stock. Salem now owns and operates 98 stations, located in 38 markets. With 60 stations in 23 of the top 25 markets, Salem has assembled one of the premier radio station groups in the nation through strategic acquisition and clustering strategies. In an industry moving rapidly toward consolidation and concentration of ownership, Salem owns the sixth largest group of radio stations overall and is the third largest operator of stations in the top 25 markets, behind only Clear Channel Communications and Infinity (Viacom). Since 1998, *Radio Ink* magazine has named Salem CEO Edward Atsinger one of the 40 most powerful people in radio, most recently at number 28 on the list. Atsinger is the only Christian radio executive included.[2]

Salem has built a national presence with an acquisition strategy focused on the top 50 U.S. markets. The approach to acquisitions does, however, vary from that of its radio broadcasting peers. For the most part, radio broadcasters purchase stations based on a price that is a multiple of current cash flows of that station. Most broadcasters are not only purchasing the radio frequency, but also the format that it broadcasts. In Salem Communications' case, there is rarely the opportunity to acquire a radio station already operating in one of its strategic formats. Therefore, the focus is on acquiring a station with a strong signal, in a large market, that based upon internally developed financial projections will deliver an appropriate return on investment. Salem then reformats the station, markets and promotes the new format to develop listenership, and cultivates the customer base to grow revenues. The start-up-to-maturity process in most cases is a span of three to five years, beginning with a period of start-up losses, moving to break even, and then growing profitability.[3]

In addition, management states that Salem is the 13th-largest radio broadcaster measured by net broadcasting revenues and leads the entire radio industry in both net revenue growth and growth in same-station operating income since 2001. For 2003, the company had total revenue of $170.5 million and operating income of $42.4 million. During the year, Salem Communications bought radio stations in Boston, Sacramento, and Colorado Springs, adding to clusters in those markets, and acquired a four-station group in Jacksonville, Florida, for a total investment of $19.7 million. In early 2004, Salem bought two more FM stations in Honolulu for $3.7 million. Atsinger commented:

> The acquisition of these two full market FM stations gives Salem three FM and five AM stations serving the Honolulu market. This addition will provide attractive economies of scale to our overall Honolulu cluster, and will significantly enhance our FM coverage of this market.[4]

Salem assets total $560 million against long-term debt of $336 million. Its stock price (listed on NASDAQ) rose slightly over the year 2003 and continued an upward trend in 2004. The value of Salem's stock outstanding is more than $500 million.[5] Any way you measure it, this is a sizeable commercial business. And its business is Christian radio.

Salem Communications is the leading U.S. radio broadcaster providing religious and family-themed radio programming, with a nationwide presence that would be extremely difficult and expensive to duplicate. Headquartered in Camarillo, California, Salem employs more than 1,400 people nationwide. Salem has built a solid reputation for offering a unique blend of Christian inspirational programming, articulate and values-driven news/talk, and uplifting music that is "Safe for the Whole Family." Its Contemporary Christian music stations, primarily known as The Fish, are delivering strong growth and represent the sixth most popular music genre in the U.S. And Salem has expanded its reach beyond radio broadcasting to Christian-content Internet sites and magazines that explore Christian music, urban culture, and youth ministry.

Radio Station and Network Operations

Created in 1993, Salem Radio Network (SRN) has grown to become the largest full-service network featuring programming content that targets the core audience. SRN syndicates talk programming, news and music to more than 1,600 affiliated radio stations throughout the United States. In addition, the company is the exclusive provider of religious talk and music content to XM Satellite Radio, produced by Salem's WAVA, one of two satellite-based radio systems with a national footprint.

SRN headquarters are in Irving, Texas, with news originating in Washington, D.C. Music network operations are based in Nashville, Tennessee, where SRN occupies a clean, modern office complex in a surprisingly quiet cul-de-sac near the municipal airport. On the music side, from its Nashville location Salem originates three radio networks and programming for its four local radio stations, including 94 FM The Fish. Salem Music Network offers three 24-hour Christian music formats and syndicates a specialty radio magazine. The availability of SRN's content menu provides Salem Communications with programming and cost benefits. The company can quickly and economically program recently acquired stations by availing itself of its own network content.

Through its contemporary Christian music format, "Today's Christian Music," Salem is able to provide a national audience with programming similar to that used on its Fish stations. This includes the words of inspirational recording artists with upbeat contemporary music. This is music that is "Safe for the Whole Family," with sounds that cross age demographics and lyrics that parents appreciate. Christian music represents approximately seven percent of total U.S. album sales and is the sixth most popular music genre. Salem Communications believes that this listener base has been underserved in terms of radio coverage, especially in the larger markets. So far, Salem Communications has launched 15 Christian music radio stations to take advantage of this opportunity.

Salem Music Network General Manager Mike Miller defines the primary demographic for The Fish stations as females ages 25–49, an attractive and desirable target for advertisers. Miller allows that within Salem and the Christian radio industry, top AC programming consultants are designing formats to appeal to this audience. "People will listen to familiar radio. We want to keep them in a comfort zone," he said.[6] The sound is bright and professional with minimal intrusions into the music.

Although Miller has worked in Christian radio for more than 20 years, most on-air personalities and sales and marketing staffers come from secular radio. "Our main competitors are mainstream Adult Contemporary (AC) stations," Miller said. "The people on air are welcome to talk and comment about life experiences and offer an occasional Scripture passage, but no preaching. We want the audience to get the message from the music."[7]

Along with Today's Christian Music, Salem Music Network provides "Solid Gospel" and "The Word in Praise" music streams for its own stations and affiliates. With uplifting Southern Gospel and a cheery on-air presentation, Solid Gospel has helped scores of radio stations develop fiercely loyal and responsive radio audiences. Broadcasting live from the heart of Nashville, Solid Gospel has its finger definitively on the pulse of the southern gospel industry, daily bringing its listeners the opportunity of participating in the lives and ministry of the artists and personalities through one-of-a-kind features, interviews, and specials. Solid Gospel, a network that Salem purchased, has a small but dedicated audience of adults ages 35-plus, located primarily in the rural South, Southwest and Midwest.

The Word in Praise features Praise and Inspiration music that is often used in contemporary church services. Its audience is adults ages

25-plus, with a slight female skew, who go to church regularly and rec-
ognize the music. The music and presentation style are more slowly paced
than Salem's other streams, much like a secular Soft AC format. Stations
use this music stream most often as sustaining programming.

In 1999, Salem started an Internet stream for teenagers called Christian Pirate Radio. The objective was to provide Christian rock and contemporary Christian music with an edge to serve this audience outside
of markets where Salem operated stations. Salem suspended its operation in May 2003, however, when copyright fees for music in Internet
streams became prohibitively expensive.

SRN Talk offers personality talk radio and SRN News, which originates from its news center in Washington, D.C., where a team of anchors
and reporters provide coverage of breaking news. News/talk programming is the second most popular radio format in the country, based both
on listenership and number of radio stations. Salem's research has shown
that news/talk is highly complementary to the Christian teaching/talk
format. Both formats express conservative views and family values.
Founder Stuart Epperson is not bashful about explaining his and the
company's political leanings:

> My partner Ed Atsinger and I founded Salem Communications Cor-
> poration, which owns and operates commercial radio stations in vir-
> tually all the major markets in this country. We are in this business
> primarily because we have a point of view. Moreover, we think our
> views are well received in the marketplace of ideas. Our editorials
> emphasize limited government, free enterprise, a strong national defense
> and traditional moral values. These principles are also, in general, the
> views of our talk show hosts. We have both local hosts and nationally
> syndicated hosts. Indeed we syndicate far beyond the reach of the sta-
> tions we own. Not only are we conservative in our politics but we also
> operate within the Judeo-Christian moral framework, as did our found-
> ing fathers.[8]

Yet Epperson is also a fervent supporter of freedom of expression and a
foe of government intrusion into broadcasters' rights to include controversial programming in their schedules.

> I deplore the current state of this immoral and debased culture. I am
> working in every way I know how to change it. I think what is being
> passed off as entertainment these days is an outrage, but I am serious

when I say we support limited government.... Mark my words, however: if impending government action can cause Howard Stern to be taken off the air, imagine a bill that would give the FCC power to so regulate content that after three fines for violating standards set by fiat, a station could lose its license.... It is my fervent hope that Conservatives, especially Religious Conservatives, won't get driven into believing that more government is the answer to this cultural problem. It will only lead to disasters ... and no bill, once passed by Congress and signed into law, is ever repealed. Today it is Stern, Bubba (the Love Sponge) and Janet Jackson in the spotlight. Tomorrow it could be Limbaugh, Dobson and Janet Parshall.[9]

The Christian news/talk format also provides Salem Communications the opportunity to use the syndicated talk programming of its network on its local stations. SRN features some of the most persuasive and familiar on-air personalities on radio.

The Mike Gallagher Show is a blend of timely political commentary, compelling talk and terrific discussions on social issues and lifestyle topics. His warmhearted perspective as a husband and father of four children has helped catapult the show to one of the fastest-growing radio talk programs in the country. *Talker's* magazine estimates that 2.25 million listeners across America tune in weekly, including those in top-10 markets like Chicago, Dallas, Los Angeles and Washington, D.C. Mike is a sought-after pundit on television and appears regularly on Fox News Channel, CNN, Court TV and MSNBC.[10]

Janet Parshall, host of *Janet Parshall's America*, is one of America's most articulate advocates for Christian values in a society that often seems to have lost its moorings. As the leading Christian syndicated talk show in the country, *Janet Parshall's America* is heard daily on more than 100 stations coast to coast. The program originates from Washington, D.C., where her guests include senators and representatives; authors and film producers; Catholics, Protestants and Jews; pro-family advocates; historians; public policy experts; and national leaders. As one of the only conservative talk shows in the nation hosted by a woman, *Janet Parshall's America* is thought-provoking and interactive radio. As a frequent guest on MSNBC, C-Span, *Focus on the Family* and Fox, Janet is quickly becoming one of the more visible conservative commentators in the media.[11]

From pop culture to politics, from religion to feminism, from American history to the fight for the family, *The Michael Medved Show* is a hard-hitting, contemporary talk show with a new style and personality. More than just another sound-alike conservative talker, Michael Medved has a unique blend of provocative dialog, incisive commentary and relatable humor. He reviews both new movies and political performances (like candidate debates and major speeches), focusing on the values and impact of our media-saturated culture. Medved's local show debuted in 1996 in Seattle. Its top ratings generated plans to take the show to a national audience; it debuted nationally in 1998 on 40 stations. By October of 1999, the show reached more than 100 markets across the country.[12]

The Hugh Hewitt Show is entertaining political talk that "aims at your head, not below the belt." Hugh's upbeat and engaging style has made his show a growing favorite of Americans across the country and can be heard on more than 40 radio stations nationwide, including the afternoon drive in Los Angeles, Phoenix, San Diego, Seattle, San Francisco and Denver. Hewitt appears frequently as a political and social commentator on CNN, MSNBC, and Fox News Channel. He is a columnist for WorldNetDaily.com and TheDailystandard.com and is the author of four books, including *In, But Not Of: A Guide to Christian Ambition and the Desire to Influence the World* and *If It's Not Close, They Can't Cheat.* He is a graduate of Harvard College and the University of Michigan Law School.[13]

The Dennis Prager Show is different from every other radio talk show in America. First, Dennis talks about everything in life. Everything. From international relations to family issues to religion to sex. Second, Dennis is not only very smart, he is very funny. Third, he brings a moral perspective to every topic. Fourth, he is relentlessly interesting. That is why, after 20 years on Los Angeles radio, he is the most respected broadcaster in Southern California. The *Los Angeles Times* has described Prager as an "amazingly gifted man and moralist whose mission in life has been crystallized: to get people obsessed with what's right and wrong."[14]

In April 2004, SRN launched a new syndicated talk program designed to fill a syndication void — Bill Bennett's *Morning in America.* Bennett is the former secretary of education under Ronald Reagan, an in-demand public speaker, national TV talk show commentator and best-selling author. His new show fills the key morning-drive slot in the network's syndicated offerings that is important to affiliate stations as well as the owned-and-operated Salem news/talk stations. The guest list for the first show included Rush Limbaugh, Donald Rumsfeld, Pittsburgh Steelers coach Bill Cowher, former New York governor Mario Cuomo, *Wheel of Fortune* host Pat Sajak, former Clinton attorney and D.C. lawyer Bob Bennett, Tim Russert, Naomi Judd and author/commentator George Will. "We are delivering a fast-paced, eye-opening national morning show with news, headline-making guests from the worlds of politics, media, sports and entertainment, and we'll open up a dialogue with listeners from coast-to-coast every morning," said Bennett.[15]

The editorial staff at SRN News is equally impressive. David Aikman is a veteran journalist who worked for *Time* as a senior and foreign correspondent for more than 23 years and has written extensively on religious freedom in Asia and the Middle East. He has served as a senior fellow at the Ethics and Public Policy Center in Washington, D.C., and is the founder and chairman of Geographa, a global fellowship of Christian journalists, and editor-at-large of the Internet-based Newsroom, which reports on the religious dimension of worldwide news. His September 1997 *Weekly Standard* cover story, "The Laogai Archipelago," was the most detailed journalistic account to date of China's prison and labor camp system.

Terry Eastland has written on legal and political subjects for publications including the *Los Angeles Times, Newsweek, World Magazine* and *Christianity Today.* He is the publisher of the *Weekly Standard,* a weekly columnist for the *Dallas Morning News* and contributor to the *Wall Street Journal.* In the 1980s Eastland was editor of the *Virginian-Pilot* and director of public affairs for the U.S. Justice Department. Eastland was also a correspondent for two PBS programs and editor of Forbes *MediaCritic* and *Media and Politics,* the online Forbes publication. Recently he was publisher and president of *The American Spectator.* His books include *Freedom of Speech and Press in the Supreme Court* and *Ending Affirmative Action: The Case for Colorblind Justice.*

Albert Mohler, Jr., serves as the president of the Southern Baptist Theological Seminary, one of the largest seminaries in the world. A theologian and ordained minister, he was listed in a 1995 *Time* magazine cover story as one of its "50 for the Future"—emerging national leaders of their fields under age 40. He came to the Southern Baptists' flagship seminary as editor of *The Christian Index.* Dr. Mohler is the host of *Truth on the Line,* a Louisville-based radio show where he brings a voice of clarity to contemporary issues. He is also a frequent guest on TV news

shows such as *Larry King Live*, representing and debating the evangelical community's viewpoint on social and cultural issues.

Phillip Johnson, a law professor at the University of California,
Berkeley since 1967, began a search to understand creation in 1987. An
adult convert to Christianity, he was troubled by the fact that the academic world is so thoroughly dominated by secular and naturalistic thinking. He became convinced that scientific evidence and logic support the
belief in a God who created the world and gave our minds the capacity
to understand truth. His books include *Darwin on Trial*, *Reason in the
Balance*, and most recently *The Right Questions: Truth, Meaning and Public Debate*. He works to disarm evolutionary theorists and proclaim the
truth of intelligent design.

At SRN, Christian teaching/talk is the foundational format.
Through this format a listener can find Bible teaching and sermons, as
well as answers to questions relating to daily life, from raising children
to religious legal rights in education and the workplace. This format
serves as both a learning resource and personal support for listeners
nationwide.

With stations that are strategically located in America's largest markets, Salem is a very important means for block programmers, radio ministries, and advertising customers to reach large audiences. As well as
generating advertising revenue, this format derives substantial revenues
from the sale of uninterrupted blocks of broadcast time (usually in 26
or 55 minute increments) to block programmers desiring an opportunity to broadcast to a specific market or across the nation. The exposure
that block programmers receive on Salem stations is very important to
their survival and growth, and, as a result, there are minimal cancellations. There are no other radio groups that provide these programmers
with a comparable national platform. There are more than 120 national
ministries purchasing broadcast time from Salem. This block programming business represents 80 percent of the broadcast day on stations with
this format and approximately 40 percent of total revenues. Focus on the
Family alone spends $3.3 million a year for airtime on Salem stations.[16]

The Contemporary Christian music (CCM)–formatted radio stations represent the single largest growth initiative for the next several
years. Christian music, in terms of album sales, grew 13.5 percent in
2001, while overall music album sales three percent, and CCM now represents the sixth largest music genre. In response to this demand, Salem

launched stations with The Fish format in a number of cities, including Dallas, Atlanta, Los Angeles, Chicago and Cleveland. This music is a major attraction to general market advertisers due to its appeal to the entire family. In the fall 2003 Arbitron ratings book, the two largest CCM stations, in Atlanta and Dallas, delivered the best ratings in their history. The performance of KLTY-FM (94.9 FM) in Dallas represented a high watermark for this station, with a 4.8 share of all listeners, ranking third in the market. KLTY-FM, the most mature CCM station, is the prototype for other CCM-formatted radio stations. These stations are delivering very strong growth as Salem continues to strive to develop them to the level achieved in Dallas and are very well positioned for continued progress in the near term.

The News/Talk format also builds on foundations laid in earlier years. Like most News/Talk radio, Salem's political slant is conservative. This format has strong appeal to the core audience and also provides the company the opportunity to showcase programs from the SRN, both reducing the overall costs of operating the radio station and increasing sales opportunities for the radio station and the national sales company, Salem Radio Representatives (SRR). In fact, with the significant growth in station acquisitions and the expansion of this new format, SRN and SRR represent very strong opportunities for growth in the years to come.

The Company established SRR in 1992 as part of a strategy to develop a national platform. SRR sells all national commercial advertising placed on SRN's affiliate stations as well as Salem Communications' owned-and-operated stations. Leveraging Salem Communications' dominant position in serving the Christian market, SRR's regional sales offices provide SRN and over 300 represented radio stations access to a variety of national advertisers. SRN is the country's largest radio advertising sales firm dedicated to helping businesses and organizations reach their target markets using Salem's Christian teaching/talk, contemporary Christian music and news/talk radio formats. Headquartered in Dallas, Texas — with offices in 12 cities across the United States — SRR offers national advertising opportunities through hundreds of individual radio stations and more than 20 network programming options. With the continued growth of Salem's O&O stations and network affiliates, SRR offers its advertising partners an unmatched level of access to this important niche market. This comprehensive coverage allows Salem to attract large new advertisers while at the same time offering the flexibility for an expanding audience to current advertisers. SRR offers an unduplicated menu of advertising and promotional opportunities to customers nationwide. Whether clients need a network strategy that reaches the entire country or one that targets a few key markets, SRR provides unique access to this important listener base.[17]

Marketing and Promotion

Since the chaotic years of the 1950s, commercial radio has been a business where consistent marketing, to both audience and advertisers, is critical to success. While Salem has national contest promotions and sponsors other special events of interest to contemporary Christian audiences, the company puts more emphasis on promotion at the local station level. Some of the local efforts are simple and inexpensive, like sending a station vehicle to local church events, publishing newsletters, and establishing websites. But others are quite elaborate and, like all effective radio promotions, assure that the existing and potential audience enjoys the association with the station and considers it an asset to the community of license.

On December 12, 2003, KPRZ 1210 AM, the Salem Communications News/Talk station for San Diego, broadcast live from the Peutz Valley Local Assistance Relief Center, as ongoing support for victims of the Southern California fires. KPRZ broadcast all its live talk shows on location from the fire. The areas of Peutz Valley and neighboring Alpine lost over 100 homes in the wildfire tragedy that damaged almost every county in San Diego. "It's tragic enough when you hear about families losing all their possessions and having to start over from scratch," commented Kimberly Bianco, promotions director for KPRZ 1210 AM and KCBQ 1170 AM. "But when it hits so close to home, and you find that you know so many people who were personally affected by the fires, it makes it even more real, and you know you just have to do something."[18] KPRZ's midday host, Dana Sturgeon, grew up in the Alpine area, so the fires personally affected her and her immediate family. Sturgeon broadcast live from the Local Assistance Relief Center in Peutz Valley from 2:00 to 3:00 P.M., and then Tim Scott, host of *Dr. Scott Live*, and Mike Law, host of *The Grapevine*, continued the coverage throughout the afternoon. "We have committed to continue our onsite coverage as long as needed,"

stressed Bianco. "Once that need is met, then we will remain committed to keeping these reparation efforts in the forefront of our listeners,
until all the needs are met, and these people can begin to rebuild their
lives."[19]

In April 2004, Salem stations KNUS-AM and KRKS-FM in Denver hosted the first ever Family Expo at the Douglas County Events Center fairgrounds in Castle Rock. More than 60 businesses and organizations
serving the Denver Metro area were on hand to provide support and
resources to meet the needs of busy parents and families. According to
Bryan Taylor, general manager of Salem Media of Colorado, the stations
were filling a need that exists in the Denver Metro area. "We hear daily
that parents are looking for resources to help them navigate parenting
and other 21st-century parenting issues. Currently, there is no Christian-
centered event supporting families in the entire Metro area. Through our
stations, we are connected to so many superior organizations that creating this event just made good family sense," said Taylor.[20] The Family
Expo included hands-on demonstrations, live broadcasts and entertainment including live broadcasts of *The Gina Geraci Show, Mr. Fixit* and
the *Mike Boyle Restaurant Show*, entertainment from S.o.K on Friday evening and KidzArk with Jay Littlefield on Saturday. Also, a special Kids
Korral provided an enclosed, secure supervised play area for children to
allow parents to attend workshops and seminars. ColoradoKids.com and
Banker's First Mortgage were co-sponsors of Family Expo.

In May 2004, H. B. London, *Focus on the Family* vice president of
ministry outreach/pastoral ministries, was the special guest speaker at the
6th Annual KKLA Pastor Encouragement Luncheon at the Anaheim/
Orange County Doubletree Hotel. The event was presented by Southern California's most listened to Christian teaching and talk radio station, Salem's KKLA-FM. Free to pastors and their staff, the 6h Annual
KKLA Pastor Encouragement Luncheon featured a complimentary luncheon, refreshing teaching, praise and worship and special gifts for all. Master of Ceremonies was former major league baseball pitcher Frank Pastore,
host of KKLA-FM's *Live from LA*. London served three decades in pastoral ministry, including a lengthy pastorship at First Church of the
Nazarene in Pasadena, CA. H. B. then accepted the invitation to become
assistant to the president for Focus on the Family. His role as vice president of ministry outreach/pastoral ministries is a liaison to pastors and
churches — a kind of "pastor to pastors." Since joining forces with Focus,

H. B. has directed the development of ministries to pastors and their spouses and given oversight to ministries affecting physicians, youth culture, the inner city, missionaries, chaplains and basketball camps for the children of single parents in many cities throughout the U.S. and Canada. He communicates with thousands of pastors and church leaders each week through *The Pastor's Weekly Briefing* (a fax network) and produces a bi-monthly *Pastor to Pastors* cassette and newsletter. Sponsors for the 6th Annual Pastor Encouragement Luncheon included Azusa Pacific University, Center for Individual and Family Therapy (CIFT), La Habra Music Center, The Master's College, Pacific Mortgage & Lending Co. and Patton College.[21]

In the summer of 2004 KFSH-FM and sister station KKLA-FM, Salem's Los Angeles CCM and Christian Talk/Teaching stations respectively, held a talent search for the next star of contemporary Christian music, and the winner had the opportunity to appear in concert with premier artists Steven Curtis Chapman, Delirious, Jars of Clay, Crystal Lewis and Jeremy Camp on the Main Stage at the third annual Fish Fest, on Sunday, July 25, at the Verizon Wireless Amphitheater in Irvine, California. The StarFish Award, sponsored by Applied Financial Planning, was chosen by music professionals as well as KFSH-FM and KKLA-FM listeners. Contestants were invited to submit one song on CD. The Salem Los Angeles music team — Bob Shaw, KFSH-FM music director; Jim Governale, weekend host; Big Wave Dave, afternoons on KFSH-FM; and Chuck Tyler, Salem Los Angeles program director — selected weekly finalists that aired Fridays on KFSH-FM's "Fresh Fish Friday," between April 23 to June 25, 2004. Listeners were invited to vote for their favorite StarFish song online on the KFSH-FM website (www.thefish959.com) or on the KKLA-FM website (www.kkla.com) from June 26 to July 4, 2004. Results were tabulated and announced on both stations on Friday, July 9. The grand prize winner appeared on the Main Stage at Fish Fest, and their CD was submitted for review and professional critique by independent label INO Records.[22]

Internet and Publishing Operations

SALEM WEB NETWORK

In 1999, Salem branched out into complementary media businesses. One such venture was Salem Web Network. It established an Internet business, OnePlace, in connection with the purchase of the assets of OnePlace,

LLC, AudioCentral, GospelMedia Network (which was sold in 2000), and Involved Christian Radio Network. OnePlace's activities enhance and support the core radio strategy by providing on-demand audio streaming for Salem's program producers. The OnePlace business model mirrors the radio station business model: revenue from ministries and advertising (banners and sponsorships). Salem then introduced Sonic-Place.com, which provides on-demand audio streaming for Salem's Christian music channels. Although it became one of the most popular websites of its kind, the cost of digital music copyright royalties forced Salem to suspend its operation and direct all SonicPlace.com traffic to a commercial website that sells Christian books, music, and videos. Individual Salem radio stations also developed their own Internet sites for promotional and informational purposes.

Salem now has some of the most visited websites for religious content and has become a leading provider of online streaming for Christian ministries, contemporary Christian and gospel music. Salem Communications' online strategy centers on creating the premiere Internet platform serving the audience interested in religious and family themes content. National websites Crosswalk.com and Oneplace.com are the clear leaders in online religious content — both text and audio. This content can be accessed not only through national portals (OnePlace.com and Crosswalk.com) but also through more than 60 radio station websites, which provide additional content of interest to local radio station listeners.

Since its acquisition in January 1999, OnePlace.com has grown to become the leading distributor of online streaming for religious ministries and radio stations. OnePlace.com serves as both a complement to, and an extension of, Salem's block programming radio business, serving more than 100 of its broadcast ministry partners. OnePlace.com provides 30-day archived on-demand audio streaming of 150 radio programs. Originally, OnePlace intended to offer "everything for the Christian community" in an easily accessible format but it soon shifted its primary focus to providing Christian audio content online. Realizing that Christian radio ministries stations provide some of the most compelling and enriching Bible-based content, Salem decided to offer a corresponding service on the Internet to allow the audience to listen to this content online any time it desired at no cost.

Today OnePlace.com is the leading provider of Christian audio content on the Internet. For the audience, that means being able to hear favorite Christian broadcasters such as James Dobson, Chuck Swindoll, Kay Arthur, and Chuck Colson any time. The Internet audience may also listen live to a choice of more than 10 Salem Christian radio stations. The site is indexed by topic and includes search services for Bible passages and, on related Salem commercial site SermonSearch.com, text of sermons on a wide variety of subjects. Technological upgrades planned for the near future will offer improvements such as faster page downloads, faster connecting speed to audio streams, higher quality audio streams, more radio programs and stations, and more biblical content, text articles, special events, and devotionals.

Salem Communications further expanded its Internet reach with the acquisition of Crosswalk.com in 2002. Crosswalk.com is the largest online destination for Christians and offers the freshest biblically based content on the Web. The aim is to offer the most compelling content to Christians who take seriously their relationship with Christ. Crosswalk.com is built around four primary content areas — faith, family, fun and community. Each category is further subdivided into areas of significance to many Christians including Bible study, devotions, marriage, parenting, music, etc. Within this framework, the site promises to provide timely, relevant, life-enhancing material from qualified, respected Christian sources, including major ministries such as Focus on the Family, Family Life Today, The Bible Answerman and Insight For Living. From the site, the audience may download the latest Steven Curtis Chapman single for 99 cents, purchase *The Passion of the Christ* on DVD, or send Bibles to the people of Iraq.

Crossguide.com is a related site that provides links to other Christian sites on the Internet. Called the place "where Christians find products, services and ministries," Crossguide.com has a directory with categories like churches, music and entertainment, education, pastor resources, events, family resources, shopping, parenting resources, kids, ministries, travel, missions, and money and finance. Banner ads plug publishers, colleges and seminaries, and Internet content filters. One recent banner across the middle of the page promoted a conference named Catalyst, a Convergence of Next-Generation Leaders, in Atlanta. Featured speakers and entertainers included John Eldredge, Third Day, Ted Dekker, Chuck Colson, Sally Morgenthaler, Joe Pine and Roadtrip Nation. Participants had a chance to win a new Mini Cooper convertible.

Crossguide.com is rapidly becoming among the largest websites for Christian classified advertising. Products, services and ministries targeted at the Christian and family-values consumer are highlighted on Crossguide.com. This enormous potential market is a significant growth opportunity for Salem Web Network.

Launched in December 2003, TheFish.com is the online home for digital delivery of Christian music. Leveraging the enormous success of Salem's contemporary Christian music format, TheFish.com offers an array of entertainment news and information of interest to consumers of Christian music. Salem's radio station websites not only promote the core radio station business, they also serve as portals allowing their listeners to access the national content provided by OnePlace.com and Cross walk.com. In 2004, Salem acquired the online employment search site ChristianJobs.com. The combination of these websites makes Salem the number one provider of Christian content online in the country, twice the size of its closest competitor. Salem Web Network generates more than 350 million page views per year and has 1.2 million unique visitors.

SALEM PUBLISHING

Salem's leadership in the distribution of Christian content also extends into print through Salem Publishing, a magazine publisher serving the Christian audience and the Christian music industry. In 1999, Salem purchased CCM Communications, Inc. CCM, based in Nashville, Tennessee, a magazine publisher that has followed the contemporary Christian music industry since 1978 and expanded from an initial magazine to five titles. Combined subscription for these magazines exceeds 150,000. The company's flagship publication, *CCM* magazine, has covered the contemporary Christian music industry for 25 years, playing an important role in the growth of contemporary Christian music. It covers Christian music, publishing and entertainment from a faith-based perspective. Each issue contains news, interviews, book and album reviews and in-depth looks at the spiritual lives of the contemporary Christian music artists. With a circulation of 70,000, *CCM* is a leader in covering Christian music. Through *CCM*, Salem is uniquely positioned to track contemporary Christian music audience trends and to use this information to make The Fish format more competitive.

Youthworker magazine is a professional journal for contemporary youth ministry. This award-winning publication delivers in-depth, no-nonsense articles that explore the unique problems that youthworkers face. It treats critical youth ministry issues in a comprehensive, candid manner designed to help youthworkers create effective strategies for their ministry. *Youthworker* reaches 18,000 subscribers.

For more than 10 years, Bill and Gloria Gaither's Homecoming video series has topped sales charts and broken box office records. In January 2003, Salem Publishing launched *Homecoming* magazine, a bi-monthly magazine full of stories and insights, sharing all the faith, friendship and fun you expect from a magazine developed by the talented and inspiring Gaither family. Within a year, *Homecoming* achieved circulation of 80,000 and reached profitability in its fourth month of publication.

Faith Talk magazines are bi-annual periodicals published with selected Christian teaching/talk radio stations that are designed to strengthen the stations' listenership and enhance sales. Using content from Salem's ministry partners as well as local radio stations, *Faith Talk* delivers content of both local and national interest while challenging the reader with timeless and inspiring messages. In 2003, Salem Publishing produced *Faith Talk* magazines for 10 radio station markets and has since expanded publication into more than 20 radio station markets.

U magazine is a quarterly publication launched in 2001 that features the best in today's rapidly expanding urban culture by recognizing the wide variety of music, books, apparel and other lifestyle products coming out of the Christian urban community.

U magazine maintains a broad editorial focus, covering the history of urban music, the impact urban culture is making outside the Christian arena, and how urban music is being used today in various Christian ministries. Circulation for this special interest publication reached 70,000 in 2003.[23]

Salem Communications Corporation is the undisputed leader in providing and distributing content to the religious and family themes audience. The core business is the ownership and operation of commercial radio stations in large metropolitan markets. Traditionally, Salem has programmed radio stations with talk programming focusing on religious and family themes. The primary format generally features nationally syndicated and local programs produced by religious, educational and non-profit organizations. Over the last 25 years, Salem Communications has become the largest U.S. radio broadcasting company (measured by number of stations and audience coverage), providing programming targeted at audiences interested in this primary format. And Salem expanded programming to include conservative news/talk and contemporary Christian music. These formats are not only complementary to the primary format, but have been successful in their own right.

Salem's acquisition strategy is straightforward: grow value by strengthening existing markets while adding new markets on attractive economic terms. Salem believes that acquisition opportunities will continue to present themselves and it continues to aggressively pursue those prospects. It currently has one of the youngest station portfolios in radio. As these stations mature as businesses in their individual markets, Salem anticipates growing revenues.

Salem Communication's broadcasting operations generate revenue from a number of sources. In addition to the traditional revenue streams consisting of local and national advertising, the company's stations derive substantial income from the sale of block programming to organizations that offer Christian teaching or talk programs. Most of these block programmers are long-term partners who provide a strong, reliable and growing stream of revenues and corresponding cash flow. Salem also operates complementary print and online business to further the service of its niche audience. Along the way Salem Communications has become a major player in the contemporary Christian music, Christian Internet, and commercial radio industries. With its entrenched position in major radio markets and dominance in network distribution of popular Christian radio programs and formats, Salem seems to have a secure and prosperous future ahead.

6. Tired of Cursing the Darkness — American Family Radio

"One evening in 1977 I sat down with my family to watch TV. On one channel was adultery, on another cursing, on another a man beating another over the head with a hammer," Don Wildmon said. "I asked the children to turn off the TV. I sat there, got angry, and said, 'They're going to bring this into my home, and I'm going to do all I can to change it.' I brooded for a while and then came up with a plan for our church to turn off the TV for a week. I sent out a press release and the national media picked up on it. Through that 'Turn Off the TV Week' I learned there were literally millions of other people around the country who felt the same way I did. That was the beginning of the American Family Association."[1]

Short of stature but long on ideas and quick intellect, Donald E. Wildmon is an ordained United Methodist minister, having earned his M.Div. at Emory College in 1965. After serving in the U.S. Army's Special Services, he pastored churches from 1965 until he founded the National Federation for Decency in 1977, which became American Family Association (AFA) in 1988. AFA and the American Family Radio (AFR) network facility occupy a low-rise building, much larger than it first seems, spread over more than an acre just off a busy highway on the western edge of Tupelo, Mississippi. Look closely and you can see where numerous additions have enlarged and improved the structure. A solid native limestone facade dresses up the otherwise ordinary construction. Above the doorway is the dignified, muted AFA logo. No other signage indicates what the business might be. On the walls of the conference room are citations of thanks and merit from Christian, conservative political, and economic development organizations, as well as autographed pictures of Don Wildmon with presidents Ronald Reagan and George Bush.

AFA promotes traditional family values, focusing primarily on the influence of television and other media — including pornography — on our society. It is an unabashedly conservative activist non-profit organization.

> AFA is for people who are tired of cursing the darkness and who are ready to light a bonfire. AFA believes that the entertainment industry, through its various products, has played a major role in the decline of those values on which our country was founded and which keep a society and its families strong and healthy. We believe in holding accountable the companies that sponsor programs attacking traditional family values. We also believe in commending those companies that act responsibly regarding programs they support.[2]

AFA supporters receive a monthly newsletter about a specific issue with a recommended action such as sending a postcard or making a phone call, as well as the *AFA Journal* with news on various moral and family issues. AFA claims that its grass-roots organization is responsible for the cancellation of the ABC sitcom *Ellen* (which featured a homosexual lead actress), the removal of *Playboy* and *Penthouse* magazines from the racks at 7-Eleven and other chain convenience stores and from the commissaries at federal prisons, Pepsi's decision to pull TV ads featuring Madonna, and sponsor cancellations from Howard Stern's syndicated radio show. It has distributed 400,000 copies of the *Fight Back Book*, a comprehensive resource guide of TV advertisers, products and addresses and organizes boycotts of national advertisers who are leading sponsors of TV sex, violence and profanity. It promotes Pornography Awareness Week and Shatter the Silence, a national observance to bring attention to religious persecution throughout the world. In 1994, AFA launched a "war on divorce," by helping develop and distribute the *Marriage Savers* video series.

When Wildmon decided to grow beyond protesting the media to create family-oriented and conservative Christian content, AFR was a logical expansion of the AFA mission. While reading *Broadcasting* magazine in 1987, he ran across an article stating that the FCC would allow non-commercial FM stations to deliver their signal to local communities via satellite. Once AFA had a Christian radio station on the air, it could create a network by building low-power translators, which Wildmon calls satellators, and feeding them the signal from the flagship station. Realizing the vast potential and relatively low economic costs of such a system, AFA filed for a station in its hometown, Tupelo. It took four years, and a tussle with the Mississippi Authority for Educational Television, to get the first construction permit.[3]

WAFR went on the air in August 1991. In February 1993, the first satellator station went on the air in Jackson, Tennessee. Then AFR added full-power stations and satellators to the network, building more stations in a shorter time than any other broadcaster in history. It did so with a mix of technical savvy, opportunism, and grass-roots marketing. Wildmon sought out unused frequencies in the non-commercial band and communities where it was likely that new ones could be allocated. He then blanketed all the churches in each town with a direct mail campaign about AFR and the advantages for that congregation to help him bring a Christian radio station to town. Whenever he got a positive response, he moved quickly to put a new station on the air. With a local church as a partner, AFR was assured plenty of promotion at no cost.[4]

In a move that brought Wildmon more controversy, he exploited an FCC policy that favors full-service radio stations over translators. Wherever he found non-commercial translators in communities that were potential AFR markets, Wildmon determined whether a full-power signal would work there or in a community nearby. If so, AFR filed the paperwork for an allocation, followed by an application for the license. In several instances, AFR was accused of bumping National Public Radio affiliates or other Christian stations off the air, leading to listener complaints. But there was nothing illegal or deceptive about this strategy. In fact, AFR lost several translators itself when other broadcasters proved they could better use the channels for full-service, full-power radio stations. Wildmon merely took advantage of the opportunity that the marketplace and regulatory structure provides and built facilities that the licensees of the translators had chosen not to construct.[5]

By June 1997, AFR had 156 stations and satellators on the air, serving people in 27 states. Now AFR has grown to 205 stations and satellators, and an additional 18 affiliates, with service to 34 states, plus an

Internet stream from the AFR homepage. The network claims that it reaches up to 15 percent of the total U.S. radio audience. Most AFR operations are in small towns, clustered in the Missouri, Mississippi, and Ohio River valleys of the American heartland. There are 25 to 30 new construction permits in the works and a similar number of construction permit applications ready to file that will broaden the AFR reach to more of the U.S. It takes only 40 full-time employees to run the operation. Most of them come from Tupelo or the surrounding area. Although the staff has grown, of the original AFR personnel hired in 1991, very few have moved on.

The AFR physical plant includes a spacious engineering shop where a team of technicians and carpenters prefabricate radio stations. They manufacture control-room furniture, build and install equipment in it, and test it before loading it on a truck. Meanwhile, in the back lot beside the satellite uplinks, another group of engineers installs transmitters, related equipment, and air-conditioning systems in standard cargo containers that can be hoisted onto the same truck and moved quickly to the designated transmission site, where the tower, antenna, and transmission line are already in place. From that point, it is only a matter of days before the new AFR radio station is on the air.

Network Programming and Local Production

All AFR stations carry their programming via satellite from the network central transmission point. Three networks broadcast from the Tupelo facility. The original AFR targeted Christian adults 35–54 with inspirational music. Later AFR added Christian classics with traditional and familiar contemporary Christian music, many selections dating from the early CCM era of the 1980s that became popular at evangelist Bill Gaither's crusades and similar venues. The target here is demographically like AFR's, but the audience differs in its taste for music. A third network, Today's Christian, targets Christian adults ages 25–39 with current and recurrent Christian adult contemporary music. None of the target marketing favors males over females or vice versa.

The AFR networks' schedules contain about 70 percent music and 30 percent spoken word. The latter is news, conservative talk, and a few teaching and preaching programs. But here AFR differs from other Christian radio broadcasters by not selling block time. Some programs, notably *Focus on the Family*, have revenue-sharing arrangements. Funding comes from donations directly to AFR or to the parent organization AFA. A typical solicitation reads like this:

> What began as a God-given vision in one person's heart is now a reality. AFR has had to clear many obstacles to get where it is today and there are still many more to clear in the future. But God is in this movement. And with His help and that of His people, AFR can reach the purpose for which God brought it into being. Listeners can help in three ways: with their prayers, their financial support and by telling others about AFR and where to find it on their dial. AFR is a grass roots ministry, supported by individuals who see what this ministry can do for their own family, their own community, and for the entire country.[6]

The *Wall Street Journal* estimates that AFR raises about $5 million per year, but General Manager Marvin Sanders says that figure is high. Operating costs for the fiscal year 2002 were about $4 million.[7] The schedule for the main network looks like this:

AFR

Program Schedule
Monday–Friday *(All times Central)*

1:00 A.M. Breakpoint with Chuck Colson, *4 min.*

1:04 A.M. Today's Issues (rebroadcast), *51 min.*

3:00 A.M. Focus on the Family, *28 min.*

4:30 A.M. Our Daily Bread, *5 min.*

5:00 A.M. The Real Life with Dr. Frank Harber, *25 min.*

5:28 A.M. Turning Point with David Jeremiah, *25 min.*

6:26 A.M. The Christian Working Woman, *2 min.*

6:30 A.M. We Hold These Truths, *5 min.*

7:00 A.M. Focus on the Family, *28 min.*

9:00 A.M. Love Worth Finding, *26 min.*

9:27 A.M. Home School Heartbeat, *2 min.*

9:30 A.M. Leading the Way, *25 min.*

10:00 A.M. Breakpoint with Chuck Colson, *4 min.*

10:04 A.M. Today's Issues (live), *51 min.*

10:30 A.M. Washington Watch, *2 min.*
10:32 A.M. Dr. Richard Land Commentary, *2 min.*

11:30 A.M. Daughters of Promise, *2 min.*

12:30 P.M. AFA Report, *25 min.*

1:30 P.M. Probe, *4 min.*

2:30 P.M. Money Matters, *25 min.*

3:30 P.M. ByLine, *2 min.*

4:30 P.M. Today's Father, *3 min.*

6:30 P.M. D. James Kennedy Commentary, *2 min.*

7:00 P.M. Turning Point with David Jeremiah, *25 min.*

7:30 P.M. Answers in Genesis with Ken Ham, *2 min.*

8:30 P.M. It's My Turn with Don Wildmon, *25 min.*

9:00 P.M. Family Life Today, *25 min.*

9:25 P.M. Family News in Focus, *4 min.*

9:30 P.M. For Faith and Family, *25 min.*

10:26 P.M. Phyllis Schlafly Report, *3 min.*

Saturday *(All times Central)*

1:04 A.M. Today's Issues (Friday's Broadcast), *51 min.*

8:00 A.M. Kid's Music, *30 min.*

8:30 A.M. The Pond, *25 min.*

9:00 A.M. We Kids, *28 min.*

9:30 A.M. Kid's Music, *25 min.*

10:00 A.M. Adventures in Odyssey, *28 min.*

10:30 A.M. Down Gilead Lane, *25 min.*

11:00 A.M. The Journey with Tom Dooley, *55 min.*

12:00 P.M. Christian Worldview This Week, *30 min.*

3:30 P.M. Money Watch, *25 min.*

4:00 P.M. Top 10 Inspirational Countdown, *55 min.*

6:00 P.M. The Parent Factor with Al Denson, *55 min.*

9:00 P.M. Soul2Soul, *55 min.*

Sunday (*All Times Central*)

3:00 A.M. Focus on the Family — Weekend, *55 min.*

6:00 A.M. Words to Live By, *30 min.*

7:00 A.M. The Real Life with Dr. Frank Harber, *25 min.*

7:29 A.M. Dr. D. James Kennedy, *25 min.*

8:00 A.M. Call to Worship, *55 min.*

9:30 A.M. Hour of Holiness, *25 min*

1:00 P.M. Family Life Today — Weekend, *30 min.*

3:00 P.M. Focus on the Family — Weekend, *55 min.*

6:00 P.M. Let My People Think, *25 min.*

6:30 P.M. Sunday Evening Praise, *3.5 hours*

10:00 P.M. Afterglow, *30 min.*

On-air personalities sound professional, but all AFR networks have a distinct small-town radio style, very much in keeping with its strategy to take the radio channels that were available in the American heartland. Many of the personalities have backgrounds in commercial radio. They talk about current events, tell jokes, and sound upbeat. Occasionally, they share a favorite Bible verse, but they avoid any preaching or disputes among doctrines on the air. Like all good radio announcers, AFR personalities address their audience one-on-one, talking to individuals rather than preaching to a large group of people. AFR requires all employees to be Christians and to profess their faith. It is common to see employees on coffee breaks or eating lunch while reading the Bible and discussing Scripture. They come from a variety of churches, both liberal and conservative. Wildmon is a Methodist; Marvin Sanders is a Baptist; General Counsel Pat Vaughn is a Presbyterian.

Marvin Sanders, a jovial man who raises tropical fish and plays golf, is in charge of AFR operations and the co-host of the daily program *Today's Issues.* Sanders has been with AFR since October 1992 and involved with Christian radio since 1978. Before that, he worked as an analyst for the Cincinnati Police Division. He served as an officer in the U.S. Navy from 1966 to 1970, including a tour of duty in Vietnam. He describes himself as "a patriotic, American Christian. I am primarily a citizen of Heaven, presently 'on assignment' in the U.S." Sanders has a masters in sociology from the University of Mississippi and has completed some doctoral work at the University of Cincinnati.[9]

Today's Issues is a live call-in program aired each weekday at 10:04 A.M. Central, repeated at 1:04 A.M. the next morning. The daily subject matter deals with the moral, social, and political issues of the day. *Today's Issues* approaches these issues from a perspective of biblical, traditional, conservative values. Usually, each *Today's Issues* program features an interview with a guest. In the past this list has included well-known authors, political figures and nationally known ministers. The second host for the show is American Family Association president and author Tim Wildmon, the second generation in the family business. AFR founder Don Wildmon hosts the nightly editorial and comment program *It's My Turn* and is a frequent contributor to *AFA Report*.

Kathy Coats is a broadcaster and producer for the AFR. Having been with the network part time since its inception in 1991, she hosted her own talk show for women called *From the Heart* until 1993. In 1995, after substitute co-hosting *Today's Issues*, she became producer of the program. She also has had an on-air broadcasting shift on both the inspirational and Christian classic networks. Currently Kathy is an on-air personality, and a contributor to both the information program *AFA Report* and the listener call-in program *Today's Issues*. She also does research and script writing for issue-oriented radio specials and musical artists specials. Originally from Birmingham, Alabama, Kathy spent a few years in central Florida with her family during her high school years. Before AFR, Kathy taught women's Bible study classes in her church and in the community. She has served as the director for Sav-A-Life of Tupelo, a Christian crisis pregnancy center, and on the board of directors for the Tupelo Christian Women's Club.[10]

Few speakers entertain and inspire an audience like AFR on-air personality J. J. Jasper. He blends his love for people, life and laughter to connect with his audience as he relates personal anecdotes and insights everybody can identify with. Laughing with him, listeners learn to take themselves a little less seriously. Whether he's speaking to a church congregation or doing stand-up comedy at a banquet, J. J. relates warmly to a crowd and makes people laugh. Some have compared his comedy to that of Mark Lowry and Jerry Clower. Wherever he goes, his enthusiasm for life, his love for people and his down-home humor leave his audiences begging for more.

J. J. is heard weekday mornings on AFR where he uses his genuine love for people and his unique ability to communicate to all age groups as he ministers to morning listeners. Born in Owensboro, Kentucky, J. J. received the highest honor awarded by the State of Kentucky when he was commissioned a Kentucky Colonel. He is a committed, spirit-filled Christian who has devoted much of his adult life to volunteer youth work. He is an athlete and a licensed private pilot, and has been in broadcasting since 1985. His first book—*Moses Was a Basket Case*—was published in 2002. His first comedy video—*J. J. Jasper World Tour: One Night Only!*—was released in 1996. He has appeared on numerous radio and television shows and is in great demand as a speaker and entertainer at churches, banquets, civic groups, college campuses, youth rallies and retreats. His repertoire of hilarious true stories and clean humor is contagious. With his whole heart he believes and lives the principle expressed in Proverbs 17:22: "A merry heart doeth good like a medicine."[11]

Program Director John Riley is also a long-time AFR employee who fits an on-air shift into his busy schedule. "It is a great privilege for me to be in full-time ministry with American Family Radio," Riley said. "I have been with AFR before it began airing for the first time in 1991. Since that time, I have worked with the music and programming of the network as well as being on-air Monday through Friday afternoon to get you home from work." Like all AFR employees, Riley readily connects his faith with his objectives for the network. "Our children are gifts from God and arrows that must be pointed in the right direction for the Lord Jesus Christ," he said. "My prayer for you is that you will know Jesus in a more intimate way day by day and that the ministry of American Family Radio will help you do just that!"[12]

Special AFR programs tend to be oriented to news and issues from a conservative Christian perspective, like the recent program "Counterfeit Marriage: An Honest Appraisal of Same-Sex Unions," which is also available for purchase on CD through the AFR website.

> The program explores the reasons behind the push for same-sex "marriages" as well as answers to many of the most common questions regarding this controversial issue. In addition to covering the current rise in homosexual activism, the program will also address the nature and causes of homosexuality; whether homosexuality is good for the individual and/or society; and dispel the myths surrounding the aberrant behavior.
>
> "Counterfeit Marriage" also discusses why Christian heterosexuals should care whether homosexuals should "marry."
>
> Special guests on the program include:

- Robert Knight, director of the Culture and Family Institute for Concerned Women for America
- Dr. Bob Scheidt, current chair of the Ethics Commission of Christian Medical and Dental Society
- Dr. Glen Stanton, Focus on the Family's senior analyst for marriage and sexuality
- Alan Sears and Craig Osten of the Alliance Defense Fund
- Star Parker, founder and president of CURE, the Coalition on Urban Renewal and Education
- Other experts as well.[13]

AFR News

In 1995, AFR started its own news department "so that our listeners could get accurate unbiased information on issues of interest to them. The news AFR listeners get is so refreshingly different from the usual liberal news sources." Initially AFR produced a weekday, conservative public affairs program, originating in its Washington studio, but now all AFR news and talk programs come from its base in Tupelo. News and information has become an important niche for AFR — a chance to present news that Marvin Sanders says "is unfiltered through anti–Christian, anti-family media and reports news that is of interest to the Christian community."[14] The Rev. Jerry Falwell said that AFR is "a primary media outlet for religious conservatives today." Network promotion makes the following claims for this service:

> Whether it's a story about prayer in public schools, workplace restrictions on Christians or battles for biblical truth within our denominations, AFR News is there to tell you what the newsmakers are saying. AFR News is a national Christian radio news service based in Tupelo, Mississippi. Our goal is to present the day's news from a Christian perspective. We not only feature the latest breaking stories from across the United States and around the world, but also news of the challenges facing Christians in today's society. On AFR, you will get your news from reporters you can trust to give the latest news without the liberal bias which characterizes so much of the mainstream media. For a refreshing and informative change in where you get your daily news, tune into AFR News. You can hear AFR News at five minutes before each hour on AFR radio stations across the country.[15]

AFR News Director Fred Jackson is a Canadian with a university degree in biology and chemistry. After a stint in the Canadian Armed Forces as a pilot, he began his career in journalism. He also attended Baptist Bible College in Springfield, Missouri, for a year of study, where he met his wife, Susy. Later, Jackson's career took a new direction. "After nearly 20 years in broadcasting in Canada, God once again stirred my heart about taking what I had learned in secular news operations and applying it to Christian broadcasting," he explained. "A meeting with Dr. Don Wildmon at American Family Radio in October 1996 led me to my present position ... News Director at AFR. God has been so good to me in so many ways over the years. I praise him for giving me the privilege to serve him."[16]

Reporter Sherrie Black was born and raised in Tupelo. After graduating from high school, she attended a local community college for two years, and from there went to Mississippi State University where she majored in broadcast communications. Her radio career, however, began when she was a junior in high school at a local Christian radio station. Sherrie has been in radio, on and off, ever since. In June of 1991, she went to work at AFR before the flagship station ever went on the air. In her time with AFR, Sherrie has been an on-air personality, production staff and writer, paperwork guru, music librarian, and "general all-around flunky." She currently anchors and reports news on the hourly AFR newscasts. "I enjoy spending time with my son as well as reading, participating in local community theatre, singing, fishing, spending time in the Word, arts and crafts, cooking, gardening, and so much other fun stuff that I just can't list it all here, Black said. "I have been saved for over 25 years, and every day, He just keeps getting better and better, and I thank God for His faithfulness in my life every day."[17]

Jim Brown was born and raised in the small town of Winnebago, Illinois. "Family has always been important to me," Jim said. "I thank God every day for my two loving parents that have always set a positive example for me to follow. I'm also extremely fortunate to have four younger sisters who love the Lord as well: Annie, Jenny, Becky, and Carrie." After graduating from Pensacola Christian College in May 2000 with a major in broadcasting, Brown joined the AFR News staff in July of that year. When away from the ministry, he enjoys running in 5-K races, lifting weights, and eating healthy food. "Serving as associate editor of AgapePress Christian News Service and as a reporter for AFR News, it is my duty to try to shine the light of God's truth, which often exposes evil in different forms and different groups," Brown said. "I believe compromise on matters vital to the Christian faith can gradually lead an individual, church, or institution away from sound teaching of the Word of God."[18]

Washington reporter Bill Fancher was born and raised in "a Christian home in Columbus, Mississippi." He attended Louisiana State University where he majored in music and then Southwestern Seminary where he obtained a master of church music degree. "For all of my adult life I have balanced two careers; leading church music programs and broadcasting," Fancher said. "I have been privileged to broadcast football, baseball, basketball, ice hockey, and NASCAR racing events. I am an avid ice hockey fan, enjoy civil war reenacting, and love to write mystery novels. I compose and arrange church music, enjoy acrylic painting and play guitar and banjo ... much to the dismay of my family." Fancher came to work for AFR in 1995 and began broadcasting news briefs. As AFR News expanded, he was assigned to Washington. "It is amazing as I look back on how God has brought together my enjoyment of radio, news, politics, and ministry into one wonderful working experience," he said. "I thoroughly enjoy the political process and I enjoy the changes taking place as Christians in America become more involved in that process. Please continue to pray for me and for all of my magnificent and wonderful coworkers at AFR. May our Father guide and bless you all."[19]

Chad Groening came to AFR News after spending more than 20 years in the secular media. "I became frustrated with the liberal bias which even permeates smaller market stations," Groening said. "Working for AFR News has given me the opportunity to tell the unfettered truth, without having to worry about some liberal producer or news executive filtering the story. Most importantly, working at AFR News gives me the opportunity to serve Jesus Christ." Groening comes from a military background (his father was an Air Force fighter pilot who served in two wars) and has a commission in the Army Reserve. "My military background is a major reason why I am responsible for keeping up with national defense issues for AFR News," he said. "My other area of concentration is politics. I dig for the Christian family perspective from newsmakers in Washington. In my free time I love to follow my favorite baseball team, the Cincinnati Reds, and help my lovely wife, Christa, with her garden. We are members of Harrisburg Baptist Church here in Tupelo."[20]

Allie Martin has been an AFR News correspondent since January of 1997. He was born December 11, 1964, in Lufkin, Texas. "My father was a television newsman which gave me a taste of the business at an early age," Martin said. "I always had an interest in journalism, worked on the high school newspaper and on the staff of *The Shorthorn* at the University of Texas at Arlington. After college I worked for eight years in the television news business, with the goal of becoming a network anchorman. Although I won some awards and accolades, I felt empty inside and ran from the Lord for years." Martin, his wife, and two daughters live in Tupelo where he enjoys "spending time with my family, working out and studying God's word. I believe it's time for Christians to stand up and be counted and share the Gospel of Jesus Christ even if we have to get out of our 'comfort zones' in the process."[21]

Rusty Pugh has spent the majority of his adult life working in broadcasting. "Since 1980, I have worked in radio — both in news and programming," he says. His career in radio broadcasting includes jobs at many radio stations around Mississippi as well as in Memphis, Tennessee. "It is a real honor to be a part of the news staff here at AFR," Pugh said. "We are allowed the unique opportunity of presenting the listener with the latest news without the liberal bias that is so prevalent today. AFR news is presented objectively, but from a Christian perspective. That perspective allows AFR news to deliver many stories that secular outlets would never air. In fact, we consider it our mission to make sure that our listeners are informed on the issues that matter to Christians." He and his wife, Caroline, live in Tupelo with their son, Matthew. "Some of my favorite leisure activities are playing golf, fishing, reading, traveling and photographing the two-lane back roads ... away from the interstates," Pugh said. "I especially enjoy traveling on and reading about old Route 66. I also love reading and studying American Civil War history. I have visited many battlefield sites. Most of all, I enjoy every minute I get to spend with my wife and son ... and our golden retriever, Pickett (named for Gen. George Pickett, CSA). I enjoy the poetry of Robert Frost. My favorite food is *anything*, because I love to eat, and I like surprises!"[22]

Mary Rettig was born in Bluffton, Ohio, and grew up in the country near Ft. Wayne, Indiana. After graduating high school in 1997, she attended Pensacola Christian College where she graduated in 2001 with a degree in broadcasting. Before joining AFR News in April 2004, she worked as a news reporter for two radio stations in Bucyrus, Ohio. Of her current position as AFR News reporter, Rettig said, "I am so grateful for this great opportunity to mix serving God with my other favorite activity — talking!"[23]

Marketing and Promotion

AFR spends very little money on advertising or printed promotional material outside of the regular AFA publications. It generates press releases to small-town newspapers in the communities with AFR stations and relies on its network of partner churches for direct mail, items in church bulletins, and word of mouth. On-air promotions are unique, often based on specific activities of the parent organization, and well integrated with the AFR website. Recently, AFR raised consciousness about the issue of gay marriage and urged a U.S. constitutional amendment to make it illegal with on-air announcements and blurbs on the website.

Massachusetts Court Legalizes Homosexual Marriage

Marriage laws in other 49 states expected to be struck down! Homosexual marriage is now legal in Massachusetts. The laws defining marriage as being only between one man and one woman in the other 49 states are expected to be struck down. There will then be no law forbidding the marriage of groups of more than two people.

Send a message to members of Congress!

The only way to keep the sacred institution of marriage from being destroyed is demand that Congress pass the federal marriage amendment!

Please join more than 1,327,525 who have already signed this petition. After you have signed it, please forward it on to family and friends.[23]

A second announcement read:

A Petition to Members of Congress

Activist liberal judges are intent on destroying the institution of marriage as being between one man and one woman. I urge you to pass the federal marriage amendment defining marriage as the union of one man and one woman only.

This is a defining moment in history. It is time for members of Congress to take a stand for traditional marriage.

Senator Wayne Allard of Colorado has given Americans a method to restore our religious liberties by introducing a bill, S. 1558, called the "Religious Liberties Restoration Act."

S. 1558 is a legislative statute which would nullify the authority of federal courts to make judgments regarding the public display of the Ten Commandments, the National Motto and the Pledge of Allegiance.

A simple majority and the signature of the President is all that's needed for this bill to pass. No constitutional amendment is needed. Urge your two senators to co-sponsor this bill![25]

Another promotion, with spots set to the *Mission Impossible* theme music, gave away trips to participate in a mission trip to an impoverished community in Guatemala. The copy read:

American Family Radio and Compassion International could be sending you on a mission trip like no other in the Guatemala Mission Adventure Giveaway. Today is the last day to visit AFR.net to register to win a Compassion Adventure Pack — a tote bag filled with a sports bottle, a book and a CD from a Compassion artist. If you're chosen as an Adventure Pack winner, you'll qualify for the drawing for the Guatemala Mission Adventure.[26]

Tim Wildmon and Marvin Sanders, co-hosts of *Today's Issues*, conduct Spiritual Heritage Tours of Washington, D.C.

Are you looking for a tour of our nation's capital — Washington, D.C. — that will be much more than looking at impressive monuments? Are you looking for a tour that will help you capture the deep, rich, Christian heritage of our country and the people who founded it? If you are, then our Spiritual Heritage Tour is for you.

Hello folks, I'm Tim Wildmon of the American Family Association and American Family Radio. Marvin Sanders, my wife, Alison, and Stephen McDowell have been organizing and leading tours of Washington and Mount Vernon for five years now. We have taken several hundred people with us over that time period and know how to get the most out of each day. I can honestly say, we have never had one complaint about the tours. In fact, we have had many people return with us for a second or third time because they learned so much and enjoyed themselves so much.

If you are looking for a stuffy trip with people who are too serious to smile — this is not your tour! But if you are looking to join other Christian brothers and sisters from across the country who want to laugh, have fun and eat well while having a wonderful time of educational and inspirational sightseeing — then you've come to the right place!

Now feel free to look around the website. It will not take you long. And if you have any questions, please e-mail me at twildmon@afa.net or phone 662–844–5036 ext. 228. We at Spiritual Heritage Tours look forward to hearing from you![27]

Like other Christian radio and media outlets, AFR is promoting the effort to control the flow of unwanted Internet content, especially where kids are involved.

> Get the reliable protection your family needs today. While the Internet is a wonderful thing, most parents are concerned with protecting their loved ones from the temptations, dangers and harmful material that gradually invades most homes. The AFA Filter by Bsafe Online has strong, always current Internet filtering software and porn blocker technology that is so easy, any novice can install a free trial right now. Endorsed by American Family Association and many other leading ministries and organizations, Bsafe Online has a passion for protecting families on the Internet.[28]

AFR intends to continue its growth, as funding allows. Because AFA has the policy not to borrow money, it is unlikely that the radio network will buy many new stations. It is currently suing to overturn an FCC policy for considering competing applications for non-commercial stations that AFR finds discriminatory. Another potential constraint on growth is competition from other Christian radio stations.[29] But AFR is well established and has consciously pursued an expansion strategy of building stations in small towns and cities in the interior of the United States where there is support from a local church, avoiding the costly and competitive urban markets. "We take what's available," said Marvin Sanders.[30] So it is likely that AFR will continue to be a strong conservative voice in both Christian media and the radio industry as long as that is Don Wildmon's vision and mission.

7. It's All About the Music — K-LOVE and WAY-FM

"We'll talk about abortion on the air, but won't come down on one side or the other," said Andrea Kleid. "We program rock music, and we could alienate listeners."[1] At the time Kleid, now national promotion manager for EMI Christian music group, was promotions director for WAY-FM in West Palm Beach, Florida. WAY-FM is one of a growing number of Christian radio stations and networks that let the lyrics and tempos of contemporary Christian music speak to the audience. Along with The Fish from Salem, WAY-FM and K-LOVE are largely responsible for developing this format strategy, one that is remarkably similar to adult contemporary or contemporary hits on commercial radio. The big difference for WAY-FM and K-LOVE is that they are non-commercial ministries with more than 80 percent of their support coming from donations by listeners and underwriters. This format, more than any other, is bringing many new listeners, especially young adult and upscale women, to Christian radio.

More Music Every Hour — K-LOVE and AIR-1

"It's simple. Do what the listener wants," said Mike Novak. "We have done research both on specific markets and on a network basis. We know what they want, in all parts of programming."[2] Novak, vice president of programming for EMF Broadcasting, oversees the on-air operations of the K-LOVE and Air-1 radio networks. EMF holds licenses for 88 full-time Christian radio stations and 169 translators and satellites in 40 states, with concentration in Pacific-coast and southwestern states, and plans to add more stations in the future as opportunities and funding permit.

Like many Christian radio organizations, the Educational Media Foundation (EMF) is a ministry that uses radio and every form of media available to reach as many people as it can for Christ. K-LOVE targets women ages 25–49 with Christian adult contemporary music and upbeat, professional personalities. "We have to go out and compete with other forms of entertainment and cut through the noise. Tell the truth, plain and simple," Novak said. "Other forms of media are doing so poorly, they are driving new listeners to us."[3] The programming and marketing philosophy stems from a simple statement of purpose:

- Vision: To communicate the Gospel message through the mass media, leading as many people as possible toward salvation and spiritual growth.
- Mission: To effectively communicate the Gospel message to those who don't know or fully understand it, through full-time contemporary Christian music and short educational elements over radio, the Internet, and other select targeted media — using modern day language and the highest professional standards.[4]

Although K-LOVE seems an overnight success story, in reality it has been the result of a sustained effort for almost a quarter century. In 1980, popular San Francisco Bay Area radio personality Bob Anthony conceived the idea of a full-time contemporary Christian radio station that would appeal to families and encourage people with its music. He sensed that traditional Christian Radio was not reaching the average person. His vision was to launch a new all-music station featuring popular Christian artists at the time such as Amy Grant and Keith Green. Although a revolutionary concept in the '80s, this new station's announcers would tell people of God's love simply, using straightforward language. This easy-to-understand approach would feature positive music that everyone could enjoy and short messages free of Christian jargon.

The first station in what would become the K-LOVE Radio Network was a small, noncommercial station in Santa Rosa, California. On

October 15, 1982, KCLB-FM, "The Positive Alternative," broadcast for the first time. Almost immediately phone calls and letters poured into the KCLB offices. The station was impacting lives, the staff was filled with excitement, and more people began tuning in. Five years later, in 1986, the KCLB board asked Dick Jenkins, K-LOVE's current CEO and president, to step in as general manager of KCLB.

On September 12, 1988, a 9,000-acre fire destroyed KCLB's main transmitter on Geyser Peak in Santa Rosa, California. Although the staff was stunned, another site on Mount St. Helena was quickly found for the transmitter. Providentially, the new location improved the signal and the staff began receiving reports from even more listeners who previously couldn't hear KCLB.[5]

KCLB changed its name to K-LOVE Radio in 1988 and a network of stations began to evolve. Dick Jenkins' personal goal is to see a non-commercial, contemporary Christian radio station in every United States city with 50,000 or more people. "Christian music reaches today's young families better than any other media. Young families are under attack from a constant barrage of unwholesome values, primarily on TV and radio, but also in magazines and newspapers," said Jenkins. "Music is a tool that penetrates barriers and reaches people wherever they are — in their cars, at home, or in the workplace. We literally have the opportunity to take the Gospel on a personal level anywhere, anytime. Someone can turn on the radio when they are totally alone, and the Holy Spirit can speak to them through the music and commentaries on K-LOVE. They may be on drugs or thinking about suicide and just one song will speak to them," he added. "The great thing about radio is that it's always available and the Lord can use it 24 hours a day, and He does."[6]

Utilizing FM translators, satellite technology and digital broadcasting, K-LOVE grew into a network of radio signals, in a scheme similar to that of AFR. All programming originates in the network's California base. The radio audience is now about 1.5 million listeners per week, more than a third of them self-described non–Christians. In 1998, K-LOVE began broadcasting live, 24-hour music without commercial advertising all over the world at www.klove.com. Currently, the network reaches about 160,000 people with more than a million hits on its website each week. In addition to offering Christian music, the K-LOVE website gives listeners up-to-date information on Christian concerts and events, as well as links to artists' websites.

The K-LOVE and Air-1 Radio networks joined forces in 1999 under the organization banner of the Educational Media Foundation and EMF Broadcasting to broadcast great Christian music to people with a wide variety of musical tastes. Air-1 plays Christian Hit music that appeals to younger adults, a perfect complement to K-LOVE's Adult Contemporary format. Listeners can hear also Air-1 on the Internet by linking through www.klove.com. In 2002, Arbitron ranked K-LOVE's web stream as the second most popular in the world, behind Britain's Virgin Radio.[7]

In September 2002, EMF introduced *Christian Music Planet* magazine. This bi-monthly magazine seeks to enrich the lives of its readers through in-depth artist interviews, insightful columns and compelling articles about Christian music, its trends and its overall impact on our culture. A national magazine, the circulation of *Christian Music Planet* magazine is over 175,000 per issue.

At the same time, EMF Broadcasting moved into its headquarters building in Rocklin, California, combining all its ministries under one roof for the first time. From consolidation came increased efficiency and the pooling of resources, as well as better service to listeners in the future. On average, it costs EMF broadcasting $40 per hour to operate each full-time station. In 2002, total revenue exceeded $33 million, with 95 percent of it from listener donations. Another two percent comes from promoting Christian concerts and seminars, and the rest from tower leases, interest on reserve accounts, and other sources. So far, the generosity of the growing audience has kept the radio ministry solvent and able to expand. EMF uses at least 10 percent of its donations to acquire new stations and to invest in new distribution technologies like the Internet. K-LOVE's listeners make donations at about twice the rate of most other Christian radio ministries. Dick Jenkins attributes this success to a revenue model that stresses the expectations that the audience has for EMF and its radio services and that, in turn, the ministry has for its audience.

> I believe the first step to increasing the amount of donor income is to discard the common perception that one to three percent of a radio station's weekly ratings cume [weekly Average Cumulative Audience Estimate] will give. That rate of giving is about half the level of a National Public Broadcasting viewer, meaning that supporting "Big Bird" has a higher value than supporting the Gospel of Jesus Christ. I don't accept

that premise. Raise your audience's expectations, and the listening audience will raise theirs. As proof of this concept, K-LOVE currently enjoys a six-percent response rate from its weekly 12 plus cume.[8]

The secret to this growth has been the programming, based on popular Contemporary Christian music combined with the personalities who, like all radio professionals, relate to both the music and the audience, establishing the image of K-LOVE as a reliable, trustworthy companion. They offer spiritual encouragement, inspiration and a deeper understanding of our Judeo-Christian heritage and promote positive, wholesome family values. While brief personal testimony is welcome, opinions, endorsement of political agendas, or other controversial statements are not because they are not what the audience tunes in to hear. Jenkins explained this strategy:

> Today's listeners compare a Christian radio station's professionalism to secular stations in that market, rather than its fellow Christian broadcasters. At K-LOVE, announcers such as Jon and Sherry Rivers, Mike Novak, David Pierce, Julie Williams, Kip Johns, and the afternoon show's J. D. Chandler and Larry Wayne strive to make a one-on-one connection with listeners. They know that non-believers don't always understand Christian terms, so they relay the gospel message in everyday language, often using their own lives as examples. This establishes a close rapport with the listener, something the K-LOVE announcers have learned through an average of 27 years of broadcasting experience.[9]

K-LOVE formulates its programming strategy with a sound basis in marketing research. It spends more than $100,000 a year on perceptual studies and music research, including phone and online surveys, auditorium testing, and music advisory panels. The programming decisionmakers also pay close attention to psychographic variables like emotion. Yet all decisions are focused on the mission: to tell as many non-believers as possible about the Gospel. Mike Novak said:

> If you have an emotional connection with something, you're far more committed to it. Another important lesson we've learned is that a lot of people say they're Christians, but they don't have a relationship with Jesus. Of course, once they do have that relationship, everything changes.[10]

To reinforce the emotional bond with loyal listeners, K-LOVE offers a variety of personal services. Each month, listeners submit nearly 9,000 prayers requests, and K-LOVE staffers get together three times a day to honor the requests. There are also three full-time pastors on the staff who are available for personal counseling and prayer around the clock. The Donor Relations center makes more than 50,000 calls a year to listeners — not to solicit donations but to thank them for their past generosity and ask if they can pray for them, their families, and friends. Director of Donor Relations Virginia Walker describes their reactions:

> Listeners are thrilled to know their radio station staff cares about them enough to pray for their needs. They love it. The people who answer the phone get so excited, they say, "K-LOVE is calling!" The people we talk to don't feel like they're just sending money anywhere — they're sending money to their radio station.[11]

And K-LOVE also lets individual listeners share their experiences as Christians with the rest of the audience, as Jenkins explained:

> K-LOVE shows listeners the value of the network through year-round, on-air listener testimonies. Through these messages, the staff attempts to prove to its listeners that the network is encouraging believers and reaching out to non-believers across the country and around the world with the message of Jesus Christ.[12]

Novak thinks the future for K-LOVE and its non-commercial business model is especially bright.

> Part of it has to be the need for God. There has never been a time where He is needed so much. With better ways of measuring what listeners really want, hopefully we will be able to serve them better.[13]

Dick Jenkins attributes the growth of K-LOVE to its professionalism, attention to core mission, and adaptability to the changing radio marketplace that includes both Christian and secular outlets.

> Ultimately the success of any station or network is determined by what comes out of the speakers. The philosophy at EMF Broadcasting is that the radio station that provides the best listening experience is the one that wins the audience. That kind of forward thinking, coupled with God's blessing, has rallied K-LOVE to celebrate 20 years of radio ministry. The unique broadcasting, managerial, and revenue model at K-LOVE is fluid, always transforming to meet the challenges of the future.

K-LOVE isn't static. It's alive. It breathes. It changes with the ebb and flow of listeners' needs. It changes to continue meeting our goal to deliver the Gospel in the language of today's culture, to people throughout the world.[14]

Christian Hit Radio—WAY-FM

In March 2003, WAY-FM founder and CEO Bob Augsburg made the following statement to his staff and supporters:

> I am so excited to inform you of a new vision for WAY-FM that has been prayed over and worked on by our leadership team for over a year. This vision begins July 2003, which marks the start of a new fiscal year for this ministry. We believe it will significantly impact our growth and outreach over the next four years and beyond. In summary, it is called *Vision 20:1* and is captured in one sentence:
>
> > Trusting God, we will partner together to expand our outreach to 20 million people by 2007, resulting in a daily, Christ-centered impact in the lives of 1 million youth and young adults.
>
> We believe this vision statement represents a key challenge God has laid on the hearts of our staff, leadership and board. It is one that encourages us to trust Him as we in turn use our energies and gifts to honor God and have real impact in His kingdom.
>
> But with this vision comes significant responsibility, which is why we have developed some specific strategies to turn this vision into reality. You'll note this vision statement has two distinct parts aimed at (1) broadening our outreach and (2) deepening of our impact.
>
> To broaden our reach, WAY-FM is setting a goal to establish a potential listening audience of 20 million people throughout America. Presently, our existing WAY-FM stations in Nashville, Tennessee; Fort Myers and West Palm Beach, Florida; Huntsville, Alabama; and our many translators and affiliate stations are reaching a potential audience of just over seven million people. However, later this year we anticipate three new WAY-FM's in Denver, Colorado; Tallahassee, Florida; and Clarksville, Tennessee, which will make our ministry signal available to a total of nearly 11 million people — an increase of 57 percent, moving us past the halfway mark to our vision of 20 million people!
>
> But we aren't content simply expanding WAY-FM's potential audience. We want to impact lives every day by increasing our stations' number of actual listeners. Presently, ratings show that WAY-FM stations combined reach 350,000 listeners every day. Our vision is challenging

us to partner with God as we seek to triple our daily listening audience to 1 million by 2007. That will take a lot of hard work on the part of our staff, but we are excited and confident this "stretch" goal will be met.

To those of you who support WAY-FM financially or are involved in volunteering or praying, please know that this vision will never go anywhere without you standing with us. This vision statement and the addition of these new stations represent just some of the ways your gifts are being used to reach new people for Christ. We hear daily from listeners about how WAY-FM is giving people hope, helping them to connect with solid local churches, and encouraging young people and young families. Please know that we are extremely grateful for everything you are doing to help this ministry reach out to the youth and young adults here in this area and in new cities very soon.[15]

By the end of the year 2003, the ambitious first phase of this expansion was complete. And due to a fortunate coincidence, WAY-FM acquired another radio station in Longview, Washington, about 40 miles north of Portland, Oregon, giving the group its first exposure in the Pacific Northwest. Vision 20:1 is well underway with further growth in 2004. Augsburg updated the status recently:

Presently WAY-FM has expanded so over 11 million can now hear this life-changing music and ministry. We now have a new WAY-FM outreach in Wichita, Kansas. The biggest change was the recent sign-on of WAY-FM in Denver, Colorado. The response thus far in the Denver area has been phenomenal. This station's coverage includes six major universities throughout Colorado's Front Range.[16]

The concept for WAY-FM is different from traditional Christian radio and from the overt connection to socially conservative politics. Its mission statement is: "WAY-FM exists to encourage youth and young adults in their Christian lives and to introduce non-believers to Christ."[17] Although this is similar to the objectives of many Christian broadcasters, it is focused on a narrowly defined target audience like secular commercial radio. And WAY-FM further details its strategies in its statement of core values:

Christ Centered

We celebrate our identity as a faith-based Christian ministry. The foundation for all we do is based on Jesus Christ as revealed in God's Word. This becomes authentic when our staff, with the help of their respetive local church, exhibits Spirit-led living.

Vision Driven

Everything we are about begins with the vision we believe God has given us, and is found in our mission statement. Vision provides the direction that moves us forward together.

Prayer Supported

From the boardroom to the stock room we want our ministry covered in prayer. We pray for one another regularly, pray for God's Hand to remain upon this ministry, and encourage others to do the same.

Clear Communication

We welcome and lovingly respond to Spiritual inquiry from our listeners. Since our very calling is to communicate to an audience, we strive to communicate clearly and honestly with each other as well.

Respect Towards Others

We acknowledge our interdependence of each other and that everyone is created in the image of God. For those reasons alone, others deserve to be treated with love, dignity and respect. We are all leaders in some way and look to Jesus as our example of the perfect servant leader.

Wise Stewardship and Accountability

We deeply appreciate all resources God entrusts us with and consider ourselves stewards of your generous gifts. We believe in being accountable to high standards so that we earn your trust.

Remain Flexible

We acknowledge that change is a part of life, and the life of an organization. By remaining flexible we are willing to shift attention and responsibilities as the need arises in order to better serve each other and our listeners.

Professionalism with Excellence

We strive to do our work using out-of-the-box creativity and cutting-edge research, believing work done with excellence honors the Lord and also exemplifies leadership in our industry.

Integrity That Is Honored and Protected

The character of our people and the ministry itself is more important to us than our reputations. Integrity is highly valued and protected so as not to disappoint the Lord and hurt His work.

Listener and Ministry Focused

Recognizing we are part of the entertainment medium, we want our primary focus to be on relevant and transparent ministry to our communities that reflects our listeners' lifestyle needs, through a caring and encouraging presentation.[18]

The final core value is the key to WAY-FM's programming strategy and its success with its target audience. By utilizing contemporary Christian music and its inherent message, WAY-FM achieves its mission with a minimum of spoken-word intrusions. Doug Hannah, former network program director in Nashville, says its approach to programming is centered on the listener rather than a dogmatic philosophy. "We're looking for a common ground among all Christians and attempt to talk to people in language they can understand," Hannah said. "We stay away from issues of theological controversy or non-essential issues that divide Christians. People have an appetite for music and entertainment that reflects their values. People want positive affirmation — in the music they hear."[19]

The other element to WAY-FM's programming strategy is a shrewdly designed and focused marketing scheme. "We do auditorium testing and call outs to select our music, but our secret weapon is Annie," said Andrea Kleid, former promotion director at West Palm Beach. "Annie is our model listener, and we all know her like an old friend. She's 31 years old, a transplant from the Midwest, married with two kids, drives an SUV, works part time and is active in the community. We know about her family, her kids, the things she cares about, what worries her. Even though Annie doesn't really exist, there are plenty of listeners like her in our market. So whenever we're making programming decisions, we ask: 'What would Annie think about this?'"[20]

WAY-FM broadcasts on eight primary full-powered stations:

WAY-FM Denver, Colorado, 89.7 FM (Signal coverage includes Front Range cities Denver, Fort Collins, Loveland, and Boulder, as well as Wyoming cities Cheyenne and Laramie)

WAY-FM Nashville, Tennessee, 88.7 FM (Signal coverage includes Middle Tennessee cities Nashville, Franklin, Murfreesboro, Hendersonville, Lebanon, and Columbia)

WAY-FM Fort Myers, Florida, 88.7 FM (Signal coverage includes Southwest Florida cities Fort Myers, Naples, Cape Coral, Punta Gorda, Sanibel Island, and Port Charlotte)

WAY-FM West Palm Beach, Florida, 88.1 FM (Signal coverage includes South Florida cities West Palm Beach, Fort Lauderdale, Boca Raton, Lake Worth, Coral Springs, Pompano Beach, Deerfield Beach, and Jupiter)

WAY-FM Huntsville, Alabama, 88.1 FM (Signal coverage includes North Alabama cities Huntsville, Athens, and Decatur)

WAY-FM Clarksville, Tennessee, 88.3 FM (Signal coverage includes North Tennessee cities Clarksville, Dickson, Springfield, Ashland City and Southern Kentucky cities Fort Campbell, Hopkinsville, and Oak Grove)

WAY-FM New Johnsonville, Tennessee, 89.9 FM (Signal coverage includes West Tennessee cities New Johnsonville, Waverly, and Camden)

WAY-FM Longview, Washington, 90.3 (Signal coverage includes Longview, Kelso, and Vancouver, and Astoria, Oregon, on 89.7)

The budget for WAY-FM exceeds $3 million per year. The stations and network raise about 85 percent of it in direct donations from listeners, during two shareathons a year. Each one lasts three to four days. The remainder comes mostly from underwriters. Concert promotions with popular Christian recording artists bring in additional revenue.[21] Most of the network-owned stations originate programming, up to eight hours a day, and WAY-FM has 17 affiliates aside from the O&O's. In the past, the group experimented with a Christian rock stream on the Internet at www.wayfm.com, targeted at males ages 18–24 as a possible radio format for some of the translators operated by the primary stations. But WAY-FM suspended this service in late 2004.[22]

WAY-FM has been extremely successful in the very competitive Nashville, Tennessee, radio market where there are 67 stations including 11 with Christian formats. Nashville is also the center for production, distribution, and marketing in the Christian music and publishing businesses. WAY-FM had more listeners than all other Christian radio stations combined in the fall 2002 Arbitron survey. Claiming to be "an industry leader in Christian and mainstream radio," WAY-FM Nashville has won two of the three Dove Awards the station group has amassed as large-market station of the year. The awards are given annually by the Gospel Music Association. In addition, the station has earned numerous Nashville AIR Awards in the local market for many aspects of its radio service. Two years ago the outstanding morning-drive show hosted by

Marcia Ware and Jeff Brown won the AIR Award as best morning show in the entire market, among all radio stations. At the time they had only been on the air together for four months.

The Marcia and Jeff Show is not only popular in Nashville but also in other cities where WAY-FM sends it live via satellite to their O&O stations. Brown is a 17-year radio veteran who worked in Muncie and Indianapolis, Indiana, before moving to Nashville for a stint on the Morningstar Network, now part of Salem Communications. In 2002 he joined the WAY-FM morning team. Brown recently said his career has gone through many transformations along the way:

> I dropped out of college the first time around. I was a music ed. major and one day decided, I can't mess with these junior high kids the rest of my life. They'll drive me nuts. Not long after I dropped out, my mom was at a career fair with my younger sister and came across a new "radio school" that was just starting up. I was the first ever student to enroll, and six months later, the first ever to graduate. Talk about a crash course.[23]

Ware grew up in Chicago, attended Anderson College in Indiana, worked briefly as a singer for Bill Gaither, then graduated from the University of Indiana in 1989 with a degree in music business. She spent a few years in Michigan trying unsuccessfully to start a music career and for a short time sold advertising for a Christian radio station. A job lead brought her to Nashville in 1995. But that job fell through, and on the advice of a friend Ware auditioned at WAY-FM for the vacant Midnight–6:00 A.M. graveyard shift. Bob Augsburg interviewed her over the telephone, liked what he heard and offered her the position, which she held for two years before moving to midday. In 2001, Ware was the obvious choice to fill the vacancy in morning drive time, the most important air shift in radio. In the meantime, she has advanced her career as a singer, working regularly in the studios and churches around Nashville. After the September 11 terrorist attacks, Ware recorded a version of "God Bless America" that WAY-FM featured for many months.[24] As one of the more recognizable radio personalities in a large market, Ware's appeal is her ability to identify with her listeners, as she explained:

> I think that's why the show does so well — because listeners can hear someone who is living the same life they are living. In Christian radio,

that's unique. There are enough people out there who are critical of things I say that keeps it real for me. I have to remember that people are going to talk to you like they know you. I don't see myself as a celebrity. To me, this is my job and my ministry. I don't see this as any kind of stardom thing ... and God help me if I do, 'cause that ain't it. Music is always going to be my first love, but I have given up on being a signed artist. I am 36, sweetheart. They are signing artists out of incubators now. But it wasn't without tears coming to that realization. I have a great job where I am touching lives and am more involved in the industry than I ever would have been otherwise.[25]

Like Ware, Brown works hard to establish his on-air personality and to relate to and entertain his listeners.

There are several roles I take on, or play, as one half of the morning show. Many people don't realize that some of those roles are sometimes exaggerated. Example: For comedic purposes, I've referred to myself a time or two as the Eternal Pessimist, usually to give me or Marcia the opportunity to deliver a well-timed line. Truth be known, I probably have a more optimistic approach to life than most of the people I know. After all, I *am* a believer.[26]

Marcia and Jeff have a bright, appealing presentation and complement each other well. While Brown is organized and professional in a formal way, Ware is emotional and improvisational. Throughout the four hours they mix the carefully selected music with banter about their lives, families, current events, and personal faith. Contests and special features keep the show lively, as with any well-programmed secular radio station. One popular recurring item is the *Family Match Game* that tests how well the members of a listener's family know each other. Another is *Morning Thoughts*, short inspirational segments that listeners may download from the www.marciaandjeff.com website. One is entitled "17 Words That Will Never Fail You."

1. Prepare: If you fail to plan, you plan to fail.
2. Care: For others more than yourself—but don't forget to see about you.
3. Believe: That God is who He says He is, and that He's creating you to be something extraordinary.
4. Forgive: This is a biggie. Start with yourself, then the ones who have hurt you ... remembering all the while that Christ came to forgive us all.

5. Change: Not something to be feared, but embraced — it's almost always for our good ... and if not, we have the power to make it so. That's the beauty of faith.
6. Risk: That's the epitome of love — go out on a limb today.
7. Listen: Don't just wait for the other person to stop talking so that you can speak your mind.... I wonder what kind of world we'd live in if we all took time to do that.
8. Choose: Today the one you will serve. Your checkbook and your calendar should be the appropriate indicators.
9. Relax: You're not perfect ... not on this side of heaven, at least. Take it a day at a time.
10. Pray: God loves you.... He wants time with you.
11. Persist: Stand your ground; hold on to your beliefs. God will come through for you if you stand up for Him.
12. Smile: People will wonder what it is you're thinking about.
13. Focus: A word for all of you multi-taskers — be aware of the big picture, but take things one event at a time.... You'll enjoy it more.
14. Act: Don't react — thinking first will save you a great deal of time for having to make apologies later on.
15. Trust: God wants you to know that He's got your back ... and there are 66 books full of stories that prove just that.... When's the last time you took it off of your shelf?
16. Wait: Tom Petty says it's "the hardest part," and it can be. But it's in the waiting that we learn grace and stamina. At least that's what I'm learning.
17. Accept: That you have limits — and God has none. We serve an awesome creator who will never fail us.[27]

Another Morning Thought is called "The Husband Survival Guide."

This is a handy guide that should be as common as a driver's license in the wallet of every husband, boyfriend, or significant other!

DANGEROUS:	What's for dinner?
SAFER:	Can I help you with dinner?
SAFEST:	Where would you like to go for dinner?
ULTRASAFE:	Here, have some chocolate.
DANGEROUS:	Are you wearing that?
SAFER:	Gee, you look good in brown.
SAFEST:	WOW! Look at you!
ULTRASAFE:	Here, have some chocolate.

DANGEROUS:	What are you so worked up about?
SAFER:	Could we be overreacting?
SAFEST:	Here's 50 dollars.
ULTRASAFE:	Here, have some chocolate.

DANGEROUS:	Should you be eating that?
SAFER:	You know, there are a lot of apples left.
SAFEST:	Can I get you a glass of wine with that?
ULTRASAFE:	Here, have some chocolate.

DANGEROUS:	What did you do all day?
SAFER:	I hope you didn't overdo it today.
SAFEST:	I've always loved you in that robe!
ULTRASAFE:	Here, have some more chocolate.[27]

On-air and special-event promotions at WAY-FM concentrate on live music from Christian artists and extensions of the ministry to support local churches and family services. In a recent month WAY-FM Nashville hosted a free concert with Rebecca St. James and another with Christian rap artists, a Back to School Sonic Pool Party, and a Love and Respect Marriage Seminar, and participated in events at a local church youth weekend and the West Tennessee Impact 2004 Youth Jamboree. WAY-FM also raises funds and solicits donations for charities like Habitat for Humanity, the Nashville Rescue Mission, the Second Harvest Food Bank, and America's Fund for Afghan Children. Listeners recently donated more than 6,000 Christmas gifts to children of Ft. Campbell (in Clarksville, Tennessee) soldiers who were on duty in Iraq and more than 500 cell phones to the Wireless Foundation to provide emergency communication for women in potentially violent living environments. In one 22-hour blitz, WAY-FM listeners agreed to sponsor more than 1,000 children through Compassion International. A recent outreach called Pennies from Heaven urged groups of listeners to collect change to support Mercy Ministries of America, which operates a safe house in Nashville for young people in crisis. The announcements read:

> Lisa was malnourished by her parents, and scarred by numerous cigarette burns. She reacted in fear at the sight of any kind of belt or rope; evidence of her horribly abusive home life....
>
> Laura was a professional patient. In five years, she'd been through five counselors, four psychiatrists, three nutritionists, and numerous medical doctors. Not one of them had been able to help her overcome her eating disorder....

Venus sat still, the words from the doctor reverberating inside her head. *"You're pregnant..."* Having a baby now would ruin her life. She was too embarrassed to tell her family. She was trapped....

These are just a few of the stories of young women who have found help, hope and healing ... but most important, a true relationship with Jesus Christ.

It all began when each of them came to Mercy Ministries of America.

You can help provide much-needed funds for the Nashville Mercy home with Pennies from Heaven all this month. Get your class, your youth, civic or church group together and collect all the loose change you can between now and most of September. The group that collects the most will win a FREE intimate concert with Grammy-winning band Jars of Clay! Your change can change a life.... [29]

The youth ministry is still at the heart of what WAY-FM is trying to accomplish with Christian radio, as Bob Augsburg explained in his quarterly message for the summer of 2004:

WAY-FM is growing rapidly this summer, thanks to the heartfelt prayers and faithful support from listeners like you. It is so encouraging to hear the stories of how God is using our radio stations to really change lives. One recent E-mail that really touched us all says:

I am 15 and I listen to WAY-FM. I have been bulimic and have been through a lot of stuff in my life. Next week I have to go to the hospital for a scope to see how bad I have messed up my system inside. It is really stressful and I've had thoughts of killing myself but I know that is not an option. I was simply going to E-mail you to tell you what a great radio station this is and I end up telling you about my life.... Hmmm, maybe it's a sign. But really, thank you, WAY-FM, for giving people like me a radio station that helps us feel better about ourselves. I appreciate this station a lot.

It's unbelievable how serious some of the issues are that our youth are facing today. So very different than when I was growing up. All of us at WAY-FM are committed to helping youth and young adults find the hope and encouragement they need in God's love. Together, we hope to be able to touch more lives in the future.[30]

In the rapidly expanding Christian radio business, K-LOVE and WAY-FM stand out as innovators who are developing programming concepts to bring new listeners to this radio genre. By concentrating on popular music, a bright sound, upbeat on-air personalities — strategies normally associated with commercial, secular radio — and eschewing traditional preaching and teaching, both groups are building loyal audiences in key demographics like young adult women. The success of these programming concepts is forcing established Christian broadcasters to re-evaluate the way they achieve their evangelistic missions and objectives. Music-centered formats are responsible for most of the growth in Christian radio, and both K-LOVE and WAY-FM are at the forefront of this programming strategy. Many other established Christian radio services are slowly moving from the traditional Christian talk and preaching and teaching formats. This shift away from spoken-word programming comes at a cost, as ministries that purchase block time represent important income for Christian radio broadcasters. But the industry seems to be large enough and its audience suitably diverse in its demographics to accommodate and support more than one Christian radio format.

It is deceptively simple, however, to evaluate K-LOVE and WAY-FM as business models for entertainment ventures. To do so misses the point of the ministries. For neither organization seeks fame or commercial accomplishments. They see Christian radio as the medium that best helps them spread the transforming message of the Gospel. As their networks and audiences grow, they become much more effective evangelists. "It's not about us, " said K-LOVE's Mike Novak. "This is our chance to do God's work. He should get all the credit."[31]

8. In the Wilderness — Heartland Radio Ministries, Joy 89.3, and WTMV

Although the growth of Christian radio can largely be attributed to the big operators who are building networks, clusters of stations, and radio groups to cover entire regions or even the whole nation, a substantial number of Christian stations are serving small towns with local radio ministries. In the United States, regulatory policy has traditionally favored establishing broadcast service in as many communities as possible, a concept known as *localism*. Half of the radio stations in the nation are in small towns, many outside of measured radio markets. Christian radio follows that pattern to some extent. While many small-town operators get blocks of programming from the networks, the needs and interests of listeners in those communities determine their focus and programming strategies. What follows are profiles of three small town Christian radio businesses.

Because It Matters What You Listen To — Heartland Radio Ministries

Hardin, Kentucky, population 564, is not the kind of place where you would expect to find a media empire. Back in the railroad days, people called towns like Hardin "whistle stops." In fact, it still has ties to that era. A few years ago, some enterprising folks bought a few miles of track and some rolling stock, reconditioned all of it, and started the Hardin Southern Railroad, running short excursion trains for tourists in the summer and at Christmastime.

Otherwise, businesses are few. Hardin is a farming community with some grain-storage facilities and used-car dealers, a convenience store or two, and a couple of pretty good restaurants that serve fried catfish, Kentucky country ham with red-eye gravy, and iced tea as sweet as pancake syrup. There's one small building that houses a service station, beauty shop, and taxidermist (an intriguing foray into horizontal diversification), but it looks closed.

But Hardin, Kentucky, is Darrell Gibson's hometown and the place he chose to make his entry into the media universe. Gibson is the co-founder of Heartland Ministries, Inc., a non-profit, non-stock Kentucky corporation that exists for the purpose of encouraging the body of Christ. Since 1988, Christian radio has been the focus of this ministry. At the time, it was easier to find and get licenses for non-commercial frequencies than commercial ones, so Heartland Ministries developed a non-commercial business plan.

Gibson had more than two decades' experience in local radio and knew his community and audience well. West Kentucky's population is conservative in its politics and religious preferences, and southern gospel music is very popular. At one time a local commercial FM had a Southern Gospel format, but by the late 1980s, it had shifted to Oldies. All-night sings — the other venue to promote this music — had faded in popularity. Yet churches and other organizations in the area continued to book gospel singing groups for services, revivals, and special concerts. Gibson believed that his radio operation could provide the promotional platform for these events and other church-related activities, while featuring the music as the fundamental programming.

Along with his partner, Randy Shelton, and longtime WVHM employee Cecil Glass, Gibson sought for and received significant donations from two anonymous individuals to get the project underway and matched those funds with pledges from local churches that wanted regular programs once the station got on the air. Additional support came in the form of *pro bono* legal and financial advice and the discounted services of a consulting engineer who believed that Christian radio was a good idea.[1] On June 19, 1989, WVHM (The Voice of the Heartland Ministries), 90.5 FM, went on the air with a format of southern gospel music and Bible teaching programs featuring nationally known and local pastors. Soon, there was demand for his programming in adjacent rural areas and small towns, so Gibson began to expand with translators and more stations. In 1995, WVHM added its first translator in Madisonville, Kentucky, operating at 94.9 FM. Shortly thereafter, WVHM added its second translator in Central City, Kentucky, at 103.5 FM. In early 1999 WVHM added its third translator, 107.7 FM, in Union City, Tennessee. These improvements extended the reach of WVHM from a signal radius of 15 miles to one of more than 70 miles.

Younger listeners began to request a different style of music. Rather than break the WVHM format into blocks for different audiences, Gibson decided to build a new radio station for this audience. In the mid–1990s, Heartland Ministries received a construction permit for a brand-new radio station featuring contemporary Christian music. WAAJ, FM 89.7, known as "The J-FM," went on the air on November 16, 1996, offering listeners a Christian Hit Radio (CHR) format called "The Real Rock." The building boom did not end with two primary signals. WTRT, FM 88.1 ("Truth 88") was the fourth station added to the roster in December 1998. WTRT serves primarily Marshall, Calloway, and Graves counties in West Kentucky with an Inspirational/Praise and Worship music format.

In July 2001, Heartland built WAJJ-FM in McKenzie, Tennessee, operating at 89.3 MHz. Although this station uses the same CHR format as WAAJ and all voice tracks come from the Hardin facility, the McKenzie operation has separate breaks and information to localize the content. In October 2003, Heartland began to provide WVHM programming to a translator in Madisonville, Kentucky. On April 19, 2004, 90.1 WHMR in Ledbetter-Paducah, Kentucky, went on the air to provide traditional preaching, teaching, and Christian worship programs. Although WHMR features spoken-word programming, the majority is soothing music that Gibson calls "Christian Easy Listening."

All programming for the five radio stations originates in the same Hardin studio. Based on the floor plan of a small ranch-style house, the interior layout is surprisingly efficient for a radio operation. Although there is little or no ambient noise from traffic or other exterior activity, except an occasional lawn mower, the control rooms are well isolated and soundproofed. Early on, Gibson operated a recording studio on the premises. Now live announcers are quickly giving way to voice tracks, hard drives, and satellite-network feeds. Remarkably, Heartland employs only five full-time and about 10 part-time people in its regular operations, although volunteers help out, especially during the two shareathons a year. Gibson and Underwriting Manager Cecil Glass are in their '50s, General Manager Justin Patton is in his '30s, but the rest of the employees are under 30. Heartland recruits and trains its staff locally. Gibson supplements the local voices with professional voice tracks from a producer in Canada. "He cuts anything we can fit on one sheet of paper for $35," Gibson said. "We e-mail him the copy, he records it, and sends us back an MP3 file the same day. Then our local people add some effects and stick it into the computer with everything else that's on the air."[2]

Gibson estimates the total investment for all station and translators and the studio facility at $350,000. The annual operating budget is approximately $400,000, most of which comes from listener and business underwriter donations. The shareathons typically run two to three days, raising the bulk of the operating budget. But very few listeners are also donors. "If we had 10 percent of our listeners making pledges, we would not have to take so much time out of broadcasting the programming they want to hear," he remarked. Heartland also sells program block time to local and national ministries, using a national representative to book the latter. "We financed our expansion out of donations and faith," Gibson said. "Always work out the world's economy using God's system. And listen to your audience. They tell you what they need. Don't worry about demographics."[3]

The overall programming concept is stated in the Heartland Ministries' mission statement:

> Chapter 4, verse 8 of Paul's letter to the Philippians says, "Finally, brethren, whatever is true, whatever is pure, whatever is lovely, whatever is right, whatever is of good repute, if there is any excellence and if anything worthy of praise, let your mind dwell on these things."
>
> Therefore, we believe that "it matters what you listen to." That's our motto, slogan, battle cry, whatever you want to call it. So, 24 hours a day, seven days a week, 365 days a year, Heartland Ministries, Inc., provides encouragement to the body through Christian radio with formats that include southern gospel, Christian hit radio, and praise and inspirational music and teaching ... all listener supported ... all to the glory of our Lord Jesus Christ.[4]

Music is a valuable component of the programming on all Heartland stations, but the message in the lyrics carries more importance for the strategy. "We're not here to promote music; music is what the audience wants to hear," said Gibson. "People want to be encouraged, and music is a very effective hook and teaching tool. Our programming is 100 percent teaching. The lyrics demonstrate biblical implications for today's life."[5] Airtime devoted to music varies among the stations. The J-FM and WTRT play music more than 80 percent of the time. WVHM is 60 percent music, and WHMR, the traditional preaching and teaching station, less than half.

There is a very professional attitude among the staff at the Heartland stations. Even part-time air personalities have extensive training and mentoring from the senior staff and conform to simple yet comprehensive protocols for performance, many of which describe good radio practice in general. Two sets of rules are posted prominently around the studios. The first one reads:

On-Air Polish

Things to remember to help you sound better!

1. Use *more* personality while saying *fewer* words. The words you *do* should communicate enthusiasm to the listener. Be sure people get the feeling you're in a good mood every time you open the mic. Be able to intro songs, give the time, etc., with personality!
2. Avoid lengthy commentaries or stories. If you think you have a *really* great thought, then: (a) keep it under 30 seconds, (b) practice it all the way through before you go on, and (c) make sure it really is good!
3. Do not espouse theology on the air. If you feel the need to comment on a song or Bible verse, do so without saying anything that the Baptists, Methodists, Presbyterians, Pentecostals, or Church of Christ-ers will disagree with. In other words, simple, well-known Gospel truth!
4. Articulate your words with care ... try to pronounce every syllable with crisp-sounding consonants. Remember to take your time, there's no rush! Also beware the West Kentucky accent on words like "try," "cry," etc. They should end with the long "ee" sound.

The second set of rules extends and clarifies the first:

On-Air Shine

Things to remember that will help you sound betterer!

1. Close all doors in WVHM when you are getting ready to read "DATEBOOK." We don't want a ringing telephone to go out over the air ... or a ringing telephone to cause you to rush through "DATEBOOK."

2. Remember that you have many listeners and that they are diverse in both age and background. Avoid the temptation to make comments that only someone in your peer group will understand. Imagine that you are talking to a group of four different persons: (a) 10 year old, (b) 20 year old, (c) 30 year old, (d) 60 year old. Be careful not to alienate any of them, particularly with college-age humor.

3. Along the same lines of "don't espouse theology on the air," try to avoid saying the words, "I think..." when talking about the truth. Truth is not determined by what you think. You either know it, or you don't. If in doubt, *Don't Say It*!

Although audience data are hard to come by in rural areas outside measured markets, there is apparently some overlap among all the Heartland stations, with the southern gospel music on WVHM appealing to a broader audience. The Christian hit music on WAAJ reaches the 18–34 demographic best, especially young parents looking for wholesome radio programming that they can listen to when the children are around. This is intentional. "We want WAAJ to encourage stronger families, especially fathers," Gibson said. "To do that, you must give Mom and Dad something to listen to."[6] Heartland takes network programming from Focus on the Family, Crown Financial Ministries, Salem Radio Networks, and others in the Christian Radio Consortium. The USA Radio network provides national and international news feeds. Local emphasis includes the on-air personalities, either live or on voice tracks, and a substantial number of public service and community and church events announcements. These notices also appear on the Heartland Ministries website. There is no local news, but there are frequent weather updates on all stations.

Recently, Heartland Ministries Radio has seen more competition. Even in this sparsely populated rural location, other Christian radio operators from nearby towns are expanding with networks of translators and bringing new signals into the listening area. And the competition is not just local. American Family Radio bought a station in Paducah, Kentucky, and is very active with local promotion and outreach. WAY-FM has applied for a construction permit to put a translator in Murray, Kentucky, 10 miles south of Hardin, to bring in its signal from Clarksville, Tennessee. Gibson does not seem to be concerned with this situation, and even welcomes the expansion of Christian radio to some extent. "The other stations are not necessarily competition," he said, "because we're all trying to do the same thing. The biggest quest for us is not what anyone else is doing, but what we're doing."[7] Heartland has worked with AFR on some joint promotions and events and has used programming from WAY-FM in the past. Gibson thinks there will be more collaboration in the future because everybody has the same basic objective. "Well, Jesus is coming back! Until then we will press on, lifting up Jesus all day, every day and growing according to His purpose."[8]

Positive Hit Radio — Joy 89.3, WMSJ

Freeport, Maine, is a Yankee village of 1,800 people that uneasily accommodates thousands of tourists every day. They come in cars and buses from all over New England, the Middle Atlantic, the rest of the U.S. and the world to do one thing: shop. Long the home of the mail-order sporting-goods icon L. L. Bean, Freeport re-invented itself in the late 20th century as one gigantic shopping center full of highbrow outlet stores, where the daily influx of bargain hunters clogs the parking lots and the narrow streets, overflows the sidewalks, and creates a traffic snarl that tries the patience of year-round residents who just want to get from one end of town to the other.

Beneath all this Visa-card madness, few local businesses and reminders of the traditions of life in Freeport remain. There's one odd intersection on Main Street with a triangular patch cut out of one corner. It was here that the horse-drawn wagons turned as they hauled timbers from the Maine woods to the shipyards at the harbor. They needed the extra room to swing the long mast poles. There is also plenty of demographic and sociological uncertainty below the surface. Outwardly, Freeport is prosperous, and the surrounding area has attracted wealthy retirees and young professionals seeking shelter from crowded cities and suburbs. But there newcomers brought escalating housing costs and property taxes with them. The divisions between haves and have-nots have gotten deeper and sharper.

Freeport is home to Downeast Christian Ministries and Christian radio station WMSJ. The history of WMSJ isn't about one person or even a few. "It's about God spurring thousands of believers to come together and be a part of His ministry in reaching New England and the world through Jesus Christ."[9] In January of 1984, the process began that would culminate in the creating of radio station Joy 89.3 WMSJ. Founders Thom Starkey and Jim Butt, along with 20 other believers, came together to form what was originally Maine-ly Music Ministries, later to become Downeast Christian Communications. The group initially launched a cable-access program aimed at gathering support for a radio station. Seven years of prayer, patience, sacrifice and determination would see this small but dedicated group through, as they waited for their vision to become reality. Their faith over the years of bi-monthly bake sales, construction delays, and the chronic shortage of funds paid off in 1992 when Downeast Christian Communications received a construction permit for a noncommercial FM channel in Freeport, the southern Maine town that is home to L. L. Bean.

After losing its planned tower on Bailey's Island in scenic Casco Bay, Downeast approached a Christian couple nearby, but the request was emphatically refused. Less than 24 hours later, the woman was on the phone insisting God had told her they were to sign a lease for the site. Then the money ran out and Downeast was close to losing its construction permit. The board held a final prayer session, and the next day, a check for $10,000 arrived, ensuring the project would move forward. In January 1993, in the midst of a period of record cold, the temperature turned a balmy 60 degrees, just in time to pour the cement for WMSJ's tower.[10]

Finally, in July of 1993, WMSJ signed on the air. The station wasn't able to broadcast 24 hours a day initially. For months, dozens of volunteers helped take turns coming in to sign the station off. Short of funds, WMSJ held its first shareathon in October of 1993, seeking to raise $40,000. It was a very emotional early victory for the board and volunteers who had given so much to bring Christian music to the airwaves of southern Maine. Sacrifices were still being made, however, as the studio would go through the winter of 1993-94 with space heaters as the only source of warmth. It wouldn't be until the following winter that a heating system was donated and installed by a team of listeners.

Early on, it became apparent to the board and staff that the original 91.9 frequency wasn't covering the area they had hoped. The signal barely reached greater Portland, the largest population base in Maine, and didn't reach much, if any, of York County. In 1994, dozens of volunteers took to the streets and roads throughout southern Maine to count houses as part of the application process for the vacant frequency at 89.3 FM. That same year, WMSJ launched its first major area of community outreach: concert promotion. WMSJ would welcome Greg Long and five other artists in 1994 and 1995. WMSJ's concert ministry continues to be one of the station's most effective means of reaching out to its audience of teens and young adult listeners.[11]

Now the programming format at Joy 89.3 is very much like a secular radio station, with upbeat disc jockeys who play the music that the Christian audience wants to hear. Some promotions are tune-ins, like the *Top 5 at 5, Tuesday Trivia,* or *Phrase That Pays.* But many others are related to some community service and station outreach, like *The Ultimate Dad, This Month's Child in Need of Adoption,* and a joint venture with Habitat for Humanity to build houses in Portland.[12]

We're the Master's Voice—WTMV, Youngsville, Pennsylvania

In northwest Pennsylvania, the Brokenstraw River valley is farming country. It flows by Youngsville just before it empties into the Allegheny. A few miles to the southwest, near Titusville, Edwin Drake touched off a new era when he sunk the first oil well in the United States. Youngsville is a tranquil town, its population less than 2,000 and almost all descendants of European immigrants. Bill and Patty Baker decided it was a good place for a Christian radio station, an enterprise with which they had experience.

The Bakers had formerly pastured churches in Tionesta, Fern, Waterford, Union City, New Holland and Titusville, Pennsylvania, before coming to Youngsville. Bill Baker was instrumental in the creation of five FM radio stations in western Pennsylvania. In addition, both Bakers previously managed Christian station WCTL in Union City, Pennsylvania, and worked in various capacities at WNAE/WRRN (FM) in Warren, WKST in New Castle, WPIC/WPIC-FM in Sharon, WWIZ (FM) in Mercer, WFEM (FM) in Ellwood City, and WGRP/WGRP-FM in Greenville, all in Pennsylvania.[13]

In December 1997, the Bakers submitted an FCC application for a non-commercial educational family radio station in the name of Living Word of Faith Christian Outreach, a ministry they inaugurated in 1982 that includes Bible studies, fellowship, Christian care-giving as well as communications. The FCC approved that application in October 1998, and the station went on the air in January 1999. The call letters are WTMV, an acronym for "We're The Master's Voice" at 88.5, "where Jesus is *alive*!" Even though the station was still conducting program and equipment testing, WTMV took on an ambitious endeavor in airing five local Christmas concerts and cantatas during the first couple of weeks of broadcasting.

It is truly a mom-and-pop business. WTMV operates out of what was once the living room of Bill and Patty Baker's home. The studio, transmitter and office are all located there. The 50-foot tower, topped by a single-bay circularized FM antenna, is located right outside in view of the back window.[14] With 100 watts of power, WTMV covers the Brokenstraw Valley in stereo 24 hours a day. One satellite dish is outside another window in the room and pulls in the signal from Tupelo, Mississippi, and the American Family Radio network and another satellite dish, located near the top of the station's broadcast tower, receives the signal of the Praise Broadcasting Network from Arlington, Texas. "Family Friendly" programming is aired, from both the satellite networks, as well as 30 hours of locally produced features. A typical weekday schedule looks like this:

WTMV

Monday–Friday
Program Schedule

*=Feature
**=Local Programs Underlined
AFR=American Family Radio

12:00 A.M.–6:30 AFR Music

[AFR News every hour at :55]

2:00–2:55 Today's Issues — Tim Wildmon & Marvin Sanders
    *Breakpoint — Chuck Colson
    *Washington Watch — Janet Parshall
    *For Faith & Family Minute — Dr. Richard Land

4:00–4:30 Focus on the Family — Dr. James Dobson
    *Our Daily Bread

6:00–6:05 Family News in Focus

6:30–6:55 Turning Point — Dr. David Jeremiah

6:55–7:00 AFR News

7:00–7:55 AFR Music — J. J. Jasper
    *Christian Working Woman — Mary Whechel
    *My Turn — Dr. Donald E. Wildmon

7:55–8:00 AFR News

8:00–8:30 Focus on the Family — Dr. James Dobson

8:30–8:55 Alive at 88-Five**— Bro. Bill Baker
    *Parent Talk Tip — Randy Carlson
    *Susan B. Anthony List
    *Business Proverbs — Steve Marr
    *Global Mission News

8:55–9:00 AFR News

9:00–9:55 Alive at 88-Five**— Bro. Bill Baker
    *Dobson Family Minute — Dr. James Dobson
    *On the Right Tract — ATS
    *4th and Goal — Coach Bill McCartney
    *Got a Minute for Your Health — Dr. Elmar Sekala
    *American Inspiration — Presidential Prayer Team
    *Outreach Alert
    *Our Daily Bread

9:55–10:00 AFR News

10:00–10:55 Alive at 88-Five**— Bro. Bill Baker
    *Promise Keepers Moment
    *Today's Child — Child Evangelism Fellowship
    *Back to Genesis — Dr. John Morris
    *Home School Heartbeat — Mike Ferris
    *Proverbs 31 Ministry — Sharon Janes
    *National Concert of Prayer — David Bryant
    *The Mediator — Dr. Larry Poland

10:55–11:00 AFR News

11:00–11:04 Breakpoint — Chuck Colson

11:04–11:55 Today's Issues — Tim Wildmon & Marvin Sanders
    *Washington Watch — Janet Parshall
    *For Faith & Family Minute — Dr. Richard Land

11:55–12:00 Noon AFR News

12:00–12:55 AFR Music — Kathy Coats
    *Daughters of Promise — Christine Wyrtzen

12:55–1:00 AFR News

1:00–1:30 AFR Music — Kathy Coats

1:30–1:55 Today's Issues — Dr. Don Wildmon

1:55–2:00 AFR News

2:00–2:55 AFR Music — Kathy Coats
    *Probe — Kerby Anderson

2:55–3:00 AFR News

3:00–3:30 AFR Music — Kathy Coats

3:30–3:55 Money Matters — Larry Burkett & Steve Moore

3:55–4:00 AFR News

4:00–4:55 Alive at 88-Five**—Bro. Bill Baker
    *Dobson Family Minute — Dr. James Dobson
    *On the Right Tract — ATS
    *4th and Goal — Coach Bill McCartney
    *Got a Minute for Your Health — Dr. Elmar Sekala
    *American Inspiration — Presidential Prayer Team
    *Outreach Alert
    *Our Daily Bread

4:55–5:00 AFR News

5:00–5:55 Alive at 88-Five**— Bro. Bill Baker
    *Promise Keepers Moment
    *Today's Child — Child Evangelism Fellowship
    *Back to Genesis — Dr. John Morris
    *Home School Heartbeat — Mike Ferris
    *Proverbs 31 Ministry — Sharon Janes
    *National Concert of Prayer — David Bryant
    *The Mediator — Dr. Larry Poland

5:55–6:00 AFR News

6:00–6:55 AFR Music — John Riley

6:55–7:00 AFR News

7:00–7:55 AFR Music — Jim Stanley
    *Dr. D. James Kennedy Commentary

7:55–8:00 AFR News

8:00–8:55 AFR Music — Jim Stanley
    *Listen America — Dr. Jerry Falwell

Friday Only

8:30–8:55 Realtime — Ron Hutchcraft

9:00–9:55 Stoked** — Tom Delp

8:55–9:00 AFR News

9:00–9:55 AFR Music — Jim Stanley

9:55–10:00 AFR News

10:00–10:30 Focus on the Family — Dr. James Dobson

10:30–10:55 For Faith & Family — Dennis Rainey & Bob Lepine

10:55–11:00 AFR News

11:00–11:26 For Faith and Family — Dr. Richard Land

11:26–11:30 Phyllis Schlafly Report

11:30–11:55 AFR Music

11:55–12:00 AFR News

Saturday

*Local Programs
AFR — American Family Radio

12:00–7:00 A.M. AFR Music

[AFR News every hour at :55]

8:30–8:55 Spotlite on Kidz** — Tiffany Chaffee & Grampie

8:55–9:00 AFR News

9:00–9:15 Patch the Pirate

9:15–9:30 Uncle Charlie's StoryTime

9:30–9:55 A Visit with Mrs. G

9:55–10:00 Kidz News

10:00–10:30 We Kids — Mr. Nick

10:30–10:55 Stories with Aunt Angela

10:55–11:00 Kidz News

11:00–11:30 Adventures in Odyssey

11:30–12:30 Toonz for His Kids — Mark Zimmerman

12:30–12:55 Down Gilead Lane

12:55–1:00 Keys for Kids

1:00–1:30 Christian World View — Tim Wildmon & Brandon Howse

1:30–1:55 Southern Gospel USA — Gary Wilson

1:55–2:00 AFR News

2:00–2:55 Good Ole Gospel Music**— Patty Baker

2:55–3:00 ARF News

3:00–3:55 Life in the Barn**— Khlare Bracken

3:55–4:00 AFR News

4:00–4:30 Warren County Christian School

4:30–4:55 Money Watch — Larry Burkett & Steve Moore

4:55–5:00 AFR News

5:00–10:00 Top 10 Inspirational Songs — Bill Gault

[AFR News every hour at :55]

10:00–12:00 A.M. Soul 2 Soul — Mike Beck

[AFR News every hour at :55]

Sunday

*=Feature
AFR News, Mission Network News or *This Week in Review* hourly at :55
AFR Music between programs
**=Local Programs

4:00–4:55 A.M.Focus on the Family — Dr. James Dobson

7:00–7:30 Words to Live By — Radio Bible Class

8:30–8:55 Truths That Tansform — Dr. D. James Kennedy

9:00–9:55 Call to Worship — Dave Kersey

1:00–1:15 Life in the Barn**— Warren County Christian School, Khlare Bracken host

1:30–2:00 Spotlite on Kidz**— Tiffany & Stephanie Chaffee and Granpie

2:00–3:30 Sunday Classics—Khlare Bracken

3:30–4:00 Hour of Decision — Dr. Billy Graham

4:00–4:55 Focus on the Family Weekend — Dr. James Dobson

7:00–7:30 Let My People Think — Ravi Zacharis

7:30–11:00 Sunday Evening Praise — Buddy[14]

The Bakers, both ordained ministers, have a wealth of broadcast experience from their nine years in management of a Christian radio station as well as three decades in all areas of secular broadcasting. Bill Baker, who is physically challenged, said WTMV affords him "the opportunity to combine my many years of broadcast experience and as a pastor to minister directly from my home at this electronic pulpit.[15] The husband and wife team are assisted by daughters Noelle Baker and Patti Chaffee and granddaughters Tiffany and Stephanie Chaffee, who have their own weekly program on the station, *Spotlite on Kidz.* Khlare Bracken, a teacher at Warren County Christian School, does a weekly program from the school called *Life in the Barn* as well as a Sunday Classics program each Sunday afternoon.

WTMV is truly a down-home station. Baker explained that while the station is airing satellite programs, they might be just a few steps away in the kitchen cooking a meal or baking. An occasional bark can be expected to be heard during some of the local programming. Noelle's Siberian Husky, LaKota Sioux, or Chimo, Phoeniz or Teka — all German shepherds — or Wylie, a red Siberian Husky, or Patti Lynn's cocker spaniel, Chloe Mae, are likely to be in the house at any given time.[16] WTMV utilizes four CD players, three cassette machines and even turntables. Operations also include broadcast software that records all of the station's ID's and announcements on the hard drive of one of the station's computers and an automation and switching system that enables the station to air programming from satellite networks or the computer hard drive without live assistance.

Baker stated that WTMV is the "biggest little radio station on the dial" from Youngsville "the biggest little town" on the map, a slogan the borough has embraced for many years. A "David in the land of Goliaths" is another way Baker described the radio station, with the low-powered facility located in an area served by many other full-power FM stations.[17] This is a faith operation with financial dependence based on listener support. Although small in size, WTMV is big in expectations and performance.

There are probably no people more dedicated to Christian radio than the ones who operate these small-town ministries. Although they must function on shoestring budgets and depend on the vagaries of donations to survive, they are closer to their audience than the urban and national Christian radio broadcasters. They know their listeners personally and thus can focus their ministries and programming on the needs of the community. That is what good radio is all about.

9. Sprouting the Seeds

It is unlikely that any book about Christian radio today would be able to cover in detail all of the dynamic organizations that contribute to the expansion of the genre. Indeed, directories like the *Broadcasting and Cable Yearbook* and the NRB's *Directory of Religious Media* have trouble keeping up with their lists, which include the mere basic facts. There are at least two atlases of Christian radio stations available, but they are both out of date almost as soon as they are printed. What follows are several brief descriptions — snapshots, if you wish — of Christian radio groups that are both interesting and important but for which neither time nor budget for this project permitted detailed descriptions.

Sharing the Gospel with a Lost and Dying World — Pillar of Fire International Radio Network

"It has been said that when the Lord has need for someone to do a special work in the world, a baby is born." And so, Nathaniel Wilson was born to Oliver and Laura Wilson, a Pillar of Fire evangelist.

The Pillar of Fire is a Methodist-based denomination founded in 1901 with the following objectives:

> The building up of the Kingdom of God in the earth through the preaching of the gospel; the publication and circulation of religious literature; the establishment and maintenance of schools for both secular and religious instructions with all necessary adjuncts for their support and efficiency; the establishment and maintenance of churches for the spreading of the Gospel; the engaging in works of education,

benevolence, patriotism, charity and missions everywhere; and the building up of Christian character among all people.[1]

The interest in radio evangelism began when Pillar of Fire's Ray White, Luther Wilson (Nathaniel Wilson's uncle) and C. T. Crawford appeared as guests on a tiny station in New England. There, they determined: "Never again could they be content until this new medium of communication enabled them to preach to multitudes, at the same time that they were preaching to an assembled congregation."[2]

Soon the organization applied for and received an FRC (Federal Radio Commission) license for a new radio station in Denver, Colorado. On March 9, 1928, KPOF-AM signed on the air. Unlike so many other early Christian radio operators, Pillar of Fire persevered and kept the station operating continuously, eventually finding a permanent home at 910 kHz, where it still broadcasts 24 hours a day. But their goals were much loftier — to establish a Christian radio network with its headquarters in New York City.[3]

Nathaniel Wilson and another student were then sent to radio school to train for their operator's license. Meanwhile, Pillar of Fire received a license for a part-time AM with the call letters WAWZ, in nearby New Jersey. In the years to come, Nathaniel would continue his preaching, serve as the first WAWZ engineer and also teach and train other young men in engineering. The first official broadcast of WAWZ occurred on March 15, 1931.[4]

WAWZ has endured through many years and many obstacles. In 1950, hurricane winds destroyed the tower of WAWZ. This allowed for a stronger tower to be built, with an upgraded directional antenna system for improved coverage. This introduced WAWZ into the world of FM radio by 1954. On September 30, 1999, Hurricane Floyd hit Zarephath, New Jersey, the headquarters of Pillar of Fire International and home of WAWZ. Ten to 16 feet of water covered the entire Zarephath campus, including the community chapel, library, elementary school, and main administrative offices. WAWZ, located on the second floor of the chapel building, remained on the air during the storm and flood. Throughout the storm, WAWZ only went off air from early Friday evening to around 8 P.M. Saturday night.

As WAWZ continues to branch out and grow, its mission remains the same:

On the air since 1931, WAWZ-FM serves the greater New York, New Jersey, Eastern Pennsylvania metropolitan region with a bright, fresh and new approach to Christian radio. WAWZ 99.1 FM is the flagship station of the first Christian radio network in the nation. It is our prayer to endure as a true sanctuary on the FM dial as we continue to share the gospel of Jesus Christ.[5]

On February 7, 1982, WAWZ and Pillar of Fire stations received the National Religious Broadcasters Pioneer Award for being the first Christian radio network. In 1996, WAWZ-FM was named the National Religious Broadcasters Radio Station of the Year.

WAWZ has recently developed some changes in programming to better update their listeners as they move forward. These changes were primarily made to allow the station to attempt to reach a greater listening audience and impact more lives for Christ. WAWZ views their location, the New York metropolitan area, as a prime mission field, as it is like no other. Through research of their own, the station discovered they only reached a relatively small percentage of the New York listening audience, given the size and reach of their facility. WAWZ realized it must become more culturally relevant in order to meet more demands. It costs WAWZ around $3 million plus to operate business in a single year, and with the station's programming changes, the goal is now to triple or quadruple the current audience in order to reach the market better for Christ.[6]

Since Christian music is the nation's fastest-growing music genre, WAWZ has developed a highly successful radio format that will best reach their target audience (females ages 25–44), through compelling new Christian music (75 percent) and spiritual programs (25 percent). Among these new additions are great teaching and Christ-centered talk programs, all added in order to present the gospel more fully to the listener. Such programs include *Sharing Jesus* with Robert B. Dallenbach, *Living a Legacy* with Crawford Loritts, and *A Word with You* with Ron Hutchcraft. The switch to more music for the listener is a big industry change for WAWZ, who prior to February 2003 had a predominately spoken-word format with only inspirational music.

In keeping with the station's new style, more live personalities will be added, along with traffic, weather and short-form features integrated with Christ-centered music to encourage and edify believers and reach unbelievers. Some promotional strategies used for listener attraction are on-air contests, guest appearances, and building the "family brand that serves not only the Christian lifestyle group but mainstream listeners as well."[7]

Scott Taylor, Program Director for WAWZ Star 99.1 FM believes that this new format change for the station will be a big improvement. Taylor believes that the Christian radio business is growing so rapidly because "there is now a commitment from Christian record companies and radio stations to deliver a quality presentation and a positive alternative to what's typically heard on most radio stations."[8]

Along with KPOF and WAWZ, Pillar of Fire also owns New Life 93.3 FM, WAKW in Cincinnati, Ohio. It offers support to missions and charities in Nigeria, Liberia and India, and operates schools and churches in Colorado, California, Ohio, New Jersey, and Pennsylvania. Furthermore, Pillar of Fire also publishes and circulates religious literature through its publishing house, The Pillar of Fire Press of Zarephath, New Jersey.[9]

Reaching the Unreached and Strengthening the Unbelievers — HCJB World Radio Network

While organizations like the Moody Bible Institute, Pillar of Fire, and the Missouri Synod of the Lutheran Church were establishing evangelistic Christian radio in the United States, the founders of HCJB World Radio Network were doing so outside the country, primarily in Spanish throughout Latin America. On Christmas Day 1931, from a makeshift studio inside a sheep shed high in the Andes of Ecuador, HCJB — the world's first missionary radio station — went on the air with 200 watts of power. Inside the shelter sat Clarence Jones and Reuben Larson, two Americans with a vision to reach the world. Together with its local partners, HCJB World Radio now has ministries in more than 90 countries and broadcasts the gospel in more than 100 languages and dialects. HCJB World Radio's mission is:

> To communicate the gospel of Jesus Christ to all nations so that people are transformed and become active, vital parts of the Body of Christ. In order to carry out this purpose through our core ministries of mass media, healthcare and education we will:
>
> • Evangelize unbelievers that they may come to know Him.
> • Educate and disciple believers that they may grow in Him.
> • Equip and mobilize believers that they may serve Him.[10]

Clarence Jones was a member of the music, youth and radio staff of the Chicago Gospel Tabernacle founded in Chicago by Paul Rader. He saw the effectiveness of the tabernacle radio ministry at WJBT and felt missionary radio could spread the Gospel around the world. In 1930, he visited Venezuela, Colombia, Panama and Cuba seeking broadcast permits without success. Back in Chicago, Jones met Reuben Larson, who had pioneered a mission in the jungles of Ecuador under the Christian Missionary Alliance. Larson said he and the other missionaries could get a permit in Ecuador, which they did. Jones got the equipment, and the pair put the low power shortwave station on the air.

The founders of HCJB were the Joneses and Larsons, along with D. S. and Irma Clark and J. D. and Ruth Clark — brothers and their wives who had come to Ecuador from Brazil with the Christian Missionary Alliance — and Paul and Bernice Young, who worked with the Bible societies. In 1939, HCJB World Radio bought property on the north side of Quito for studios and operations. Towers and antennas were built on the grounds. Clarence Moore built the first 10,000-watt transmitter at the LeTourneau plant in Peoria, Illinois. It went on the air in Quito on Easter Sunday 1940. To use its power more effectively, Moore invented the Cubical Quad Antenna, now famous around the world.[11]

Shortwave signals began to reach far corners of the world, and programs in languages other than Spanish and English began. During World War II, NBC made a contract for HCJB to re-broadcast news and commentary programs in Spanish to the local Ecuadorian audience. The income from that helped build the broadcast center that is still in use today. In 1949, HCJB became partners with HOXO in Panama, a relationship that continues today.

In 1956, the 25th anniversary, a 50,000-watt, band-switching shortwave transmitter, built by missionary engineers and national technicians, was installed. In the 1960s, HCJB added FM radio and moved the main transmitting facilities to Pifo, 15 miles east of Quito. In 1969, HCJB World Radio added three 100,000-watt shortwave transmitters made by RCA. The HC500 (500,000 watts) was built in the late 1970s by a team at facilities provided by Crown International in Elkhart, Indiana. It went on the air in 1981. The Elkhart team continues to build 100,000-watt transmitters that have replaced the older RCAs and are used by other missionary broadcasters. They also design and assemble the "suitcase FM radio station" being used by partner ministries in many countries where

HCJB assists local groups in establishing radio stations and recording studios.

HCJB established a cooperating ministry, World Radio Network, in Texas in 1976. It was led by Dr. Abe Van Der Puy after he had served 20 years as president of HCJB World Radio, with the objective to build and operate FM stations along the United States–Mexico border from Texas to Arizona. The mission's international headquarters moved from Miami to Colorado Springs, Colorado, in 1992. In a joint project with Trans World Radio, HCJB World Radio established the ALAS satellite network for all of Latin America in 1993. The mission's first official office and studio in Eastern Europe was established in 1994 in Kiev, Ukraine.[12]

At present, the largest area of expansion in the ministry is what HCJB calls "radio planting," working in partnership with local churches or Christian groups to help develop Christian radio for their community. Projects of every size and shape are under way throughout North and South America, Africa, Europe, the former Soviet world, North Africa and the Middle East, Central and Southeast Asia. With radio planting, HCJB World Radio works through the local partners. HCJB provides equipment, technical support and training while local partners run the stations. These local radio ministries have already been established in more than 30 countries. Local AM and FM stations reach the growing urban areas where shortwave listening is less common.

HCJB World Radio now operates shortwave radio stations with an immense coverage area, potentially reaching nearly 80 percent of the world's population. Broadcasts go out from Quito, Ecuador, in 12 languages and 22 dialects, and the station receives thousands of letters from listeners in 115 countries each year. HCJB works with other missionary broadcasters around the globe to make gospel broadcasts available to everyone in languages they can understand. Programs are also aired from other international broadcasting sites including the Seychelles, Swaziland and the U.K.

The transmitter site in Pifo, Ecuador, features 11 shortwave transmitters, ranging in size from 10 to 500 kilowatts. Making the broadcasts from Ecuador possible is a highly qualified engineering staff. A hydroelectric plant in Papallacta that harnesses energy from Andean lakes and rivers provides power for the shortwave broadcasts. The Loreto Hydroelectric Project, which is presently under construction, will add to the generating capacity. Staff at the Engineering Center in Elkhart, Indiana, continues to design and build antennas, high-power shortwave and low-power FM transmitters as well as recording studios. These are shipped to and installed at sites around the world. HCJB World Radio operates seven local stations in Ecuador, reaching a potential audience of five million.

The World Radio Network has AM and FM stations in Panama and 12 FM outlets along the United States–Mexico border where four million people live, including three million in Mexico. In the United States, World Radio Network has Spanish-language stations in Bisbee, Douglas, Nogales, and Yuma, Arizona; Brownsville, Eagle Pass, El Paso, and Laredo, Texas; and Hood River, Oregon. There are English-language stations in Sierra Vista, Arizona; Corpus Christi and Eagle Pass, Texas; and a satellite uplink facility in McAllen, Texas. This group of stations, with their multiple repeaters and affiliates in urban areas like Chicago and Dallas, has a potential reach of 12 million listeners. It distributes Spanish-language versions of popular Christian radio programs like *Focus on the Family* and *Insight for Living* and produces many programs in house.

Among the World Radio Network productions is *Al Despertar,* a two-hour live daily program from McAllen that includes national and border news, financial issues, sports and music. *Linea Abierta* is a one-hour daily talk show that offers news, interviews, roundtable discussions, special series and listener calls. Topics include health, immigration, education, and culture. Another live talk show, *Bienvenidos a América,* is a once weekly discussion of issues that affect immigrants. Nationally recognized guests include high-ranking government officials and immigration attorneys with details of policies and special programs available to the Hispanic community.

At the heart of HCJB World Radio's ministries is the international headquarters in Colorado Springs. The corporate office gives overall direction and leadership to the organization, overseeing efforts such as resource development and communications. The International Radio Group helps coordinate broadcast relations and radio planting around the world. Offices and studios in 12 countries have been established to represent the mission, assist local ministries and recruit missionaries. Some offices are used to produce radio programs and train local Christians in radio operations. Representation sites in eight countries also help make the mission known. Field direction in Quito oversees the ministries of over 250 missionaries and 430 Ecuadorian employees.

HCJB World Radio Network is a sizeable operation with a multi-million-dollar annual budget, funded by donations and program time-purchase contracts. The staff includes paid professionals, missionaries from various Christian denominations, and thousands of volunteers.[13] In addition to Christian radio stations, HCJB operates a television ministry and has established churches, hospitals, and medical clinics in Quito and in the Amazon rain forest.

Quality Bible Teaching—Bott Radio Network

The Bott Radio Network (BRN) began more than 40 years ago with a vision for a full-time Christian talk radio station and has since expanded into 21 stations in eight states. President and CEO Richard "Dick" Bott became interested in the inner workings of radio as a child. This is partly due to the fact that he sang on the radio in Minneapolis, Minnesota, for the state director of child evangelism while he was younger. Bott attended Souls Harbor, a church in Minneapolis with a daily radio program while in high school. Here he spent many hours behind the scenes, watching and learning all he could about radio.

Bott met and married his wife, Sherley, at St. Paul Bible Institute (now Crown College) and they moved to San Francisco to work at her father's radio station. Bott began working in sales and marketing, and proceeded to work himself up to general manager. In 1957, Bott learned that a station was for sale in Salinas Monterey, California. He and the family decided to take the offer and paid off the station in three years. This station groomed Bott for his next vision, creating a Christian station targeted specifically to the Christian community. At this time, most Christian programs were carried by secular stations. The nation boasted only a few Christian radio stations and Dick was focused on the idea of a fully commercial station offering only Christian programming.

In 1962, a country and western station came up for sale in Kansas City, Missouri, and on November 12 KCCV, Kansas City's Christian Voice, was born. This station became a large success due to it being a Christian station paid for completely by advertising and selling airtime, and also in formatting the station as Christian talk. After the Kansas City purchase, other stations were bought in Oklahoma City, Oklahoma; Fort Wayne, Indiana; and St. Louis, Missouri. BRN serves 15 markets, which are located primarily at the heart of the nation. Through these stations, the BRN now spreads the gospel to millions of people. The non-denominational network is not affiliated with any church, nor does it accept donations from listeners. It is supported wholly by its program producers and by local businesses that advertise on the network and sponsor its programming.

Critics have complained that Bott stations are against modern Christian radio, but Bott believes it's only "a matter of knowing your target audience and what they like. We're designed right now to be talk radio. I feel our format is carefully constructed to reach and audience that enjoys reading."[14] Bott stations offer teaching and talk radio 24 hours a day, 7 days a week. Besides offering "good food" in the talk-only format, the BRN is also innovative in helping local listeners stay abreast of local issues, as well as national issues that concern the morality of our nation. The mission of the BRN is based upon:

> Renewing your mind daily with quality Bible teachings, strengthening your family with God's Word — all day — everyday, presenting the power of God's Word to change lives, and providing America's best Bible teachers to help you grow and Christian news to help you know.[15]

"Music programming typically sits in the background of a listener's realm of attention," said Jack Houghton, director of advertising sales and marketing for the network. "Our talk-intensive format is a foreground medium, attracting more listener attention as they learn from the talk shows and teaching programs. This is a benefit to our advertisers because it provides greater recognition and retention of advertising messages from a quality audience."[16]

BRN is based upon integrity, service, quality and strength and uses these to better serve their listeners and to gain new listeners everyday. They especially love the feedback of individual listeners whose lives they have helped to change. Program Services Manager Beth Huisman believes that Christian radio is popular because "I believe people are hungry for truth, and since our stations share the truth of the Word of God, people listen."[17]

As the network's coverage and listening audience continue to grow, BRN's commitment stands firm: to help people grow in their faith and apply it in their daily lives. In addition to the effect the programming has on this mission, community outreach continues to play a vital role.

BRN regularly sponsors local and regional events such as Promise Keepers, Women of Faith and Worldview Weekend conferences in addition to supporting local non-profit pro-life and relief organizations.

Future projects for Bott include developing an Internet ministry to support its radio outreach. In April 2003, Bott signed a deal with ChristianNetcast.com, a company specializing in providing quality, affordable streaming services for Christian radio stations. This streaming enables radio networks and churches to go beyond the limited reach of airwaves by broadcasting their programs via the Internet. Now listeners all over the world can "tune in" on their computers and hear the Good News that the network is offering for those in need. Today, BRN broadcasts 24 hours a day nationwide on Sky Angel's direct broadcast satellite (DBS) service and worldwide over the Internet at www.bottradionetwork.com. The Internet broadcast has listeners on six continents.[18]

BRN is a pioneer in the development of Christian talk radio and is dedicated to the quality Bible teaching and Christian news and information format it has broadcast for more than 40 years. Today BRN is one of the nation's leading Christian radio networks and the only radio group headquartered in Greater Kansas City. The network has plans to add more stations that will increase its service area and enable the network to continue its steady growth. "The Christian radio audience has grown dramatically over the years," says Richard Bott II, executive vice president, who has an MBA from Harvard Business School, "and we are as committed to our format as we were more than 40 years ago when KCCV began broadcasting."[19]

Seeing "The Light"—The Sheridan Gospel Network

The Sheridan Broadcasting Corporation was developed in Pennsylvania in 1972, and acquired WILD in Boston, WUFO in Amherst-Buffalo, and WAMO AM/FM in 1973. The National Black Network (NBN) was also formed in 1973. This made it the first black-owned radio group and the largest black-owned broadcast firm. In 1976, Sheridan acquired 49 percent of stock of the Mutual Black Network (MBN) and gained operational control. This left the only two black network companies — Sheridan and NBN. By 1978, MBN had 91 affiliates and revenue of about $3 million a year — placing it just slightly ahead of its rival network, NBN, which had 80 affiliates and earnings of about $2.5 million.

In 1979, Sheridan acquired the remaining 51 percent of MBN, changed the name to Sheridan Broadcasting Network (SBN) and provided listeners with news, sports, and featured programming to urban-oriented radio stations across the country via satellite. In 1991, in what was the biggest deal in the history of black radio, Sheridan Broadcasting Corporation came together with NBN to form what is now American Urban Radio Networks (AURN).

AURN provides over 300 weekly programs to 400 affiliate radio stations — with satellite capacity to reach over 94 percent of the U.S. African American population. AURN produces more urban programming than all other broadcasting companies put together; that's in television, cable, and national radio. AURN has currently 15,000 shows produced annually and has been in the business for 30 years.

In 1997, Sheridan Broadcasting created and financed a 24-hour, satellite-distributed gospel radio format called "The Light" and founded a new corporate division, Sheridan Gospel Network.[20] The Light is now heard in over 50 markets and in the Virgin Islands. Headquarters for the Sheridan Broadcasting Corporation is located in Pittsburgh, Pennsylvania, with offices in Atlanta, Georgia, and Buffalo and New York, New York.

Affiliates of The Light include 22 radio stations, all of AM format, stretching from Buffalo to Richmond, California, to Jacksonville, Florida. The Light Alliance has also formed strategic partnerships with industry professionals such as *Bobby Jones Gospel, Gospel Flava* magazine, *Gospel Industry Today, Gospel Today* magazine, *Gospel Truth* magazine, Terry Manufacturing Co., Inc, and The Word Network. Alliance with The Word Network was developed in August of 2001 in order to highlight each other's programming and offer other promotional items to its listeners.

The Light is described as the urban adult radio format for the new millennium, playing the best gospel hits from the best artists of the day. This includes a special blend of traditional classics and contemporary hits combined with specialized programming elements to inspire, uplift and encourage listeners.

The Light offers its listeners a variety of different programs and information for their everyday lives. The Light promotes their announcers to be the best in black gospel music today, with featured slots such as *The Morning Blend* and *The Afternoon Drive*. In 2002, at the 10th Annual American Gospel Quartet Convention, The Light was voted Favorite Gospel Radio Network for the second year in a row. Rick Joyner, announcer for *The Afternoon Drive,* was also voted Favorite Syndicated Personality for 2002.[21]

The target audience of The Light is females ages 25–54. They are an all-music network that features trained professionals and on-air personalities. The Light strives to stay on the cutting edge and always provide their listeners with improvements to better serve their needs. Promotional strategies to keep listeners and gain new ones include concerts, featured guests, conferences, sweepstakes, prizes and attention. National Program Director Jacquie Haselrig said that in her opinion the Christian radio business is growing so rapidly "because there is a need for it. This format offers solutions to problems and other types of music stations are not giving their audience what it needs."[22]

All Christian Radio, All the Time — Bible Broadcasting Network

On May 28, 1968, Lowell Davey, president of the Bible Broadcasting Network (BBN), made an offer to purchase a radio station in Norfolk, Virginia. As he stated in that letter, "We sense the need of a quality station that is Christian oriented and has quality music, both classical and Christian. We are, therefore, in the process of looking for the availability of such a station."[23] That was the beginning of the BBN. Davey was not able to purchase that station but the idea of BBN was underway. Official incorporation took place about a year later on March 28, 1969, when BBN purchased a radio station that had gone bankrupt and was off the air. BBN began when WYFI, Norfolk, signed on October 2, 1971, at 5:00 in the evening. Since that beginning so many years ago, BBN stations have played their theme song every morning at 5:57 A.M.—"To God Be the Glory."

The stated purpose for BBN is "to get God's word into the hearts and minds of people using the most efficient means at our disposal." Radio and the Internet remain the most cost-effective tools for reaching the audience 24 hours a day. For BBN, radio is not a business. It is a ministry. "We believe the programming must be warm, friendly and informative and must present the Truth. The microphones of the Bible Broadcasting Network are as sacred as any pulpit in the world so we broadcast daily prayer times, children's programs, Bible teaching, teen programs and family guidance programs."[24]

BBN uses the tools of technology along with a blend of ministry-focused, mostly spoken-word programming.

> The truth of the Gospel has not lost its power, but has often lost its audience because of poor or inadequate presentation. We may only have one chance to share the Gospel message with a person. Our message must always be right and honoring to the Lord and be presented in a way that doesn't take away from its importance. Our desire is that many will come to Christ, homes will be built up, and Christians will go forth to evangelize in fulfillment of the Great Commission.[25]

BBN now owns and operates more than 30 full-power stations and more than 100 low-power stations in 29 different states. Every radio station carries the same network programming, which originates in the BBN studios in Charlotte, North Carolina. Potential reach for the network is 50 million people each day in the U.S. BBN also owns, operates or has helped to build radio stations in 14 different countries, plus shortwave to several others. All these stations carry the same type of music and programs heard in America. There are now more than 100 foreign radio stations with a potential listening audience of over 100 million people. In the past few years, BBN has added one new station every 11 days. BBN also has websites in English, Spanish, Portuguese, Chinese, Japanese, Korean and German. E-mail response comes in from all over the world. Missionaries, businessmen, students, and a host of others have written or called.

The Bible is the standard for network programming. BBN features broadcasts from "some of the finest Bible teachers and preachers heard anywhere. Our policy is that a broadcaster must be ethically, morally, and theologically right to be on BBN."[26] Featured personalities include David Jeremiah, J. Vernon McGee, James Dobson, Irwin Lutzer, John MacArthur and Chuck Swindoll.

Through careful planning and preservation BBN has one of the most unique collections of Christian music found anywhere. With more than 10,000 songs that have been digitally preserved to choose from, the conservative music is mixed and cycled in a systematic blend for "the best sound this side of Heaven." Much of this collection is not available today anywhere else.

BBN is a 100 percent listener-supported, not-for-profit organization. "We do not sell anything including radio time. We don't offer gimmicks or gadgets or promises of wealth and health ... just all Christian radio, all the time."[27] Each fall BBN has a four-day shareathon to raise the operating funds for the following year. Then, in the spring, BBN hosts a three-day shareathon for special projects. During each shareathon, listeners call and share "faith promise commitments" until the goal is reached. When BBN reaches its goal, the shareathon ends and the network returns to regular programming. But with a rapidly expanding ministry, the financial burden grows greater each year.

The Bible Alone and in Its Entirety — Family Stations, Inc.

Family Radio aired its first broadcast on February 4, 1959, over radio station KEAR-FM in San Francisco, California. Since then, the ministry, based in Oakland, California, has established 48 powerful AM and FM stations in the U.S. with many in major metropolitan markets, a shortwave facility, and several smaller educational facilities and translators. Family Radio also shares programming with local TV Stations in San Francisco and Newark, New Jersey, and broadcasts the Gospel via the Internet, around the clock and around the world.

Family Radio, established in 1958 under its official name, Family Stations, Inc., is a non-denominational, non-commercial, non-profit, listener-supported, 24-hour Christian ministry with the express purpose of sending the Gospel into the world. It is supported entirely by gifts from listeners, solicited over the air and on the Family Radio website. Its president and general manager, Harold Camping, is a full-time volunteer, receiving no salary or financial compensation. "In reality, Family Radio regards the Lord Jesus Christ as its Chief Executive Officer because it operates altogether under the authority of the Bible, says Camping. "The Board of Directors and all of its employees are regarded as servants who serve Jesus Christ as their King."[28]

Family Radio has an intensive desire to be altogether faithful to the teachings of the Bible, both in the conduct of its employees, and in the biblical messages it sends into the world. Therefore, the programs sent out by radio broadcast, the Internet, and other technologies are constantly reviewed to make certain that the messages being aired are faithful to the Bible. The broadcasts originate in most of the major languages of the world "so that as many people as possible can hear the true Gospel in their own language."[29] Family Radio's International Department began broadcasting its first programs in 1973 with transmissions in English and Spanish. Since then, nine more languages have been added to its international outreach, making a total of 11 languages. Family Radio currently broadcasts Christian programming in English, Spanish, Chinese, Russian, German, French, Hindi, Arabic, Italian, Portuguese, and Turkish and is in the process of developing service in Polish, Korean, Indonesian and Vietnamese.

Family Radio sponsors a correspondence School of the Bible. Anyone may join free of charge to learn biblical Hebrew, biblical Greek, and receive instruction in many books of the Bible. The curriculum includes courses that are designed to help students minister the Word of God more accurately and effectively. School of the Bible operates on the principle of Matthew 10:8: "Freely ye have received, freely give." In accordance with this principle, the school does not charge tuition; it is dependent upon the support of its students and friends. For most of the years of its existence, Family Radio has also served as a great help in building up local churches. Because the Bible indicated that these local churches are divinely mandated to send the Gospel into the entire world, Family Radio has undertaken their support as part of its mission and outreach activities for the radio service.

Most of the programming on Family Radio stations is traditional preaching and teaching, in keeping with their mission to spread the biblical message far and wide:

> At Family Radio, we emphatically teach that the whole Bible is the Word of God; so that, in the original languages in which the Bible was written, every word was from the mouth of God, and consequently, is never to be altered and must be obeyed. The Bible alone, and in its entirety, is the Word of God. Therefore, we reject the phenomena of tongues, visions, voices, etc., as having any part in the true Gospel since the Scriptures have been completed.
>
> On Family Radio, we clearly teach the Biblical truth that all mankind

are sinners, and therefore, are subject to God's righteous wrath. We further teach the sad truth that because man by nature is spiritually dead, he will not and cannot come to God on God's terms. However, God in His wonderful love has chosen a people for Himself for whom the Lord Jesus Christ did all the work necessary to save them. This is the Bible's grand message of salvation that Family Radio wishes to send to every nation of the world.[30]

To God Be the Glory — Family Life Network

The Family Life Network began as a dream in 1977 when Executive Director Dick Snavely was first presented with the idea of radio. Dick, the founder of Family Life Ministries, and his son Rick attended a regional National Religious Broadcasting (NRB) convention. They went looking for new video equipment that would be used to tape some of the ministry's Saturday-night programs. They had envisioned airing these programs on local cable channels. However, during the three-day convention an acquaintance encouraged them to look into radio instead of television.

A short time later Snavely hired a consulting engineer to conduct a frequency search for a new station. The consulting engineer discovered a frequency that could be reallocated to Bath, New York, home of Family Life Ministries. The ministry immediately began the protracted legal process of petitioning the FCC to have 103.1 FM moved from Dubois, Pennsylvania, to Bath. Once the channel was reallocated, Family Life Ministries applied for and was granted permission to build the new FM station.[31]

On August 29, 1983, listeners got their first chance to hear WCIK when the station began broadcasting at 6:00 A.M. WCIK had a weak signal at 790 watts, and it only reached a small community. Though most of those involved with the station had little or no experience in radio, they had a passion for serving the Lord and wanting to do things right. A number of months passed and the operation began to run more smoothly. Now it was time to formally ask the listeners for their support.

WCIK was a commercial license but the management of the station chose not to seek underwriting through commercial advertising. Some businesses desired to buy spots on the station initially, but no sales department was ever established to solicit commercial sponsorship. Instead a shareathon was scheduled the following May for the purpose of raising $100,000 to help WCIK stay on the air for the next year. The goal of $100,000 was quite ambitious, but it was the amount that was needed. At one minute after midnight the final day of the shareathon, the goal was exceeded by a few hundred dollars.[32]

The Family Life Network now consists of 10 stations and 27 translators. Of the full-powered stations that the network operates they range in power from 380 watts to 17,000 watts. The more powerful stations will broadcast a signal 50–60 miles in each direction. Most of its operation is in and around western New York state.

Faith, Learning, and Living— Northwestern College Radio

Northwestern College in St. Paul, Minnesota, integrates the educational philosophy of "faith, learning and living" through two focuses: higher education and media. The higher education focus offers a vast array of opportunities within a strong academic program. Northwestern offers 44 bachelor degrees ranging from elementary education and pastoral studies to broadcasting and electronic media and psychology. The core component is the traditional day-school program, which enrolls over 1,700. Alternative education programs, serving over 800 students, include FOCUS degree completion, Center for Distance Education, Urban Bible Institute, MacLaurin Institute serving University of Minnesota students, and the Christian Center for Communications in Quito, Ecuador.[33]

Northwestern's campus encompasses 107 acres and 12 buildings. The newest is the $10.5-million state-of-the-art Mel Johnson Media Center completed in summer 2003. It houses the media ministry, FOCUS and the academic department of communication. Northwestern College is under the leadership of Dr. Alan S. Cureton, who began his duties as president in January 2002. Employing a total of 600 full-time and part-time employees, Northwestern is an independent nonprofit enterprise that takes a biblically Christian ethical and moral position and is theologically conservative in doctrine.

Northwestern is a community in which all learning is framed within the context of a Christian worldview. Every student who completes a four-year degree receives the equivalent of a second major in Bible in addition to the major of choice. Daily chapel is an integral part of the program where students hear world-renowned speakers and participate in praise and worship.

The media focus began in 1949 when Twin Cities' radio station KTIS went on the air thanks to $44,000 generated by Northwestern students. President William F. "Billy" Graham gave the first on-air prayer. Northwestern now owns and operates 15 noncommercial listener-supported Christian radio stations in Minnesota, North and South Dakota, Iowa, Wisconsin and Florida with a combined audience of half a million listeners a week. The SkyLight and SkyII satellite networks sell Christian programming to 300 Christian radio stations around the country. LifeNet.FM, an Internet contemporary Christian music station, has an audience potential of 88 million people.[34]

The programming is primarily praise and inspiration music. In addition, Northwestern College Radio devotes approximately five hours per day, Monday through Friday, to spoken-word programming, including popular features like *Insight for Living*, *Focus on the Family*, and *Breakpoint*. The weekend programming includes long music sweeps with a few continuity breaks for traditional preaching and teaching programs, notably Billy Graham's *Hour of Decision*.

The list of Christian radio groups goes on to include many broadcasters new and old, urban and rural, who have taken advantage of the opportunities of the 1990s to build or expand operations. Crawford Broadcasting of Blue Bell, Pennsylvania, has 30 stations including ones in Los Angeles, Chicago, San Francisco, Detroit, St. Louis and Denver. CSN International of Santa Ana, California, operates a group of 20 stations in small to medium cities that stretches from Hawaii to the West Coast to Texas and the Midwest and on to Massachusetts and Maine. The Good News Network, based in Grovetown, Georgia, has 11 stations in rural Georgia, South Carolina, North Carolina, and Alabama. Mortenson Broadcasting in Lexington, Kentucky, has 17 stations primarily in Kentucky and West Virginia, but also outlets in Dallas, Pittsburgh, and Nashville. The Pilgrim Radio Network, a service of Western Inspirational Broadcasters based in Carson City, Nevada, has 50 stations and translators throughout Northern California, Nevada, Wyoming and Montana. The Positive Radio Group, founded by Vernon Baker and his family in Blacksburg, Virginia, has 38 stations throughout the Appalachian region of Virginia, West Virginia, North Carolina, and Tennessee.

The Radio Training Network from Lakeland, Florida, has 15 stations in resort and retirement communities in Florida, North Carolina, South Carolina, and Missouri. Toccoa Falls College in Northwest Georgia maintains a network throughout the state and into parts of Florida.[35]

It is an understatement to say that Christian radio is no longer limited to the backwaters of the South, Southwest, and rural American heartland.

10. A Bountiful Harvest

At 7:30 Monday morning several thousand people stood in a line that spread throughout the gracious interior of Nashville's Opryland Hotel. They waited patiently, making small talk, for their turn with security screening. Hotel employees stood by to collect all bags, briefcases, and cameras, passing out red claim checks in turn. Everyone had to be in the hall by 9 A.M. when the doors would close. President George W. Bush was due at 10:00 to address the 2003 convention of the National Religious Broadcasters (NRB).

The closest seat to the stage was about two-thirds of the way toward the rear of the enormous ballroom. For a time, a well-dressed young man in the next seat, an administrator for one of Nashville's largest independent Baptist churches, chatted about his congregation. He seemed surprised that the pastor was unknown outside the Nashville area. After a while, the crowd ran out of conversation. The noise decreased noticeably. People anxiously began to check their watches. Ten o'clock came and went, but the restless murmur that filled the room remained subdued.

A little before 11:00, a live picture filled the giant TV screens on either side of the stage, the house lights dimmed, and the stage lights came up. An enthusiastic announcer introduced Sarah Paulson, pre-recorded on video, who sang a heartfelt version of *America the Beautiful*. After a brief pause, contemporary Christian star Michael W. Smith took the stage, sat down at the Steinway, and performed three songs whose lyrics deftly mingled praise, inspiration, and patriotism. The pictures on the screens faded between pastoral scenes with horses moving gracefully in slow motion, Americans saluting a waving Stars and Stripes, and shots of Smith's live performance. In between songs, he talked about his personal relationship with God, his loving family, and his visits with the president on his Texas ranch. The crowd was standing and swaying in rapturous delight throughout his concert. After Smith left the stage, the restless murmur returned. The crowd waited reverently.

It was almost 11:30 when the announcer introduced NRB Chairman Glen Plummer, a lean, energetic black man and one of the few people of color in the room. He brought the crowd to its feet for President Bush and embraced him for the pictures that would illustrate this event to media audiences around the world. To his credit, the president noticed the homogenous audience and gently chided the group for its lack of racial diversity, calling 11:00 to noon on Sunday mornings the most segregated hour in America. That statement didn't make it into most of the news stories about the speech.

Instead, the president and the media concentrated on the impending war in Iraq. He thanked the audience for its patience and explained that he was meeting members of his prayer team, seeking guidance for pursuing the war on terror, getting the faith-based initiative through Congress, and restoring family values in the country. Overcome by the moment, the audience stood transfixed, waving hands in the air, lapsing into thunderous applause and choruses of "Amen." Couples hugged. Women wept with joy.

Notes from the 2003 NRB Convention

The political interests and influence of Christian broadcasters was apparent elsewhere at the 2003 NRB Convention. During the Public Policy Breakfast the morning after President Bush's appearance, Stuart Epperson of Salem Communications began his address by stating: "Nothing is more controversial than the Gospel of Jesus Christ."[1] From there, he went on to extol the efforts of Christian radio in its efforts to get out the vote in the 2002 elections that saw Republicans seize control of both houses of Congress, with an acknowledgment of help from the Catholic church in Texas to win the governor and Senate races for pro-life candidates. In addition to asking where candidates stand on abortion, Epperson suggested that Christian broadcasters learn their positions on moral issues like homosexuality and traditional marriage and on public religious expression before offering support. The last proposition brought enthusiastic applause from a crowd that largely considers itself persecuted for publicly professing its faith. On the subject of regulation, Epperson brought up the fight to reduce copyright fees on audio and video web streams.

By contrast, in the Radio Boot Camp educational sessions, Christian radio professionals heard that the audience they want to reach does not want to hear political diatribe or, for that matter, radio evangelism. In a survey of 5,000 Christians conducted by the Audience Development Group, only half listened to Christian radio. Most often, popular contemporary Christian music, with formats like WAY-FM or K-LOVE, was the draw. Turnoffs included unfamiliar music and too much preaching and praying. Nevertheless, crusaders and evangelicals, the two smallest segments of the Christian Radio audience, were the most dedicated listeners.[2]

More interesting still were the comments from Christians who did not choose Christian radio. They describe it as "profit driven" and "aimed at exploiting needy folks." It's radio for "white Republicans" with "sappy hymnlike music played by evangelical, fake-sounding disc jockeys."[3] They can't relate to the stations because they think the concept of Christian radio is out of touch with their daily lives. Most of these listeners don't realize how much the genre has changed in the past decade.

The advice that came from this research was simple: If Christian radio stations want to attract a mainstream Christian audience, they have to be more like mainstream radio stations. They must target listeners with marketing schemes. They must create tight playlists of likeable, familiar music with fewer stop sets and less preaching. They must sound professional and upbeat. The personalities must relate to the listeners as people without talking in code, making judgments, or demanding that they change their behavior. They must reach out to the audience through churches and other venues, tell them they exist, they care, and their programming is unexpectedly good. Virtually all the audience growth in the past two years has come from Christian AC or CHR stations. The only talk show that works with this audience is James Dobson's *Focus on the Family*. To grow, Christian radio must become radio for Christians, both the saved and the sinners.[4]

There's an important paradox here. On one hand are traditional Christian broadcasters, their small but dedicated audiences, and the evangelical organizations who purchase program time to provide revenue. Lumped together with conservative political news and talk, this comprises a programming strategy that, while waning in influence, is still viable. Many of these broadcasters fail to see how they can go mainstream without losing sight of their missions or lowering their standards.

Meanwhile, CCM, Christian AC, CHR, Praise and Inspiration, and other music-based formats are spreading the Gospel through song lyrics and attracting new listeners. These Christian radio broadcasters find affinity with the music industry, like their counterparts in secular, commercial radio. They feel more at home at the Gospel Music Association convention than at the NRB. They have a friendly but somewhat uneasy coexistence with the traditional Christian broadcasters.

However, if the Christian radio audience grows — and with it financial support for stations — there should be room for diverse programming strategies. That means more specialization and narrower target audiences and fewer Christian stations with block formats. This transition happened years ago in mainstream radio. Groups like Salem and Bott are poised to profit from becoming the sources for preaching, teaching, and conservative news/talk radio. K-LOVE, WAY-FM and The Fish, also a Salem venture, stake their claims to the young adult and teen audiences who want more music. And AFR is carving out its niche with political advocacy through conservative church congregations.

What's most important is that Christian radio stations are developing new listeners, something the rest of the radio industry is having problems doing. This is a very healthy trend that ought to be good for radio in general. Since most of this new audience is young, Christian radio should be able to count on a new generation of loyal listeners.

What They Say About Themselves

This seems like an appropriate time to return to two questions posed in the first chapter and get answers to them from the people who are involved in Christian radio today.

WHY IS THE GROWTH IN CHRISTIAN RADIO HAPPENING NOW?

Mike Miller, Salem Radio Network:

The big groups — K-Love, AFR, Salem — made a commitment to growth. When The Fish was a success in Dallas, it got attention in the radio business.[5]

Marvin Sanders, American Family Radio:

The industry became professional. We produced good radio and competed better with other radio stations. The availability of a variety of Christian music created an opportunity for format radio. In 1989, the FCC relaxed the main studio location rule, creating satellite translators. God has said it is time.[6]

John Hayden, WMBI Chicago:

How much growth has there really been?[7]

Doug Hannah, WAY-FM:

People have a growing appetite for music and entertainment that reflects their values. People want positive affirmation in the music. Christian radio has gotten its act together. Companies like Salem have forced it. Radio is radio. If you want credit in Arbitron, there are things you do on the air.[8]

Jim McDermott, Spirit FM, Camdenton, Missouri:

Probably two main reasons: (1) A significant number of Christian music stations are now using the methods that mainstream radio has used for years — i.e., setting focused audience targets, music research, focus groups, proper formatics. If Christian stations will provide programming that serves the listener in the way that listener expects to be served, the potential audience is quite large. (2) The rise of organizations such as Educational Media Foundation (K-LOVE) and Salem's Fish stations. These two groups are the first to have the money to acquire the big signals in the major markets, and to be able to market those stations effectively.[9]

Joe Polek, WMSJ, Freeport, Maine:

Listeners of the radio are getting tired of the "junk" that is on mainstream radio stations. They are tired of songs that talk about sex and drugs. They are tired of having the change the station when their kids are around. They are tired of DJs who make rude comments or jokes. Christian radio is a positive alternative to mainstream radio. We promise to be family friendly. We promise to talk about things that are fun for the whole family, meaning you never have to be embarrassed about what you are hearing. The songs we play encourage you throughout your day and uplift your spirit. Who wouldn't like that?[10]

Mike Weston, WMHK, Columbia, South Carolina:

The music is of a much higher quality now and, as a result, more and more people are becoming familiar with it and finding they enjoy it. Along with that, more and more songs from CCM artists are crossing over to mainstream radio charts. CCM radio will continue to grow and expand as long as good, solid radio stations with a clear vision sign on and execute well. Also, as more secular radio stations continue to degrade as to what lyrics and messages they allows on their air, Christian radio's genuine family and clean-air emphasis will become more and more attractive to listeners who are tired of blue humor and hearing messages on secular radio that are destructive to their families and their values.[11]

WHERE IS CHRISTIAN RADIO HEADED IN THE FUTURE?

Alan Mason, Audience Development Group:

Christian broadcasters tend to see things from their perspective. But now they have to go for a target-rich environment. You can't say: "We are the beacon. Come to us." You can't force them to listen. Missionaries have to learn to speak [the audience's] language.[12]

Erik Rhoads, *Radio Ink* magazine:

Can most Americans relate to Christian radio broadcasters? For people to relate to you, you must reflect the culture without being part of the culture. Christian radio stations are not substandard citizens. They use secular techniques of high quality broadcasting. But Christians tend to spend time within their own subculture and not enough time outside it. If we don't understand them, we can't relate to them. You have to ask: "How are we perceived? To whom do we appeal? Are we fun, cool, relatable?"

If listeners find Christianity on the radio, thousands are lost because they don't know what to do next. Maybe they try church and don't like it. Maybe the Bible is too overwhelming or unfamiliar. Maybe they are embarrassed. Christian radio needs a hand-off system that teaches the Gospel in simple terms, introduces listeners to the church family, and teaches the next step. The system must be demographically and psychographically based, localized, and integrated with the World Wide Web.

Relate, study the culture, and don't be dull. The future of Christianity is in the hands of Christian broadcasting. It must lead a movement of relatability and repair a broken image. [13]

Mike Miller, Salem Radio Network:

The Internet may be a problem, and so might satellite radio. Audiences are migrating to music stations. Conservative news/talk will continue to remain strong, but will traditional radio ministries continue to be able to afford air time?[14]

Marvin Sanders, American Family Radio:

More competition will mean some will not survive. We need to have more Christian radio for teenagers with backing from large donor grants.[15]

Darrell Gibson, WVHM, Hardin, Kentucky:

I forget I even have a website. Our primary function is Christian radio. We have been here 16 years, and people have begun to take us for granted. Giving is down in general across Christiandom. Our future depends on making sure the bills are paid and continuing to operate with integrity.[16]

John Hayden, WMBI Chicago:

Digital broadcasting and the Internet are factors. But local market emphasis is more important. There is pressure on program providers to shorten their programs, cut them in half, and create breakaways for spots. There are too many good programs for too few slots in the schedule.[17]

Doug Hannah, WAY-FM:

The numbers are going up in general except for the stations that are not audience focused. Christian talk and preaching and teaching block-time stations are on the decline. Demographics favor music formats. You don't have to be one-stop Christian radio.[18]

Sal DiGuardia, KDUV, Visalia-Fresno, California:

At some point, the many great owners and managers of Christian radio stations will come together and aggressively pursue excellence in our industry financially, creatively, and really hiring the absolute best talent in the industry. I would really like to open the doors of a company like Clear Channel, to embrace Christian radio, and give guys like me, and a handful of very talented programmers, the chance to take it to the next level. We have an amazing industry on our hands and it would be great to have that kind of backing to really program these stations as well as anything Clear Channel currently owns.[19]

Jim McDermott, Spirit FM, Camdenton, Missouri:

It will continue to get better as more stations focus their programming to aim at one demographic target instead of trying to be all things to all people. The danger is that as our stations become more professional in their presentation, they can lose their spiritual edge. If we are going to be radio for Christians, we will always have to be about challenging Christians to live out their faith. Unfortunately, the number of stations that buy into the above model is still the minority. That is the challenge for this format, to overcome the bad stereotype of religious radio that still exists in many, many towns and cities across America.[20]

Joe Polek, WMSJ, Freeport, Maine:

I think more Christian stations will be showing up in the commercial frequencies on the radio dial, making them more competitive to the major mainstream stations. I think it can only keep getting better.[21]

Mike Weston, WMHK, Columbia, South Carolina:

I think the music will continue to improve even more and eventually surpass secular music in quality, inspiration, and creativity. It will continue to attract more and more excellent on-air talent who are ready to leave the world of corporate radio. I think the stations that want to be successful will need to realize that the Christian radio listener of today is not the same as even five years ago. They will need to stay in constant touch with not only the listeners they have now, but with those who might sample their product. It will also become better at meeting the needs of the culture where it is "at." Finally, I think Christian radio will become less religious and inward focused, using inside language, and begin to be simply the best thing on the radio dial ... Christian or otherwise. It will do all of this without losing its primary vision to spread the Gospel and support believers.[22]

George Cooper, Transworld Radio:

Missionary and Christian radio struggle with the issue of audience. While desiring to be evangelistic, how do we get the unsaved (read: uninterested) to listen to the message? Some broadcasters spice it up with contemporary music and trendy speech. More often than not, broadcasters satisfy the supporting constituency with Bible-teaching programs, yet wonder who really listens. However, by identifying the intended audience as God-fearing people, we are able to satisfy believers and interested unbelievers. This includes unsaved church members as well as members of non–Christian religions. These are seekers whom God draws in to listen. Our primary task as Christian broadcasters is to unapologetically teach God's Word, which He has promised to bless: "It will not return to me void" (Isaiah 55:11). For me, Proverbs 9:8 sums it up: "So don't waste your time on a scoffer; all you'll get for your pains is abuse. But if you correct those who care about life, that's different; they'll love you for it."[23]

Tom Atema, Blue Ridge Broadcasting:

There is a difference between what is cultural and what the Bible says is truth. For some strange reason, many Christians tend to fight change, even though God is in the business of changing us daily. We tolerate irrelevance. It is all about the numbers — and it has nothing to do with numbers! Numbers are my scorecard. Numbers let me and you know where we are, how to set up the next play, how far we have come and how far we need to go. Numbers have even become a sign of success, but nothing could be farther from the truth! The number of songs we do or do not play, the number of programs we do or do not carry, an increasing budget, better annual Arbitron numbers, etc., can convince us that we are in the center of God's will — but this is not true. The greatest indicator of our relevance is the impact we have on the culture. The true measure of success is what is happening with our listeners.[24]

Specific Challenges for Program Producers

Veteran Christian radio producer Robb Hansen sees many changes ahead for traditional preaching and teaching, and other forms of spoken-word programming. Among them are more emphasis on preachers and teachers as radio personalities, improved production values with the end result of capturing listeners, more cross traffic between radio programs and the Internet with interactive functions eventually moving to the Web, shorter features and other modifications to accommodate spot breaks and limited attention spans, and the unforeseen impact of new digital and wireless technologies. Hansen says:

> In the fourth quarter of 2002, for the first time in history, the audience share of Christian talk radio dipped below that of Christian music. Many factors led to this shift, including the expansion of contemporary music outlets by Salem Communication Corporation's Fish stations, the K-LOVE network and a host of smaller entities.
>
> Clearly, many factors play a role in this development and we should seek to understand them. But it is just as important to identify and make needed changes. For if those involved in Christian talk are united in anything, it is their desire not only to maintain but also to grow their impact on the church and culture.
>
> Christian talk radio will be around for a long time. There are simply too many people committed to the format for it to go away. Station owners, both individual and institutional, have deep convictions about the importance of making such programming available for anyone who goes looking for it or happens upon it. They deeply believe that God uses radio teaching to draw people to Himself and that He will continue to do so — and they're right. The fundamental issue is what Christian teaching and talk radio will look like in the years ahead. Will decision-makers continue to hold to the structures and forms of times past, or will they boldly ask the hard questions about what will make their offerings most effective? Change isn't always bad. God can richly bless new approaches to presenting the timeless truth of the Gospel. As always, the difficulty will be implementing new methods without faltering in commitment to the message.
>
> Audiences today seem to expect higher quality in all of their church-related experiences, from worship to parking to childcare. The trend is entirely a result of the consumer mindset that has permeated the culture. Determining which innovations in production are most helpful in enhancing effectiveness is more difficult. David Jeremiah's longform

teaching program, *Turning Point*, regularly uses on-air drama and sound effects reminiscent of radio from a bygone era, but featuring content as up-to-date as the evening news. The dramatic clips grab listener attention by their unique flavor and focus that attention on the subject matter of the teaching that follows. Finding the right mix of production elements that fit best with the ear of today's audiences can be tricky, but with careful planning it can be accomplished.

Programs with the right draw will develop a growing cadre of dedicated Internet-only listeners — the wave of the future. The availability of teaching through online streaming portals has already revolutionized the audience cultivation process for Christian talk. Casual listeners who might never bother to go to the hassle and expense of ordering a copy of a message by contacting a ministry now regularly return to a ministry's Website to catch whatever portion of a message they may have missed on a traditional broadcast. Ministries have yet to move decisively to maximize impact because of this increased traffic.[25]

For the most part, long-form programmers and syndicators have been hesitant to embrace the idea of chopping up the programs. But significant changes are only a matter of time. As some have pointed out, sermons are already broken into pieces to make them fit the 24- or 26-minute window. Would further editing the content truly damage the potential for impact? Devin Eckhart, executive director for Chip Ingram's 24-minute daily program, *Living on the Edge*, is troubled by the trend:

> While assembling the programs could be done in some other way, it seems as though the personal connection with listeners that occurs during a teaching program, where the Holy Spirit may be working to convict or challenge a listener, would be poorly served by a sudden interruption of a spot break.[26]

Bob Butts, head of Alistair Begg's *Truth for Life*, agreed.

> One of the trends in our culture is a move toward quick doses of information, sort of a *USA Today* approach to communication. Sometimes people may not want to listen to the full length of programs because the teacher just doesn't have enough to say. I believe five words describe what it takes to succeed in the current radio industry: remain, rule, raise, relate and rely.
>
> 1. Remain committed to Christ and the truth of His Word, to your call and to your family.

2. Rule your kingdom. Control the products of your organization as much as you can by using internal talent, then outsource the rest to likeminded people.

3. Raise a lot of money, raise the bar and raise your ministry to donors. Starting a broadcast is not for the faint-hearted; it takes a lot of time to develop and sustain a broadcast. Don't necessarily do just what works; do what God has called you to do. And remember, your donors commit financially to your ministry because they believe in what you're doing, so develop a ministry to them.

4. Relate with other ministries. Fraternize with your peers and get more deeply involved in the NRB family. Learn from others who are farther along the road and be a part of the fraternity that sharpens one another.

5. Rely on God. Pray about everything. Is this what God wants you to do or is it what you want? Ask for wisdom in everything.[27]

Roger Kemp at Salem Communications said the emphasis has to remain on the objectives of the ministry, the nature of the contemporary Christian audience, and the realities of the Christian radio marketplace:

There's been a lot of talk in our industry about reformatting — or rethinking — the way we package the long-form program. It's shaken the tree a little bit and has garnered some healthy dialogue this year about our teaching format and how we need to be going out to a new era and a new generation. Let me give you four points stations are looking for in radio programs.

1. Programs Produced for Radio

We listen to radio one person at a time and that makes it an intimate medium. We do a lot of media things in groups, but with radio, it's different. That's one of the reasons it's so spiritually powerful: people are left alone with their thoughts, undistracted, and use their imagination. Preaching programs originally meant for groups need to be repackaged for radio. In some cases, you need to do extra things to the program to make it user-friendly for radio, such as asking the personality to do something special in the beginning of the program or the closing. Radio is all about connecting and often, it takes a person addressing a person heart-to-heart.

2. Relationships

We look for ministries behind the program that know how to develop a relationship with their listenership. Ministries on the air often know more about their audience than the radio station knows. The ministry answers 800-number calls and mail. There is a level of sophistication about how you treat and respond to those listeners. It must be relational and there must be a flow back and forth.

3. Innovative Packaging

One of the formats we have suggested — not imposed — is a 25:00 net broadcast broken into segments. In the midst of those segments, the station has the right to retain spot time. The way it currently stands, in a 26:00 or a 25:00 program, we have 4:00 per half hour or 8:00 per hour to be a radio station apart from the block program, with no access to parts of the hour on the clock. Some programs are conducive to having program breaks. It is a difficult program to produce because it takes a lot of creativity to know where to break the program, how to break the program and how to continue to drive the listenership forward. Our desire is to have the spot breaks at different parts of the hour and be able to identify ourselves and brand ourselves so there is appropriate attribution when listeners call or write to your ministry. The first programs that are experimenting with the new format are increasing their response level, which is no surprise, because every time they leave for a break or return from a break, they tell the listener who they are. One ministry is 50 percent above its previous response rate; another is even greater. I know there is a lot of controversy and strong feelings and we certainly are not suggesting that every ministry consider this, but we are suggesting it for new programs and believe it is going to be the way of the future for many programs. The traditional ideal listener in our minds as we prepare programs — the female 25–54 sitting at the kitchen table with a cup of coffee, her Bible, your study guide, a pen and her checkbook — is probably not the norm.

We are presumptive as programmers and think everybody in the world knows who we are, but in most programs, if the listener hasn't caught the first few minutes of the program, they don't know who they're listening to until the end of the program. There are many advantages to this concept and it is something to consider.

4. Content: Still King

We're looking for great content, people who are connecting with the culture by way of Scripture and application. If you don't have content, you can't package it, manipulate it or break it into pieces — it'll never work. If God's hand is not on it, it won't work. The first thing we look at with potential programming is: show us the fruit. Show us where it is working before we consider putting it on the air. If it isn't powerful already, it's doubtful it would be powerful on the radio.[28]

Steve Reinke at *Focus on the Family*, perhaps the most successful program producer and distributor, said the challenge is mutual and requires an open mind where technology is concerned.

Stations and program providers need each other. *Focus on the Family* needs radio stations. You may not necessarily need *Focus on the Family*, but you need programming of some sort. It's your content. What eventually costs the ministry is going to in some way cost you. The ministry needs to watch its money the same way stations do. The Lord has not given Christian broadcasting an infinite amount of money.

Satellite Delivery
Satellite is by far one of the cheapest ways of doing programming once your program reaches more than 250 stations. Some ministries still deliver in cassette and CD. A trend is beginning to deliver programming online via FTP. There are major advantages to satellite delivery, including higher quality,

selection choices, and timely, direct delivery. Of course, there are also a couple of disadvantages. It's the station's responsibility to get the program; if it comes down from the satellite at 2:00 A.M., you have to make sure the equipment is ready to receive it. You also have to deal with misfeeds. If something happens, you have to call the network's head end and resolve it.

Internet Delivery

Internet delivery's advantages include 24/7 availability, high-speed access supplying it more quickly than real-time, and assured delivery. The Internet's disadvantages include equipment and download failures, file-format incompatibilities, corrupt data, limited server connections, non-automated downloads and cost. It is an expensive proposition to do Internet delivery. Monthly fees are associated with the Internet. Let's say a station downloads from your FTP site an average of five programs a day, at 30 MB per program, for a total of 150 MB per day. At the same time, 999 other stations may be downloading the same files at 150 MB each. Over an average of 20 days per month, the total space required is three terabytes — the equivalent of 10 hard drives, each holding 100 GB. Since most network providers charge per MB, you can see why many program providers question that Internet delivery is a good thing to do ... it's expensive! Our budget is going to be reflected in what you do.

Combined Satellite and Internet Delivery

If we can combine Internet and satellite delivery, we can take the best of both worlds and save money. It works like this:

1. The programmer transfers the file from the FTP to the satellite.
2. The satellite transfers the 150 MB file to a station, which can be faster than real-time. The data for a half-hour program can transfer in less than a minute, writes to a hard drive, can be downloaded while other programs are airing, and, with a feedback channel, can alert the uplink to missing packets, which are then resent and automatically repair a file you never knew had a problem.
3. The satellite simultaneously transfers the same 150 MB to all the other stations. It still is only 150 MB and is not multiplied by each transfer.
4. By month's end, 20 days, the total file transfer is only three GB, a scale 1,000 times less than the Internet download. You also can use a high-speed Internet connection to request a missing file, which you can drag and drop to a web page on your network, or move between hard drives.[29]

But ultimately, said Michael Shelley at In Touch Ministries, the program producers must remember that a radio ministry is still a ministry, an effective way to spread an evangelical message to a widely separated audience and to raise funds for other outreach efforts.

Nobody does radio or does programming just for the sake of doing it. At In Touch, we do radio to fund ministry initiatives. Paul didn't go to Turkey and Europe just for the sake of it, and he wasn't funded by the people he went to. The church in Jerusalem funded him.

At In Touch, we have an initiative to go into 100 languages in 10 years. We're at 43 after three years and we had 35 three years ago. The work that stations do on our behalf is for those in Vietnam, because Vietnamese is one of the new languages of our program. We have to get over the mentality that "It's only the United States." Our world is so much bigger than what we think it is. We are commanded to go into all the world. My job is to get the message of Jesus Christ to as many people as possible, and I do that through your radio station, and you do that through what we do outside of the United States. It is so important that we understand that.

Another initiative we're doing is discipleship. How do we work within your community? It's more than just giving you a program and saying, "Good luck." There is a responsibility on my part to make sure you are given the right amount of promotion material and teaching materials. How many of our listeners use radio for their discipleship throughout the week? Christian radio is more than entertainment and information. We are taking God's Word and helping believers walk more closely with the Lord. As Christian broadcasters, our primary directive is to reach people with the Gospel of Jesus Christ.[30]

If one considers the 1990s as the era of rebirth for Christian radio, the time when the medium forged ahead in new directions while still attempting to retain the traditions of the past 70 years, the present seems full of growing pains common to adolescence. While there is general consensus on why this rebirth has happened now and on the nature of the continuing evangelical mission, there is simmering disagreement on what paths Christian radio should and must follow to become a mature and significant segment of the larger radio industry without losing sight of the fundamental objectives of a radio ministry. And with an expanding audience of younger listeners that could become a loyal core for many years ahead, there is the temptation to discard many programming concepts that have defined Christian radio up to this point and replace them with market-driven strategies. How to provide the programs, formats, entertainment, information, and companionship that this audience wants to hear while giving it the spiritual encouragement it needs is the key programming issue that everyone in Christian radio today faces. How to accomplish those objectives on what is primarily a non-commercial medium funded by donations from the audience, in a marketplace that is ever more competitive, is the challenge.

11. Revelations

This research began with seven questions about Christian radio. Now it is time to revisit and to attempt to answer those questions and offer some conclusions.

What Is Christian Radio?

Christian radio is a large, vibrant segment of the radio industry that has emerged dramatically over the past 10 to 15 years. While Christian radio has been around since radio began service in the 1920s, its growth and appeal to a wide audience has waxed and waned throughout most of its existence. Changes in regulatory policy, technology, public attitude toward evangelical Christianity, and the emergence of popular contemporary Christian music and a new generation of Christian radio entrepreneurs and professionals have fostered the recent rebirth

The programming on Christian radio stations and networks is surprisingly diverse. There are traditional outlets with evangelical preachers and Bible teaching, using inspirational music as sustaining programming. But the new breed of Christian radio is centered on music and formatted very much like secular pop stations. There are now at least four distinct Christian music formats for radio. In addition, there is a successful blend of evangelical Christian programs with politically conservative news/talk shows for a spoken-word format that sometimes includes overt and fervent social activism. And there are still many stations with an eclectic mix of programs. Christian radio serves audiences that include the smallest communities, urban and suburban areas, and nationwide listeners with this menu of choices.

Christian radio is not without critics. William Martin claims that James Dobson and his organization Focus on the Family, for which Christian radio is a primary media platform, is "quietly building what may become, if it is not already, an even more powerful and cultural influence" than the Christian Coalition, the Family Research Council, or similar religious conservative political causes. In the civil war of values between secular humanists on one side and religious conservatives on the other, Dobson is a "professional soldier on the traditionalist side, [who] fights this war every day with his radio programs and publications" and works behind the scenes of the Republican Party to advance his social and political agenda.[1] Julia LeSage credits Dobson and other Christian radio personalities like Beverly LaHaye of Concerned Women for America with using their broadcasts to encourage political activism on subjects like abortion, gay rights, and banning objectionable books from local libraries.[2]

Describing a more subtle and insidious approach to using Christian radio to advance a conservative social agenda, Meryem Ersoz writes that KRKS-FM, a popular Christian station in the Denver-Boulder Colorado market operated by Salem,

> maintains a conservative "traditional family values" message while appropriating the format of an adult contemporary station, a practice that makes the messenger station more visible, higher profile, more available, and yet makes the message itself less visible. This repackaging of Christian radio makes it less discernable from its secular, adult contemporary counterparts and unhinges it from the formatting precedents established by prior religious broadcasting programming.... To a listener running the tuning dial in search of a conventional, secular rock music station, the audible difference is virtually indistinguishable.... As the message itself is cloaked in contemporary imagery and broadcast practices, the station itself, the messenger, is rendered more visible to a broader consumer base.[3]

Yet there is surprisingly little analytical criticism of Christian radio. And some of it is oddly constructed, like an essay on Rush Limbaugh, the bombastic right-wing star of commercial talk radio, in a volume titled *Media, Culture, and the Religious Right*; or an extended essay that equates Christian radio listening with Catholic ritual and attempts to explain its popularity in terms of the political theories of Theodore Adorno.[4] Limited in scope to a particular personality, program, or radio station, and devoted to political, rhetorical or semantic analyses, these critiques reflect a narrow perception of what Christian radio is and little insight into how it operates. Besides, most Christian radio broadcasters and their listeners are oblivious.

In fact there is still little understanding of what Christian radio is today outside of the relatively small group of people who work in Christian radio and in related businesses like contemporary Christian music. While the major trade periodicals in the music business have included Christian music in their regular profiles of popularity, rarely does Christian radio receive similar treatment from the publications that cover broadcasting. The best source for information is still the NRB, its publications and conferences. When commercial and public broadcasters do mention Christian radio, it is usually in passing.

How Did It Develop Into What It Is Today?

In the late 1980s, several factors coincided to create a favorable climate to develop Christian radio. Chief among these were the growing number of Americans who proclaimed themselves Christians, the evangelical movement that attracted them, and the growing audience for Christian media like films, television, books, magazines, interactive services, and especially music. But changes in federal regulation of the radio industry and emerging technology that made it easier to find new frequencies and operate groups of radio stations from a central network transmission point are also important.

A small number of people had the insight, energy, and perseverance to seize the opportunity that the coincidence presented. Many of the leaders in Christian radio today had pursued the concept devotedly for many decades. But just as many have moved over from secular radio or had little or no prior experience with the medium.

Christian radio uses mainstream programming and marketing strategies to attract mainstream audiences in important demographics and often in large radio markets. One of the first impressions one gets from conversations with the owners, managers, and staff at Christian radio stations is how much they know about radio and how savvy they are about target audiences, market research, and the basic economic structure of the industry.

How Has the Mission of Christian Radio Changed Over Time?

The mission of Christian radio remains remarkably faithful to the original objectives of the early radio evangelists. Everyone consulted for this study considers him or herself to be involved in a ministry to bring the Word of God, the teachings of Jesus Christ, and the message of the Gospel to believers and non-believers alike.

Radio is still an effective medium for Christian evangelism because it is less expensive that other media alternatives and establishes a personal bond between individual listeners and their favorite radio personalities, programs, and stations. This listener loyalty is consistent with the deep personal faith of Christians, especially those in the growing Pentecostal, evangelical, and Charismatic movements.

What has changed is the way these ministries use radio to accomplish their objectives. The most obvious example is the reliance on the lyrics of contemporary Christian music instead of traditional preaching and Bible teaching as the primary means of reaching and communicating with the audience.

What People and Organizations Are Responsible for This Development?

This question is difficult to answer in a short space because there are so many Christian radio entrepreneurs who are advancing the concept in all sorts of market situations. They include traditional evangelical organizations, shrewd and opportunistic Christian business people, establishments whose goals are social and political change, groups that take advantage of the time-honored ties between radio and popular music, and many small operators who want wholesome radio alternatives in their local communities.

While the current lot of Christian radio station operators come from a variety of motivations and have divergent ideas on how best to accomplish their basic evangelical mission, one cannot help but be impressed by their overall sincerity, dedication, professionalism, and — most important of all — deep, abiding faith.

Why Is the Growth in Christian Radio Happening Now?

One answer is clear. Christian radio is growing because the people and organizations behind the concept want the growth to happen. They have seen and seized the opportunity to expand Christian radio service into nearly every radio household in the United States. No doubt most of them feel that God has provided this opportunity, but growth of this dimension nevertheless depends on the concerted effort of many dedicated people and access to the funds to build Christian radio ministries from the ground up.

What is not so clear is why the audience is responding to the concept. Some listeners seek spiritual solace, some want wholesome radio programming that their kids can listen to, some just like the music, and others are devoted followers of a particular minister or Christian radio personality. But are they loyal listeners who will form a core upon which Christian radio can grow and build for the future?

Is Christian Radio a Momentary Fad or an Important Trend for the Mainstream Radio Business?

Christian radio is a fixture in the radio industry and is more prominent now than at any time since the very early days of radio broadcasting in the 1920s. There is every reason to believe that it will remain popular with a significant minority of the radio audience as long as the programming is focused on what the audience wants and needs to hear.

The growth in Christian radio, in terms of the number of stations on the air, is unlikely to continue. In fact, competition may very well force some station operators to change formats or to go dark. While the number of stations may decline, there is no reason to believe that the audience will do so as long as listeners like what they hear.

Where Is Christian Radio Headed in the Future?

Christian radio has established a workable, non-commercial, non-profit business model for now. But the pressure of growth continues to stretch funding to its limits. Since most of the stations are on non-commercial frequencies, selling commercial airtime is not an option. And secular commercial radio broadcasters are unlikely to subsume the format and concept, no matter how popular they become. They simply do not understand it and lack the personal involvement with religion to make it work. But commercial broadcasters are interested in buying Christian stations on commercial frequencies and changing the programming.

In the near future, Christian and secular radio stations must convert to digital audio broadcasting, an expense of more than $100,000 for many stations. Networks and stations with many translators will be especially hard pressed to raise the funds for the conversion. Most of these operators lack access to commercial credit and capital markets. It will surely be difficult, perhaps impossible, for some to achieve the level of donations necessary.

A major challenge for traditional preaching and teaching Christian stations and the producers and distributors of the programs is declining audience for this format and the correspondent loss of revenue from donations. Short-form, more polished programs with improved production values may be the solution for some but not all the vast array of offerings in this genre.

To some extent, the future of Christian radio is tied to the continuing popularity of contemporary Christian music and the strength of the latest evangelical movement in America, but this relationship is based on mutual benefits. All forms of popular music eventually hit a plateau where audience growth declines. Future expansion depends on the ability of that genre, and the artists, composers, and producers within it, to appeal to new generations of music consumers. So far contemporary Christian music is continuing to grow, but that growth is to some extent due to the rapid increase in Christian radio stations with music formats. Once one or the other ceases to increase its audience base, both arrive at the plateau. Generally, this means some sort of economic shakeout.

The current evangelical movement is harder to gauge. Unlike music sales or radio listeners where there are facts, figures and regular surveys to provide data on who and how many people are in the audience, church attendance records are not as readily available. While there seem to be many new and large evangelical churches going up all around the United States, it is unclear whether the congregations are filled with new

Christians or people who have changed denominations. Nevertheless, there is an evangelical movement in place. In the past, such events have come about every 100 years and lasted for several decades, with each successive one leaving behind large numbers of converts and new Christian institutions.[5] One might reasonably speculate that both contemporary Christian music and Christian radio are such institutions that will remain as part of the American media culture after the present evangelical movement subsides. On the other hand, whether they will be significant features or specialized niches with small, dedicated audiences remains in doubt.

Although Christian radio often targets young adult females and the growing Hispanic population, it is still a business run mainly by white men. Where women are involved in decision-making roles, they are often the wives, children, or other relatives of the white men in charge. Hopefully, management in Christian radio will become more gender balanced as women work their way up from the many position they hold in programming, fundraising, public relations, and ministry outreach. But the pathway is by no means clear.

Christian radio is missing the opportunity to reach a large African American audience that already listens to a segregated form of the genre. While there are local broadcasters in many communities and at least one national network, the Sheridan Gospel Network, that target this audience, there is no apparent attempt to integrate programming and outreach from most Christian radio services. Considering the large portion of adult African Americans who enjoy hearing the message of the Gospel on the radio, this seems to be a shortsighted strategy.

Teenagers also represent a challenge for Christian radio. On one hand they represent the future generation of listeners, But they are hard to reach, will not or cannot contribute substantial donations during shareathons, and are not the primary targets for most advertisers and ministries. It is instructive that both WAY-FM and Salem have suspended programming experiments that target this audience in recent years and that AFR is wrestling with a way to afford a Christian radio service for teenagers.

Perhaps now is a good time to turn back to the professionals in Christian radio for one last look into the future. At the 2003 NRB Convention, a panel that included commercial, non-commercial and international perspectives looked at looming challenges for Christian radio broadcasters and came up with the following forecast.

JOE DAVIS, EXECUTIVE VICE PRESIDENT FOR RADIO, SALEM COMMUNICATIONS

Last year [2002] was the best year ever for some major national ministries. Some have the most new stations; some have the most new givers; some have the largest gift aggregate ever; some have the largest income year ever. So there are ministries that are in tune with where the public is.

The Christian market is a large and attractive market. It's a target audience of 100 million people, many of them above average in the demographic traits that advertisers like to buy and ministries want to reach. But the audience share of Christian talk and teaching is still pretty small. Commercial and non-commercial stations alike are leaving the format for music, driven by some of the economic realities. We have to develop an economic model that will allow us to grow and survive. The cost to establish a new broadcast ministry is $3 to $5 million. FM stations in major markets can sell for as much as $250 million. There is substantial pressure to sell stations and put the money to other uses.

This is not the first time Christian broadcasters have faced a real challenge. Christian broadcasting was born in an environment of challenge. The earliest broadcasters had open access to the general market. Formatted radio began to come in, and stations that were once broadcasters became narrowcasters. Today's Christian broadcasting was born when it lost access to the general audience. It was fueled by really big challenge. They had to find ways to get the message on the air. And we're going to have to do that again.[6]

DICK JENKINS, EMF BROADCASTING, K-LOVE AND AIR 1

We are in an era of unprecedented change. The five looming challenges we see are audience erosion, audience fragmentation, increased competition, decreased coverage, and increasing station prices.

The percentage of adults who are considered unchurched is growing. Another factor is the rising non-attendance among Baby Boomers and women — most Christian ministries are targeted at women — Hispanics and the residents of the Northeast and the West Coast. This is not a good trend.

We're doing about $200,000 worth of research a year and one of the shockers that we found is that 40 percent of the listeners to Christian radio are Democrats. So when you come on the air and start sounding like a right-wing crazy, instead of trying to offer an educated approach or maybe not take political sides, you're alienating 40 percent of your audience.

One of our mottos for this year is "High Touch." I believe that one of the worst things you can do in a society that's becoming more and more technical, where people are feeling more and more isolated and more and more hurried and more and more busy, is when they call you radio station and get: "Thank you for calling WXYZ. If you'd like sales, push one." That's not bonding with people. That's not High Touch. And we can stand out as Christian broadcasters as people who care about our listeners by just giving that personal touch.

Christians in general are not signing up for digital transmitters. When digital comes on and we're still analog, we're going to lose coverage. When we start losing audience, some of us will wake up. We need to wake up now.

If we're going to compete, we're going to have to reach out to new and expanded audiences in a post–Christian America. That means we can't do programming like we've done it in the past. We're going to have to develop new funding sources. We're going to have to operate more efficiently. In this changing electronic marketplace with more and more narrowcasting, fragmentation is going to be a bigger threat. Continued deregulation and higher station prices are a big challenge to Christian broadcasters.[7]

Ron Cline, Chairman, HCJB

Opportunities to broadcast are becoming more expensive. It's becoming harder and harder and harder to start a radio ministry. You go to some city and say you want to start a Christian radio station, I think you'll find it costs more money, there are many more restrictions and you need to be aware of the cost. Also the value of the station is going up. You're sitting on what many consider a gold mine. The temptation to sell that gold mine is becoming more realistic. And the people who pay the bills are diminishing. I think in five years, we're going to see some real money crunches. We're going to have to find some alternate ways to pay our way in radio. It's not going to be the same as it is today.

Government regulations could change. It might be difficult to get a frequency. It might be difficult to maintain the freedom to speak the way you want without offering equal time to those who opposes those points of view. There are no guarantees. The things that we have been enjoying these days may change. It's going to be a struggle. We see that globally. I think the good days are behind us where we've been protected and it's been fairly easy. It's going to take a deeper level of commitment to go forward from this day on. It's going to mean doing a lot of things you've haven't done before, like rub elbows with government officials and get out and raise money.

Think of the competition for the mind today. How do we get their attention? They're on the cellular phone; they're on their headphones listening to music; they're on the computer; they're driving by you in a car that makes your car vibrate as it goes by. How are you going to get the attention of the listener? What do you do on your program today that causes new listeners to want to listen to you? What are we doing that's new that's going to attract new listeners? Because they're just not foaming at the mouth looking for Christian stations.

Go out on the street in front of your station and look for about six teenagers. Bring them into your station, and let them listen to a program, and ask them what they think. You probably won't like what they say, but you're going to hear where you have to go if you're going to have an audience in five years because that's the crowd we're looking at, and that's the crowd we're trying to reach. We're not entertainers. We're ministers, and we've got to figure out how to touch them in five years. You have people out there who think that Christians have a crutch. Or that Christians are extreme Republicans. Or Christians are whacko. How are you going to get past that?[8]

Christian radio is an important component of the larger radio industry. It reaches a unique audience — people who are largely dissatisfied with programming on secular commercial and non-commercial stations and networks and who would probably not listen to radio at all if Christian stations were not there. And there is some evidence that Christian radio is creating new radio listeners, a matter that needs further investigation. If this is so, then Christian radio is good for the radio industry. The next 10 years will be different for Christian radio. The present rate of growth cannot continue and audience fragmentation will force retrenchment and perhaps a few failed ministries. But this looks like something that is here to stay, a regular feature of the American media environment taking its place alongside Sunday School, the YMCA, and other surviving institutions from past American evangelical movements.

As this manuscript nears completion, there are two recent occurrences that bear mention. The first is the result of the 2004 U.S. elections and the role that evangelical Christians and Christian media, including radio, apparently played in the Republican victory. While it is easy to claim that this triumph for moral values and conservative social and political agendas is the result of activism and media endorsements, it seems just as likely that all these events are merely correlated, representing different aspects of the same cultural phenomenon.

The second item of note is more specific: Salem Communications, the subject of Chapter 5, has made some significant changes in its operation in Chicago, one of the nation's largest radio markets. In a transaction announced October 4, 2004, Salem is trading two FM radio stations — including Chicago area WZFS-FM, which currently airs The Fish contemporary Christian music format — to Univision, the nation's leading Hispanic broadcasting company, for four radio stations, including WIND-AM in Chicago. Salem also gives up a San Francisco FM and gets new stations in Dallas, Houston, and Sacramento. With the swap that should become final early in 2005, Salem will cease its attempt to build a music audience in Chicago, concentrating instead on expanding its conservative talk radio format. Salem President Ed Atsinger said of the transaction:

> This station swap presents a unique opportunity for Salem to expand our presence in four very attractive major markets. We can now bring our syndicated news/talk format into both Chicago and Houston, which are both ideal markets for this format.... Effectively, in a single transaction we will be able to upgrade our station group, maximize our return from two under-performing radio stations, make significant improvements to our strategic formats and to our syndicated talk network, as well as strengthen our clusters in four important top-25 markets. We are now better positioned for long-term growth and have done so without using cash or debt and without issuing equity.[9]

Does this switch indicate a decline in audience interest in CCM formats? Probably not, for CCM is still one of the ongoing success stories in the music industry. More likely, Chicago is a tough sell for the format. Prior to this format change, three other Christian music stations have failed to sustain audience there in the past 20 years.[10] But the on-air staff at WZFS-FM did something unique, an indication of how strong the bond is between Christian radio stations and their audiences. For the week leading up to the November 1 changeover to a new format, WZFS aired a series of heartfelt farewells and thank-you messages from the announcers and actively promoted other Christian radio stations in the Chicago area, including the K-LOVE affiliate, whose music programming is similar to The Fish.[11] It's hard to imagine a commercial radio station with any other format taking those steps in this situation.

Even though Christian radio is now part of the mainstream radio business and in the future more decisions will be based on tough economic factors, it retains this distinctive relationship with its listening audience. It's as if the listeners readily transfer faith in the Gospel to devotion to their favorite station. This has been an important aspect of Christian radio since the beginning and through the lean years. Now that the Christian radio audience is growing, this provides an enviable asset in an industry that measures success in average quarter hour maintenance and other calculations of listener loyalty.

Chapter Notes

Chapter 1

1. Darrell Gibson, conversation with author, June 17, 2003.
2. Ed Shane, "Foreword: Challenges Facing the Radio Industry," *Journal of Radio Studies*, December 2002, iii.
3. *Broadcasting and Cable Yearbook* (Newton, Mass.: Reed Elsevier, 2003), 661–662.
4. "Christian Mass Media Reach More Adults with the Christian Message Than Do Churches," The Barna Group, July 2, 2002, http://www. barna.org (accessed November 19, 2003).
5. "Format Trends Report," Arbitron, http://wargod.arbitron.com/scripts/ndb/fmttrends2.asp (accessed August 4, 2004).
6. *Ibid.*
7. "Salem's 94.9 KLTY-FM Dallas Sets Ratings Record," *Christian Radio Weekly*, November 4, 2002, 1.
8. *Black Radio Today* (New York: Arbitron, Inc., 2004).
9. Jeff Miller personal website, "U.S. Radio Stations as of June 30, 1928," http://members.aol.com/jeff560/1928am.html (accessed March 8, 2002).
10. Quentin J. Schultze, "Evangelical Radio and the Rise of the Electric Church, 1921–1948," *Journal of Broadcasting and Electronic Media*, Summer 1998, 289.

Chapter 2

1. James R. Goff Jr., *Close Harmony: A History of Southern Gospel* (Chapel Hill, N.C.: University of North Carolina Press, 2002), 55–79.
2. Ben Armstrong, *The Electric Church* (Nashville, Tenn.: Thomas Nelson Publishers, 1979), 19–46.
3. Quentin J. Schultze, "Evangelical Radio and the Rise of the Electric Church, 1921–1948," 292.
4. Ben Armstrong, *The Electric Church*, 24–25; Dennis N. Voskuil, "The Power of the Air: Evangelicals and the Rise of Religious Broadcasting," in *American Evangelicals and the Mass Media: Perspectives on the Relationship Between American Evangelicals and the Mass Media*, ed. Quentin J. Schultze (Grand Rapids, Mich.: Academia Books, 1990), 69–95; Mark Ward Sr., *Air of Salvation: The Story of Christian Broadcasting* (Grand Rapids, Mich.: Baker Books, 1994), 31–39.
5. "U.S. Radio Stations as of June 30, 1928."
6. Quentin J. Schultze, "Evangelical Radio and the Rise of the Electric Church," 22.
7. *Ibid.*, 23.
8. Hal Erickson, *Religious Radio and Television in the United States, 1921–1991:*

The Programs and Personalities (Jefferson, N.C.: McFarland, 1992), 4–7.

9. Dennis N. Voskuil, "The Powers of the Air" in *American Evangelicals and the Mass Media*, 82.

10. Hal Erickson, *Religious Radio and Television in the United States, 1921–1991*, 2–5.

11. Dennis N. Voskuil, "The Powers of the Air" in *American Evangelicals and the Mass Media*, 83–85.

12. *Ibid.*, 70–71.

13. Ben Armstrong, *The Electric Church*, 19–20.

14. *One Timeless Message, 1926–2001*, audio recording (Chicago, Ill.: Moody Bible Institute, 2001), disc 1, track 2.

15. Tona J. Hangen, *Redeeming the Dial: Radio, Religion, and Popular Culture in America* (Chapel Hill, N.C.: University of North Carolina Press, 2002), 43–56.

16. *Ibid.*, 46–47.

17. Hal Erickson, *Religious Radio and Television in the United States, 1921–1991*, 95–96.

18. Mark Ward Sr., *Air of Salvation*, 49–51.

19. Hal Erickson, *Religious Radio and Television in the United States, 1921–1991*, 82–84; Tona J. Hangen, *Redeeming the Dial*, 85–88; Mark Ward Sr., *Air of Salvation*, 51–56.

20. Tona J. Hangen, *Redeeming the Dial*, 102–111.

21. Mark Ward Sr., *Air of Salvation*, 47–49.

22. Hal Erickson, *Religious Radio and Television in the United States, 1921–1991*, 120–121.

23. Ben Armstrong, *The Electric Church*, 36–40.

24. Hal Erickson, *Religious Radio and Television in the United States, 1921–1991*, 126–128.

25. Tona J. Hangen, *Redeeming the Dial*, 65–66.

26. *Ibid.*, 73.

27. *Ibid.*, 61–62.

28. Janet Simonsen, electronic mail to author, September 21, 2004.

29. William Martin, *With God on Our Side: The Rise of the Religious Right in America* (New York: Broadway Books, 1996), 18–19.

30. *Ibid.*, 19–20.

31. *Ibid.*, 20–22.

32. R. Alton Lee, *The Bizarre Careers of John R. Brinkley* (Lexington, Ky.: The University Press of Kentucky, 2002), 61–89.

33. James R. Goff Jr., *Close Harmony*, 109.

34. *Ibid.*, 117–119.

35. *Ibid.*, 131–135.

36. *Ibid.*, 129–143.

37. *Ibid.*, 158–171.

38. *Ibid.*, 130.

39. *Ibid.*, 157–167.

40. *Ibid.*, 221–242.

41. *Ibid.*, 209–211, 268.

42. *Ibid.*, 221–242.

43. *Ibid.*, 252–252.

44. *Ibid.*, 248–278.

45. Ben Armstrong, *The Electric Church*, 48–62.

Chapter 3

1. Lorraine Ali and Marc Peyer, "Jesus Rocks: Christian Entertainment Makes a Joyful Noise," *Newsweek*, July 16, 2001, 38; Barry Alfonso, *The Billboard Guide to Contemporary Christian Music* (New York: Watson-Guptil Publications, 2002), 7–47; Jay R. Howard and John M. Streck, *Apostles of Rock: The Splintered World of Contemporary Christian Music* (Lexington, Ky.: University Press of Kentucky, 1999), 4–45; William D. Romanowski, "Contemporary Christian Music: The Business of Music Ministry," in *American Evangelicals and the Mass Media: Perspectives on the Relationship Between American Evangelicals and the Mass Media*, ed. Quentin J. Schultze (Grand Rapids, Mich.: Academia Books, 1990), 143–169.

2. Cameron Crabtree, "Music Industry Exec Notes Impact of Contemporary Christian Music," Golden Gate Baptist Theological Seminary, http://www/ggbts.edu/events/crabtree33.html (accessed July 2, 2004).

3. James R. Goff Jr., *Close Harmony*, 251–252.

4. *Ibid.*, 276–277.

5. Cameron Crabtree, "Music Industry Exec Notes Impact of Contemporary Christian Music."

6. Michael Janke, "A Decade of Difference," Christian Music Central, http://www. cmcentral.com/features/63.html (accessed July 2, 2004).

7. Mark Allan Powell, "Contemporary Christian Music: What Can We Learn?" Evangelical Lutheran Church in America, http://www.elca.org/lp/conmu sic.html (accessed July 2, 2004).

8. H. T. Spence, *Confronting Contemporary Christian Music* (Dunn, N.C.: Companion Press, 1997), quoted in Allie Martin, "Church Debates Relevancy, Message of Contemporary Christian Music," LifeWay, http://www.lifeway.com (accessed July 2, 2004).

9. John Ashbrook in H. T. Spence, *Confronting Contemporary Music*, quoted in Allie Martin, "Church Debates Relevancy, Message of Contemporary Christian Music."

10. "Bible Guidelines for Christian Music," Dial-the-Truth Ministries, http://www.av1611.org (accessed July 6, 2004).

11. Mark Allen Powell, "Contemporary Christian Music."

12. Hal Erickson, *Religious Radio and Television in the United States, 1921–1991*, 1–17; James Davidson Hunter, *American Evangelicalism: Conservative Religion and the Quandary of Modernity* (New Brunswick, N.J.: Rutgers University Press, 1983), 23–48; Erling Jorstad, *Popular Religion in America: The Evangelical Voice* (Westport, Conn.: Greenwood Press, 1993), 4–15.

13. John C. Green, "The Christian Right and the 1996 Elections: An Overview," in *God at the Grass Roots: The Christian Right in the American Elections*, eds. Mark J. Rozell and Clyde Wilcox (New York: Rowan and Littlefield, 1997), 1–14.

14. David Gates, "The Pop Prophets," *Newsweek*, May 24, 2004, 44.

15. Patrick Kampert, "James Dobson the empire builder," *Chicago Tribune*, July 14, 2002.

16. Hal Erickson, *Religious Radio and Television in the United States, 1921–1991*, 69–70.

17. Patrick Kampert, "James Dobson the empire builder."

18. James Dobson, "The State of the Family in 2003: A Study in Navigation," *NRB* (May 2003), http://www.nrb.org (accessed June 10, 2004).

19. *Ibid.*

20. *Ibid.*

21. "About Crown Financial Ministries," Crown Financial Ministries, http://www.crown.org (accessed June 21, 2004).

22. "Howard Dayton Biographical Information," Crown Financial Ministries, http://www.crown.org (accessed June 21, 2004).

23. "Larry Burkett Biographical Information," Crown Financial Ministries, http://www.crown.org (accessed June 21, 2004).

24. "About Crown Financial Ministries."

25. "Steve Moore Biographical Information," Crown Financial Ministries, http://www.crown.org (accessed June 21, 2004).

26. "J. David Rae," Crown Financial Ministries, http://www.crown.org (accessed June 21, 2004).

27. How to Manage Your Money, "Financial State of the American Household." MP3 file, Crown Financial Ministries, http://www.crown.org.

28. How to Manage Your Money, "God's Financial Principles," MP3 file, Crown Financial Ministries, http://www.crown.org.

29. A Money Minute, "Riches without Righteousness." MP3 file, http://www.crown.org.

30. A Money Minute, "Harry Slade, Private Accountant," MP3 file, Crown Financial Ministries, http://www.crown.org.

31. "About Truth for Life," Truth for Life, http://www.truthforlife.org (accessed July 29, 2004).

32. *USA Radio Network*, promotional

brochure (Dallas, Tx.: USA Radio Network, 2003).

Chapter 4

1. "Dwight Moody Bibliographical Information," Moody Broadcasting Network, http://www.mbn.org (accessed Jun 29, 2003).

2. *One Timeless Message, 1926–2001*, disc 1, track 2.

3. *Ibid.*, disc 1, track 13.

4. Phil Shappard, conversation with author, September 23, 2004.

5. *One Timeless Message, 1926–2001*, disc 1, track 4.

6. *Ibid.*, disc 1, track 6.

7. *Ibid.*; Phil Shappard, electronic mail to author, August 3, 2004.

8. Phil Shappard, conversation with author, September 23, 2004.

9. *One Timeless Message, 1926–2001*, disc 2, track 2.

10. *Ibid.*

11. *Moody Bible Institute of Chicago*, 66 FCC 2d 162–169 (1977).

12. *One Timeless Message, 1926–2001*, disc 3, track 1.

13. *Ibid.*, disc 2, track 10.

14. *Ibid.*

15. *Ibid.*, disc 3, track 3.

16. *Ibid.*

17. *Ibid.*, disc 3, track 7.

18. John Hayden, conversation with author, August 7, 2003; Phil Shappard, conversation with author, September 23, 2004.

19. John Hayden, conversation with author, August 7, 2003.

20. *One Timeless Message, 1926–2001*, disc 3, track 13.

21. John Hayden, conversation with author, August 7, 2003.

22. *One Timeless Message, 1926–2001*, disc 3, track 13.

23. John Hayden, conversation with author, August 7, 2003.

24. *One Timeless Message, 1926–2001*, disc 3, track 13.

Chapter 5

1. Stuart Epperson and Edward Atsinger, *2003 Annual Report* (Camarillo, Calif.: Salem Communications, 2004), 4–5.

2. *Ibid.*, 11–13.

3. *Ibid.*, 13.

4. Salem Communications, "Salem Communications to Acquire Two Hawaii FM Stations," press release, May 4, 2004.

5. Salem Communications Form 10-K for Fiscal Year Ended December 31, 2003 (2004), 45–49.

6. Michael Miller, conversation with author, July 23, 2003.

7. *Ibid.*

8. Stuart Epperson, "Law of Unintended FCC Consequences," *Washington Dispatch*, May 6, 2004, http://www.washingtondispatch.com (accessed June 7, 2004).

9. *Ibid.*

10. The Mike Gallagher Show, http://www. mikeonline.com/bio/index.html (accessed July 31, 2003).

11. "Janet Parshall's America," under "Syndicated Talk Shows," Salem Communications, http://www.salem.cc (accessed June 7, 2004).

12. "Michael Medved's Official Profile," Michael Medved Show, http://www. michaelmedved.com/bio/shtml (accessed July 31, 2003).

13. "The Hugh Hewitt Show," under "Syndicated Talk Shows," Salem Communications, http://www.salem.cc (accessed June 7, 2004); Denise Davis, electronic mail to author, September 21, 2004.

14. "The Dennis Prager Show," under "Syndicated Talk Shows," Salem Communications, http://www.salem.cc (accessed June 7, 2004).

15. Salem Communications, "Bill Bennett Radio Show 'Morning in America' Launches Today on 66 Stations Across the Country," press release, April 5, 2004.

16. Salem Communications Form 10-K for Fiscal Year Ended December 31, 2003 (2004), 8.

17. *2003 Annual Report*, 13–19.

18. Salem Communications, "KPRZ 1210AM Takes Talk Shows on the Road to Peutz Valley for Fire Victims," press release, December 12, 2003.

19. *Ibid.*

20. Salem Communications, "First Family Expo Features Fun on April 2–3; KNUS-AM 710 AM and KRKS-FM 94.7 FM Host Event in Castle Rock," press release, March 25, 2004.

21. Salem Communications, "KKLA-FM Hosts 6th Annual Pastor Encouragement Luncheon; 'Focus on the Family's' H. B. London to Address Area Pastors," press release, April 20, 2004.

22. Salem Communications, "Salem Communications Hosts Summer 2004 Concert Series: Celebrate Freedom, Fish Fest, Big Splash," press release, June 19, 2004.

23. *2003 Annual Report*, 16–19.

Chapter 6

1. "About AFR: A God-given vision comes to life," American Family Radio, http://www.afr.net (accessed June 9, 2004).

2. *Ibid.*

3. *Ibid.*

4. Marvin Sanders, conversation with author, July 24, 2003.

5. Laurie Cohen, "Radio Evangelist Finds a Deft Way to Expand While Muscling NPR," *Wall Street Journal*, August 14, 2001; Marvin Sanders, conversation with author, July 24, 2003.

6. "About AFR."

7. Laurie Cohen, "Radio Evangelist Finds a Deft Way to Expand While Muscling NPR"; Marvin Sanders, conversation with author, July 24, 2003.

8. "AFR Program Schedule," American Family Radio, http://www.afr.net (accessed June 9, 2004).

9. "AFR Staff," American Family Radio, http://www.afr.net (accessed June 9, 2004).

10. *Ibid.*

11. "J. J. Jasper Biography," American Family Radio, http://www.afr.net (accessed June 9, 2004).

12. "AFR Staff."

13. "About AFR."

14. Marvin Sanders, conversation with the author, July 24, 2003.

15. "AFR News," American Family Radio, http://www.afr.net (accessed June 9, 2004).

16. *Ibid.*

17. *Ibid.*

18. *Ibid.*

19. *Ibid.*

20. *Ibid.*

21. *Ibid.*

22. *Ibid.*

23. *Ibid.*

24. *Ibid.*

25. *Ibid.*

26. *Ibid.*

27. "AFA Filter," American Family Radio, http://www.afr.net (accessed June 9, 2004).

28. Marvin Sanders, electronic mail to author, September 21, 2004.

29. Marvin Sanders, conversation with author, July 24, 2003.

30. *Ibid.*

Chapter 7

1. Andrea Kleid, conversation with author, January 4, 2003.

2. Mike Novak, fax to author, December 19, 2003.

3. *Ibid.*

4. "Our Vision," K-LOVE, http://www.klove.com (accessed October 1, 2003).

5. "Our History," K-LOVE, http://www.klove.com (accessed October 1, 2003).

6. *Ibid.*

7. Dick Jenkins, "K-LOVE: Broadcasting Quality," *NRB*, February/March 2003, 178.

8. Dick Jenkins, "6 Steps to Strategic Radio Planning," *NRB*, June 2003, 10.

9. Mike Novak, conversation with author, October 6, 2004.
10. Dick Jenkins, "K-LOVE Broadcasting Quality."
11. *Ibid.*
12. *Ibid.*
13. Mike Novak, conversation with author, October 6, 2004.
14. Dick Jenkins, "K-LOVE Broadcasting Quality."
15. Bob Augsburg, "Vision 20.1: WAY-FM's New Vision for the Future," WAY-FM, http://www.waym.wayfm.com (accessed September 29, 2003).
16. Bob Augsburg, "WAY-FM Grows Like a Weed This Summer," WAY-FM, http://www.waym.wayfm.com (accessed July 31, 2004).
17. "Core Values," WAY-FM, http://waym.wayfm.com/corevalues.html (accessed September 29, 2003).
18. *Ibid.*
19. Doug Hannah, conversation with author, September 29, 2003.
20. Andrea Kleid, conversation with author, January 4, 2003.
21. Matt Austin, conversation with author, September 29, 2003.
22. Dusty Rhodes, electronic mail to author, October 8, 2004.
23. "Start Your Day," 103.7 FM, http://www.fishfm.com/onair.asp (accessed July 31, 2004).
24. Melonee McKinney, "Community Profile: WAY-FM announcer connects with audience," *Tennessean*, January 5, 2003, http://www.tennessean.com/williamsonam/archives/03/01/27285821.shtml (accessed July 31, 2004).
25. Rachel Murphy, "Good Morning, Nashville!" *Christian Single*, November, 12.
26. "Start Your Day."
27. "Morning Thoughts," http://www.marciaandjeff.com (accessed July 31, 2004).
28. *Ibid.*
29. Melonee McKinney, "Community Profile."
30. Bob Augsburg, "WAY-FM Grows Like a Weed This Summer."
31. Mike Novak, conversation with author, October 6, 2004.

Chapter 8

1. Darrell Gibson, conversation with author, June 17, 2003.
2. Darrell Gibson, conversation with author, October 13, 2004.
3. Darrell Gibson, conversation with author, June 17, 2003.
4. "About Heartland Ministries Radio," Heartland Ministries Radio, http://www.heartlandradio.org (accessed June 15, 2004).
5. Darrell Gibson, conversation with author, June 17, 2003.
6. *Ibid.*
7. Darrell Gibson, conversation with author, October 13, 2004.
8. Darrell Gibson, conversation with author, June 17, 2003.
9. "History of the Station," Joy 89.3, http://www.wmsj.org (accessed June 15, 2004).
10. *Ibid.*
11. *Ibid.*
12. "On-Going Contests," Joy 89.3, http://www.wmsj.org (accessed June 15, 2004).
13. "Mom and Pop Station Goes on the Air," WTMV Radio, http://www.wtmv.com/history.htm (accessed June 10, 2004).
14. "WTMV Program Schedule," WTMV Radio, http://www.wtmv.com/program%20schedule.htm (accessed June 10, 2004).
15. "Mom and Pop Station Goes on the Air."
16. *Ibid.*
17. *Ibid.*

Chapter 9

1. Pillar of Fire, International, http://www.pillar.org (accessed June 21, 2003).
2. Gertrude Metlen Wolfram, "History of Star 99.1 WAWZ Radio," Star 99.1 FM, http://www.star991fm.com (accessed July 1, 2003).

3. Pillar of Fire, International, http://www.pillar.org (accessed June 21, 2003).

4. Gertrude Metlen Wolfram, "History of Star 99.1 WAWZ Radio."

5. "WAWZ: Mission Statement," Star 99.1 FM, http://www.star991fm.com (accessed June 23, 2003)

6. S. Rea Crawford, "Behind the Scenes at WAWZ," Star 99.1 FM, http://www.star991fm.com/star_progexplan.html (accessed July 1, 2003).

7. Scott Taylor, electronic mail to Andrea Keen, July 25, 2003.

8. Ibid.

9. Pillar of Fire International.

10. "HCJB World Radio at a Glance," HCJB World Radio, http://www.hcjb.org (accessed June 10, 2004).

11. Hal Erickson, Religious Radio and Television in the United States, 1921–1991, 95–96.

12. "HCJB World Radio at a Glance."

13. Ibid.

14. Jeanette Gardiner Littleton, "A Family Legacy: Bott Radio Network," Bott Radio Network, http://www.bottradionetwork.com/aboutBRN_history.asp (accessed July 12, 2003).

15. "BRN History and Purpose," Bott Radio Network, http://www.bbnradio.org/bbn/who_are_we_pages/who_are_we.htm (accessed June 17, 2004).

16. Jack Haughton, conversation with author, February 9, 2003.

17. Beth Huisman, electronic mail to Andrea Keen, July 25, 2003.

18. "BRN Stations," Bott Radio Network, http://www.bottradionetwork.com/brnstations.asp (accessed July 15, 2003); Kelly Crane, electronic mail to author, August 5, 2004.

19. Richard Bott, III, quoted in Kelly Crane, electronic mail to author, August 5, 2004.

20. "Our History," American Urban Radio Networks, http://www.aurnol.com/company_information/history.asp (accessed June 28, 2003).

21. "About the Light," Sheridan Gospel Network, http://www.sgnthelight.com/aboutthelight.asp (accessed June 25, 2003).

22. Jacquie Haselrig, interview with Andrea Keen, June 29, 2003.

23. "BBN History and Purpose."

24. Ibid.

25. Ibid.

26. Ibid.

27. Ibid.

28. "Who or What Is Family Radio," Family Radio Worldwide, http://www.familyradio.com (accessed June 10, 2004).

29. Ibid.

30. "Statement of Faith," Family Radio Worldwide, http://www.familyradio.com (accessed June 10, 2004).

31. "History of the Family Life Network," Family Life Ministries, http://www.fln.org (accessed June 17, 2004).

32. Ibid.

33. "Northwestern College and Radio Doctrinal Statement," KTIS, http://www.ktis.org (accessed June 12, 2004).

34. Christian Radio Atlas (Madison, Wis.: Scribe Media, 2003); Directory of Religious Media (Manassas, Va.: National Religious Broadcasters, 2002).

Chapter 10

1. Stuart Epperson, "Public Policy Update" (presentation to Public Policy Breakfast, 2003 NRB Convention, February 11, 2003).

2. Alan Mason, "Christian Radio Listener Exposed" (presentation to the Radio Bootcamp, 2003 NRB Convention, February 11, 2003).

3. Ibid.

4. Ibid.

5. Michael Miller, conversation with author, July 23, 2003.

6. Marvin Sanders, conversation with author, July 24, 2003.

7. John Hayden, conversation with author, August 7, 2003.

8. Doug Hannah, conversation with author, September 29, 2003.

9. Jim McDermott, electronic mail to author, May 1, 2003.

10. Joe Polek, electronic mail to author, April 30, 2003.

11. Mike Weston, electronic mail to author, May 1, 2003.

12. Alan Mason, "Christian Radio Listener Exposed."

13. Erik Rhoads, "Reinventing Christian Radio" (presentation to the 2003 NRB Convention, February 11, 2003).

14. Michael Miller, conversation with author, July 23, 2003.

15. Marvin Sanders, conversation with author, July 24, 2003.

16. Darrell Gibson, conversation with author, October 13, 2004.

17. John Hayden, conversation with author, August 7, 2003.

18. Doug Hannah, conversation with author, September 29, 2003.

19. Sal DiGuardia, electronic mail to author, May 1, 2003.

20. Jim McDermott, electronic mail to author, May 1, 2003.

21. Joe Polek, electronic mail to author, April 30, 2003.

22. Mike Weston, electronic mail to author, May 1, 2003.

23. George Cooper, "Who or What Is Our Audience?" *NRB*, March 2004, http://www.nrb.org (accessed June 10, 2004).

24. Tom Atema, "11 Essentials for Today's General Managers" (panel discussion, 2003 NRB Convention, February 11, 2003).

25. Robb Hansen, "9 Trends in Christian Talk Radio," *NRB*, September, 18.

26. Devin Eckhart, Bob Butts, Roger Kemp, Steve Reinke, and Michael Shelley, "Programming Strategies for the 21st Century: An NRB 2004 Educational Session Highlight," *NRB*, April 2004, http://www.nrb.org (accessed June 10, 2004). Transcript of a conference session.

27. *Ibid.*

28. *Ibid.*

29. *Ibid.*

30. *Ibid.*

Chapter 11

1. William Martin, *With God on Our Side: The Rise of the Religious Right in America*, 341–345.

2. Julia LeSage, "Christian Media" in *Media, Culture, and the Religious Right*, eds. Linda Kintz and Julia LeSage (Minneapolis, Minn.: University of Minnesota Press, 1998), 21–49.

3. Meryem, Ersotz, "Gimme That Old Time Religion in a Modern Age: Semiotics of Christian Radio" in *Media, Culture, and the Religious Right*, eds. Linda Kintz and Julia LeSage (Minneapolis, Minn.: University of Minnesota Press, 1998), 211–226.

4. Paul Apostolidis, *Stations of the Cross: Adorno and Christian Right Radio* (Durham, N.C.: Duke University Press, 2000); Linda Kintz and Julia LeSage, eds., *Media, Culture, and the Religious Right* (Minneapolis, Minn.: University of Minnesota Press, 1998).

5. James Davidson Hunter, *American Evangelicalism;* Erling Jorstad, *Popular Religion in America*.

6. Joe Davis, Dick Jenkins, and Ron Cline, "Into Thin Air: The Looming Challenges for Christian Broadcasters," audio recording from 2003 NRB Convention, February 11, 2003.

7. *Ibid.*

8. *Ibid.*

9. Salem Communications, "Salem Communications and Univision to Exchange Radio Stations in Key Markets," press release, October 4, 2004.

10. Patrick Kampert, "Christian radio station was a Fish out of water."

11. *Ibid.*

Bibliography

Books and Articles

Alexander, Yvonne. *Count It All Joy.* Georgetown, Del.: Fruit-Bearer Publishing, 2001.

Alfonso, Barry. *The Billboard Guide to Contemporary Christian Music.* New York: Watson-Guptil Publications, 2002.

Ali, Lorraine, and Marc Peyer. "Jesus Rocks: Christian Entertainment Makes a Joyful Noise." *Newsweek,* July 16, 2001, 38.

"The American Church Today." *NRB,* November/December 2003, 6.

Apostolidis, Paul. *Stations of the Cross: Adorno and Christian Right Radio.* Durham, N.C.: Duke University Press, 2000.

Armstrong, Ben. *The Electric Church.* Nashville, Tenn.: Thomas Nelson Publishers, 1979.

Black Radio Today. New York: Arbitron, 2004.

Broadcasting and Cable Yearbook. Newton, Mass.: Reed Elsevier, 1992.

Broadcasting and Cable Yearbook. Newton, Mass.: Reed Elsevier, 1997.

Broadcasting and Cable Yearbook. Newton, Mass.: Reed Elsevier, 2003.

Broadcasting Yearbook. New York: Broadcasting Publications, 1973.

Broadcasting Yearbook. New York: Broadcasting Publications, 1979.

Broadcasting Yearbook. New York: Broadcasting Publications, 1989.

Butts, Bob. "Programming Strategies for the 21st Century: An NRB 2004 Educational Session Highlight." *NRB,* April 2004, 26.

Christian Radio Atlas. Madison, Wisc: Scribe Media, 2003.

Cohen, Laurie. "Radio Evangelist Finds a Deft Way to Expand While Muscling NPR." *Wall Street Journal,* August 14, 2001.

Cooper, George. "Who or What Is Our Audience?" *NRB,* March 2004, 16.

Davis, Joe. "Program Formatting Redux." *NRB,* June 2003, 21.

Directory of Religious Media. Manassas, Va.: National Religious Broadcasters, 2002.

Dobson, James. "The State of the Family in 2003: A Study in Navigation." *NRB,* May 2003, 23. Online at www.nrb.org.

Elfstrand, Mark, and Ed Shane. "2 Vital Elements of Christian Talk Radio." *NRB*, September, 2002, 15.

Erickson, Hal. *Religious Radio and Television in the United States, 1921–1991: The Programs and Personalities.* Jefferson, N.C.: McFarland, 1992.

Gates, David. "The Pop Prophets." *Newsweek*, May 24, 2004, 44.

Goff, James R., Jr. *Close Harmony: A History of Southern Gospel.* Chapel Hill: University of North Carolina Press, 2002.

Hangen, Tona J. *Redeeming the Dial: Radio, Religion, and Popular Culture in America.* Chapel Hill: University of North Carolina Press, 2002.

Hispanic Radio Today. New York: Arbitron, 2004.

Howard, Jay R., and John M. Streck. *Apostles of Rock: The Splintered World of Contemporary Christian Music.* Lexington: University Press of Kentucky, 1999.

Hunter, James Davidson. *American Evangelicalism: Conservative Religion and the Quandary of Modernity.* New Brunswick, N.J.: Rutgers University Press, 1983.

Jenkins, Dick. "K-LOVE: Broadcasting Quality." *NRB*, February/March 2003, 178.

_____. "6 Steps to Strategic Radio Planning." *NRB*, June 2003, 10.

Jorstad, Erling. *Popular Religion in America: The Evangelical Voice.* Westport, Conn.: Greenwood Press, 1993.

Kampert, Patrick. "Christian Radio Station Was a Fish Out of Water." *Chicago Tribune*, November 7, 2004.

_____. "James Dobson the Empire Builder." *Chicago Tribune*, July 14, 2002.

Killingsworth, Rick. "The Financial Future of Christian Radio: Non-traditional Revenue." *NRB*, September 2000, 21.

Kintz, Linda, and Julia LeSage, eds. *Media, Culture, and the Religious Right.* Minneapolis: University of Minnesota Press, 1998.

Lee, R. Alton. *The Bizarre Careers of John R. Brinkley.* Lexington: The University Press of Kentucky, 2002.

Martin, William. *With God on Our Side: The Rise of the Religious Right in America.* New York: Broadway Books, 1996.

McDermott, Tim. "10 Non-Profit Radio Myths." *NRB*, September 2003, 7.

Moody Bible Institute of Chicago. 66 FCC 2d, 162–169 (1977).

Murphy, Rachel. "Good Morning, Nashville!" *Christian Single*, November 2002, 12.

One Timeless Message, 1926–2001. Audio recording. Chicago, Ill.: Moody Bible Institute, 2001.

Pederson, Wayne. "Long Live Radio." *NRB*, April 2001, 4.

Radio Today. New York: Arbitron, 2004.

Reinke, Steve. "Programming Strategies for the 21st Century: An NRB 2004 Educational Session Highlight." *NRB*, April 2004, 26.

Sanders, Jim. "All Aboard! Radio's Ride Into the 21st Century." *NRB*, September 2000, 18.

Schultze, Quentin J. "Evangelical Radio and the Rise of the Electric Church, 1921–1948." *Journal of Broadcasting and Electronic Media*, Summer 1988, 289.

_____, ed. *American Evangelicals and the Mass Media: Perspectives on the Relation-*

ship Between American Evangelicals and the Mass Media. Grand Rapids, Mich.: Academie Books, 1990.

Seward, Matt, and Duncan Dodds. "Christian Music Radio: Out of the Closet and Into the Spotlight." *Religious Broadcasting*, February 1993, 70.

Shane, Ed. "Foreword: Challenges Facing the Radio Industry." *Journal of Radio Studies*, December 2002, iii.

Shelley, Michael. "Programming Strategies for the 21st Century: An NRB 2004 Educational Session Highlight." *NRB*, April 2004, 26.

Spence, H. T. *Confronting Contemporary Christian Music*. Dunn, N.C.: Companion Press, 1997.

"Therapy of the Masses." Survey of America in *The Economist*. November 8, 2003, 12.

2002 Annual Report. Camarillo, Calif.: Salem Communications, 2003.

2003 Annual Report. Camarillo, Calif.: Salem Communications, 2004.

Ward, Mark, Sr. *Air of Salvation: The Story of Christian Broadcasting*. Grand Rapids, Mich.: Baker Books, 1994.

Useful Websites

American Family Association. www.afa.net.
American Family Radio. www.afr.net.
Arbitron.www.arbitron.com.
Barna Research Online. www.barna.org.
Bible Broadcasting Network. www.bbnradio.org.
Bott Radio Network. www.bottradionetwork.com.
Crown Financial Ministries. www.crown.org.
Educational Media Foundation. www.klove.com.
Family Life Network. www.fln.org.
Family Radio Network. www.familyradio.com.
Focus on the Family. www.focus.org.
HCJB World Radio Network. www.hcjb.org.
Heartland Radio Ministries. www.heartlandradio.org.
Moody Bible Institute. www.moody.edu.
Moody Radio Network. www.mbn.org.
National Religious Broadcasters. www.nrb.org.
Northwestern College Radio. www.ktis.org
Pillar of Fire, International. www.star991.com.
Salem Communications. www.salem.cc.
Sheridan Gospel Network. www.sgnthelight.com.
Truth for Life. www.truthforlife.org.
WAY-FM. www.wayfm.org.
WMSJ. www.wmsj.org.
WTMV. www.wtmv.com.

Index

205